D1268576

Building to Impact

Building to Impact

The 5D Implementation Playbook for Educators

Arran Hamilton

Douglas B. Reeves

Janet M. Clinton

John Hattie

Foreword by Dylan Wiliam

CORWIN

FOR INFORMATION:

Corwin
A SAGE Company
2455 Teller Road
Thousand Oaks, California 91320
(800) 233-9936
www.corwin.com

SAGE Publications Ltd.
1 Oliver's Yard
55 City Road
London EC1Y 1SP
United Kingdom

SAGE Publications India Pvt. Ltd.
B 1/I 1 Mohan Cooperative Industrial Area
Mathura Road, New Delhi 110 044
India

SAGE Publications Asia-Pacific Pte. Ltd.
18 Cross Street #10-10/11/12
China Square Central
Singapore 048423

President: Mike Soules
Associate Vice President and
  Editorial Director: Monica Eckman
Publisher: Jessica Allan
Senior Content
  Development Editor: Lucas Schleicher
Content Development Editor: Mia Rodriguez
Editorial Assistant: Natalie Delpino
Project Editor: Amy Schroller
Copy Editor: Christina West
Typesetter: C&M Digitals (P) Ltd.
Cover Designer: Scott Van Atta
Marketing Managers: Deena Meyer and
                    Olivia Bartlett

Copyright © 2022 by Corwin

All rights reserved. Except as permitted by U.S. copyright law, no part of this work may be reproduced or distributed in any form or by any means, or stored in a database or retrieval system, without permission in writing from the publisher.

When forms and sample documents appearing in this work are intended for reproduction, they will be marked as such. Reproduction of their use is authorized for educational use by educators, local school sites, and/or noncommercial or nonprofit entities that have purchased the book.

All third-party trademarks referenced or depicted herein are included solely for the purpose of illustration and are the property of their respective owners. Reference to these trademarks in no way indicates any relationship with, or endorsement by, the trademark owner.

Printed in Canada

Library of Congress Cataloging-in-Publication Data

Names: Hamilton, Arran, author. | Reeves, Douglas B., 1953- author. | Clinton, Janet M. (Janet May), author. | Hattie, John, author.

Title: Building to impact : the 5D implementation playbook for educators / Arran Hamilton, Douglas B. Reeves, Janet May Clinton, John Hattie.

Description: First edition. | Thousand Oaks, California : Corwin, [2022] | Includes bibliographical references and index.

Identifiers: LCCN 2022004775 | ISBN 9781071880753 (paperback) | ISBN 9781071880760 (epub) | ISBN 9781071880777 (epub) | ISBN 9781071880784 (pdf)

Subjects: LCSH: School improvement programs. | Educational innovations.

Classification: LCC LB2822.8 .H34 2022 | DDC 371.2/07—dc23/eng/20220310
LC record available at https://lccn.loc.gov/2022004775

This book is printed on acid-free paper.

MIX
Paper from
responsible sources
FSC
www.fsc.org   FSC® C103567

22 23 24 25 26 10 9 8 7 6 5 4 3 2 1

DISCLAIMER: This book may direct you to access third-party content via Web links, QR codes, or other scannable technologies, which are provided for your reference by the author(s). Corwin makes no guarantee that such third-party content will be available for your use and encourages you to review the terms and conditions of such third-party content. Corwin takes no responsibility and assumes no liability for your use of any third-party content, nor does Corwin approve, sponsor, endorse, verify, or certify such third-party content.

Contents

List of Figures

Foreword

*From *schools don't make a difference (wrong), to *schools (can) make
a big difference, to *schools aren't (yet) making enough of a difference, to *school improvement requires systematic and highly exacting
implementation*

For much—perhaps most—of the last century, educational policy
in many countries was underpinned by two assumptions. The first
was that "intellectual capacity was *wholly* or *very largely* determined
by genetic endowment and was therefore fixed, unchanging, and,
in addition, accurately measurable by group intelligence tests"
(Chitty, 1997). The purpose of schools was therefore not about
"providing an enriching and creative environment, but should be
adjusted to the function of sorting out and selecting the 'bright'
from the 'dull,' as determined by nature, and as basically reflected
in the existing social hierarchy" (Lawler, 1978, p. 3).

While some such as Arthur Jensen continued to argue that general cognitive ability was inherited, others such as Basil Bernstein
argued that the child's environment mattered far more. Either way,
many believed that students' academic achievement was largely
predetermined and schools could do little to change this. As
Bernstein (1970) put it, "Education cannot compensate for society."

The second assumption was that the quality of schooling had
little impact on student achievement. In other words, as long as
students attended school, which school they attended had little
impact on how much they learned. As Chitty (1997) notes, Jensen
and Bernstein undoubtedly contributed to the general mood of
"educational fatalism" that pervaded policy debates in England
and in the United States in the early 1970s, but perceptions about
the influence of schools on educational achievement were also
strongly supported by two large-scale surveys conducted in the
United States (p. 49).

The Equality and Educational Opportunity Study (Coleman, 1966)
surveyed over 600,000 first-, third-, sixth-, ninth-, and twelfth-
grade students in 3,000 US elementary and secondary schools.
While the original remit of the study was to describe the level of
inequality across US schools by focusing on "inputs," the study
team broadened the scope considerably, collected information
about the attitudes of teachers and administrators, and assessed
students using standardized tests of ability and achievement.

The report's conclusion was stark:

> Taking all these results together, one implication stands
> out above all: Schools bring little influence to bear
> on a child's achievement that is independent of his
> background and general social context; and that this very
> lack of an independent effect means that the inequalities
> imposed on children by their home, neighborhood,
> and peer environment are carried along to become the
> inequalities with which they confront adult life at the
> end of school. (Coleman, 1966, p. 325)

Six years later, Christopher Jencks and his colleagues reanalyzed
the data from the Coleman report together with data from a range
of other sources and came to a similar conclusion that "equalizing
the quality of high schools would reduce cognitive inequality by
one per cent or less" (Jencks et al., 1972, p. 109).

While many academics, policymakers, and educators seemed
happy to accept such strong claims, others pointed out that the
datasets analyzed by Coleman and Jencks were cross-sectional
rather than longitudinal, and therefore cast little light on the *progress* made by students in school. Even with better data, if it was
shown that some students did not make much progress in schools,
this would tell us little about what might be, not least because many
practices in schools—such as grouping students by ability—were
based on the assumption that ability was largely fixed. Therefore,
the observed results were likely to be as much a product of pre-
existing assumptions about students than about what schools
might be able to achieve.

The idea that schools *could* make a difference received support from
early international comparisons of student achievement, such as
the First International Mathematics Study (Husén, 1967a, 1967b).
A special issue of *Forum* magazine in 1974 directly challenged Basil
Bernstein's earlier claim with the title "Schools *can* make a difference" (Simon & Whitbread, 1974).

Strong empirical support for the idea that schools did in fact make
a difference—and that some schools were significantly more effective than others—came toward the end of the 1970s. A study of
eight schools in Michigan by Brookover and Lezotte (1977) found
clear differences between six schools where student performance
was increasing and two where performance was declining. In the
more successful schools, teachers believed that all students could
master basic objectives, were less satisfied with their achievements, and held higher and increasing expectations of their
students (Edmonds, 1979).

Perhaps even more influential was the publication of *Fifteen
Thousand Hours: Secondary Schools and Their Effects on Children* by

Rutter and colleagues in 1979. Beginning in 1970 with a convenience sample of 10-year-olds in London who had taken nonverbal reasoning and reading tests in the final year of primary schools, the research team tracked approximately two-thirds of these children into secondary schools and followed their progress until they reached the end of compulsory schooling 5 years later. While the study report produced a range of useful findings, perhaps the most important was the conclusion about the impact of schools on academic achievement:

> [T]he differences between schools in outcome were systematically related to their characteristics as social institutions. Factors as varied as the degree of academic emphasis, teacher actions in lessons, the availability of incentives and rewards, good conditions for pupils, and the extent to which children were able to take responsibility were all significantly associated with outcome differences between schools. All of these factors were open to modification by the staff, rather than fixed by external constraints. (Rutter et al., 1979, p. 178)

In the three decades following the publication of *Fifteen Thousand Hours*, as more and better data on school effects have become available, it has become widely accepted that schools differ in their effectiveness and, more importantly, that the factors that cause these differences are amenable to change. That said, there remains considerable disagreement about how much schools differ in their effectiveness, the factors that affect school effectiveness, and how schools can be supported in becoming more effective.

For example, while differences in student outcomes vary greatly from school to school, much of these differences appears to be attributable to factors outside the school's control. For many years, in addition to publishing the average results of students on England's national school-leaving examination, the General Certificate of Secondary Education (GCSE), for each school, the UK government also published a measure of "contextual value added" (CVA) that took account of the prior achievement of the students attending that school together with demographic characteristics (gender, ethnicity, socioeconomic status). For the 4,158 schools that had students taking GCSE examinations in 2007, the correlation between the average GCSE grades and the CVA measure was 0.27, suggesting that only around 8% of the variance in average student outcomes is currently attributable to the school (Wiliam, 2010). Analysis of data from the 2006 cycle of the Programme for International Student Assessment (PISA) examining variance in achievement *not* explained by the PISA index of economic, social, and cultural status of schools yields similar estimates for many countries:

Australia	7%
Denmark	6%
Finland	4%
New Zealand	4%
Spain	6%
Sweden	6%
United Kingdom	7%
United States	8%

Now, it is important to note that these figures tell us nothing about how good the education systems in different jurisdictions are. If all the schools are uniformly excellent, the achievement of students will be high, but the variation between schools will be small—as long as you go to school, it won't matter much which school you go to. However, these figures do tell us that similar students fare differently in different schools within the same system. More importantly, while school effects might only be 4–8% of the variation in student achievement on average, they can be hugely important for individual students.

Perhaps even more importantly, recent work on teacher quality suggests that one of the reasons that the variation between schools is small is because good teachers are fairly randomly distributed within the system, not least because it is rather difficult to identify more effective teachers with any accuracy (Wiliam, 2016). Schools can become much more effective if they support their teachers in improving.

In addition to data on the relative effectiveness of schools, PISA and other programs such as Trends in Mathematics and Science Study (TIMSS) and Progress in International Reading Study (PIRLS) have provided a wealth of information about the contextual factors influencing school performance. With all of this information about what makes schools more or less effective and with the undoubted desire of everyone working in education to make things better, we should have seen dramatic improvement in educational outcomes around the world. But we haven't.

Obviously, many—and heroic—assumptions are needed to compare results across the different cycles of PISA. But given the efforts that are made to secure the comparability of scores over time, the broad-brush conclusion from the seven cycles conducted so far (starting in 2007) is that—despite widespread, and often well-funded efforts to improve student achievement—there has been little net improvement in student achievement across the rich countries of the world.

The main reason is not, as might be assumed, that we don't know what to do. As the authors of this book point out, "We have more evidence about *what works best* for student outcomes than at any time in human history" (p. xx). As writers like Michael Fullan, Tony Bryk, Marc Tucker, and many others have pointed out, the reason is rather that most attempts to improve education have failed to address the simple fact that education systems are just that; they are *systems*. Knowing what to do is of no use if you can't implement your findings. Worse, changing one part of a system is likely to have little impact if the benefits of that change are offset by consequent changes in other parts of the system.

And this is why *Building to Impact* represents a step-change in thinking about educational improvement. Policymakers, leaders, and teachers—indeed, all of us—are, unsurprisingly, drawn to simple solutions. But as H. L. Mencken (1917/1949) wrote over 100 years ago, "there is always an easy solution to every human problem—neat, plausible, and wrong" (p. 443). Rather than pretending that school improvement is straightforward and easy, the authors face head on the inevitable complexity of improving schools. Drawing on a vast range of resources—implementation methodologies and processes, systematic reviews of research, and decades of "on the ground" experience working with teachers, leaders, and administrators—the authors present a rigorous approach that I believe represents the state of the art in school improvement.

As the authors themselves acknowledge, the 5 stages and the 18 key processes of *Building to Impact* are complex and can be challenging to implement, but that complexity should be a sign of their authenticity. After all, if there were easy solutions, we would have found them by now.

The work is not easy. As Seymour Sarason (1995) has pointed out,

> The decision to undertake change more often than not is accompanied by a kind of optimism and rosy view of the future that, temporarily at least, obscures the predictable turmoil ahead. But that turmoil cannot be avoided and how well it is coped with separates the boys from the men, the girls from the women. It is . . . rough stuff . . . it has no end point, it is a continuous process, there are breakthroughs, but also brick walls. And it is indisputably worthwhile. (p. vii)

Right now, I know of no better guide to this process than the book you have in your hands.

—**Dylan Wiliam**
UCL Institute of Education

Preface

You've got to be very careful if you don't know where you are going, because you might not get there

Yogi Berra (1998)

Education takes you places.

The relationship between access to quality schooling and longer life expectancy, greater happiness, greater earnings, and a whole host of other good things is long established and rarely disputed (Hamilton & Hattie, 2022; World Bank, 2018). The reverse leads to the reverse. A two-way street.

It's brilliant, then, that governments should invest so much in education. We deploy a global army of more than 84 million teachers to take children places. The effect of this investment has also been relatively strong. In 1920, only 32% of the world was literate; over the following 100 years, this has risen to 86% (Roser & Ortiz-Ospina, 2016). Surely this is one of the greatest achievements of human history, greater than the Pyramids and all the other wonders combined. Maybe the greatest of all.

So why the need for this book?

Because it's still not enough. Despite the global investments in education, the returns are remarkably lumpy—among countries, between schools in the same country, and even teachers in adjacent classrooms in the same school! In the predominantly English-speaking world (e.g., the United States, United Kingdom, Canada, Australia, and New Zealand), performance on international student assessments is only moderately better today than in 1970. Yes, things are improving. But the incline is too shallow, and with ever larger financial investment and increasingly overworked teachers.

Often the proposed answer to this question of educational lumpiness is more research and the design of shiny new programs to close the equity gap. However, we are going to speak sacrilege: maybe there is already enough research to be getting on with?

By our count, if you wanted to consume *all* of the existing publications on education improvement, you would need to work through 68 books and journal articles *per day* to do it in a single lifetime. This wouldn't give you enough spare time to put any of it into practice, and the research continues to grow by the hour. There are also already thousands of programs and protocols based on the existing evidence, many of which have extremely strong evidence of impact. They really do shine.

Ergo, we think the era of evidence *collection* is (largely) over. It's the era of *systematic implementation of the existing evidence* that now needs to begin. In other words, what we really need most are good implementation processes and procedures. We need processes that enable systems, schools, and teaching teams to systematically discover their most pressing needs; to systematically select, localize, or design locally appropriate high-impact approaches, based on that vast existing evidence on effective shiny things; to then deliver to the designs systematically; and to then double-back (i.e., evaluate) in order to double-up (i.e., sustain and scale thy impact).

The idea is that these processes help schools and systems to bring the (truckloads of) pre-existing evidence to life, in a manner that supports locally relevant improvement, with locally available resources and local capabilities. For the avoidance of all doubt, this also includes local evidence collection in order to check that there was indeed impact.

Most of the existing research on effective implementation comes from outside education. There is a long history of it in industry, going back more than 100 years to the work of Frederick Winslow Taylor, Henry Gantt, and James O. McKinsey. Much of it is scientific—not in terms of generating complex formulas, but in how the thinking is done (i.e., in a stepwise fashion, with checking and cross-checking against data at each stage). It's systematic to the core. Albeit the system is applied to different contexts, with different needs and that it inevitably (and desirably) leads to different initiatives and different (positive) outcomes. Same, same but different.

Despite the growing evidence that the approach to implementation (i.e., whether you have an approach, whether it is "good," and whether you actually follow it) is a major predictor of whether your improvement agenda is successful. Education has been a relative latecomer to the party. The first major handbook on education implementation did not hit the shelves until 2012 (i.e., Kelly & Perkins, 2012). Many more works have since been produced and this is strongly welcomed by us. However, they seem to fall into two broad camps:

- **Camp 1:** academic texts that wax lyrical on implementation process theory but that have limited practical application to schools and systems. Another variant of this camp is written in Malcolm Gladwell–like delicious speak. This may be a good (and fun) summer read but is challenging to put into action without developing your own process map and tools.

- **Camp 2:** practical primers that showcase *some* tools and approaches but not in enough detail that you could pick up the book and run with it. You still need to hire in the writer(s) or their teams to tell you the hidden extras or conjoin their processes with another body of knowledge.

What we felt was missing was a practical (but rigorous) step-wise process that takes educators all the way from discovering a pressing need to evaluating the impact of their selected high-probability interventions, and one that is crammed to the rafters with tools needed to support implementation and not just a couple of samples. So, we thought, why not write *that* book? And we did. And now you have it!

Building to Impact 5D is explicitly designed to be a field manual or playbook, something that you can pick up and use end to end or adapt to help you implement with rigor and impact. It combines the following:

- **Processes and practical tools** that we four (and our respective teams) already employ in our design, delivery, and evaluation work with systems, districts, and schools; and

- **A wide sweep of the global implementation science literature,** including a review of 50 implementation models and their respective tools as well as analysis of the available systematic reviews and meta-analysis on implementation success factors.

We think you will find our 5D playbook most useful if you are working at a school system, school district (i.e., overseeing several schools), schoolwide, or within-school level, seeking to generate sustainable improvement at scale. If you are part of a teaching team or a professional learning community, there's also plenty within for you to draw from. But you may not have the time or resources to follow the process from A to Z, so we also offer guidance on which elements you can undertake in a lighter-touch way.

We are not at all precious about the specifics of how you undertake local inquiry and implementation activity using the *Building to Impact 5D* playbook. You obviously need to localize to your context, resourcing level, culture, and time constraints. What we are more precious about is that you have to stop and ask each of the questions detailed within the framework before deciding what to do next—and the answers to those questions need to be generated by far more than a hunch, instinct, intuition, or gut feeling. You need to find and use data, and you need to explicitly look for disconfirming data, not just selective facts that (conveniently?) fit your preintended course of action. We are very strict about this.

As you will soon discover, there are 18 separate questions and/or processes you need to work through to properly implement *Building to Impact 5D* but you can flex the duration of each to your context. This could mean that a district-level team might spend several weeks digging and exploring one or two of these questions and/or process areas, whereas a school-level team might push forward much sooner (e.g., after a quick brainstorming session), provided everyone comes with their data! You might also move back and forth between different steps and questions, reconsidering earlier decisions as new information comes to light. This is to be expected and is completely normal. We do it all the time.

> *It takes great resolve and discipline to think and act systematically and not slip back into intuitive, hunch-based ways of operating.*

Despite this flexibility, the systems, districts, and schools that we work with often say that "it's really hard to continuously work like this." Amen to that. It takes *great* resolve and discipline to think and act systematically and not slip back into intuitive, hunch-based ways of operating. Effective implementation isn't easy. The deliberateness of thought is the important part, but it is also the cognitively fatiguing bit. It really does make your head hurt. That's why we think there is perhaps a missing role in schools and school systems: the implementation specialist or implementation scientist. This is someone whose sole job (or main job) is to support their colleagues with the mental heavy lifting and who is deeply trained in these processes. You might think of them as a cross between an educational strategy consultant, a project manager, and a formative evaluator—all in one. Other forms of specialists already exist in our world: data specialists, governance specialists, leadership improvement specialists, assessment specialists, and so on. So, why not implementation specialists? Think about it.

And now to the credits. Many people have supported and enhanced our thinking as we codified the *Building to Impact 5D* framework. These include Arran's colleagues (past and present) at Cognition Education: Shaun Hawthorne, Mary Sinclair, Brian Hinchco, Phil Coogan, Mel Sproston, Helen Butler, Lindsey Conner, Jenna Crawley, Christophe Mullins, Nigel Bowen, Durgesh Rajandiran, and Tina Lucas.

John thanks all the consultants and implementers within the Corwin Visible Learning team who have taught him about implementation and their enablers and barriers, and he thanks the team within the Australian Institute for Teaching and School Leadership (AITSL) who show him so often what it means to translate evidence into action.

Janet thanks her evaluation team at the Centre for Program Evaluation and the leadership team at the Melbourne Graduate School of Education where so much implementation occurs.

Doug thanks his colleagues at Creative Leadership Solutions, Arran for orchestrating the book, and John for his continued global impact on education.

We all thank Dylan Wiliam, who took the time to go through our manuscript to help us buttress and improve and who also wrote the foreword! And the brilliant team at Corwin who brought this project to life, especially Jessica Allan, Lucas Schleicher, Amy Schroller, and Christina West.

Obviously, our thinking didn't emerge from the ether. It very much builds on and from the heavy lifting done by others, including Michael Fullan, Thomas Guskey, Abraham Wandersman, Sir Michael Barber, Russell Bishop, Viviane Robinson, Lant Pritchett, and (the aforementioned) Dylan Wiliam. We owe these folks a great intellectual debt. They may not agree with all in this book but their words and actions have been a major inspiration.

And now back to the start.

In addition to being one of the greatest catchers in baseball history, Yogi Berra was something of a sage, renowned for his "Yogi-isms." When he said, "You've got to be very careful if you don't know where you are going, because you might not get there," he was 10,000% right. And that's the whole point of *Building to Impact 5D*: to help you systematically decide on the destination, to then explore the different ways you could undertake the journey, to put one or more of those journey plans into action, to check whether it is working, and then to decide what to do next.

When you know where you are going, when you have a plan, and when you systematically check and revise, you will get there—albeit with unexpected twists and turns along the way.

If you want business as usual, move along. But if you seek deep and delicious impact, read on.

—Arran Hamilton
Kuala Lumpur, Malaysia

—Douglas Reeves
Boston, Massachusetts, USA

—Janet Clinton
Melbourne, Australia

—John Hattie
Melbourne, Australia

About the Authors

Dr. Arran Hamilton is Group Director of Education at Cognition Education. Previously, he has held senior positions at Cambridge University Press and Assessment, Education Development Trust, the British Council, Nord Anglia Education, and a research fellowship at Warwick University. His core focus is on translating evidence into impact at scale, and he has overseen the design, delivery, and evaluation of education programs across the Pacific Islands, East Asia, the Middle East, the United Kingdom, Australia, and New Zealand. Arran's recent publications include *The Gold Papers* and *The Lean Education Manifesto*.

Dr. Douglas B. Reeves is the author of more than 40 books and more than 100 articles on leadership and education. He has twice been named to the Harvard University Distinguished Authors Series and was named the Brock International Laureate for his contributions to education. His career of work in professional learning led to the Contribution to the Field Award from the US National Staff Development Council, now Learning Forward. He was also named the William Walker Scholar by the Australian Council of Educational Leaders. His recent books include *Deep Change Leadership*, *Achieving Equity and Excellence*, *From Leading to Succeeding*, and *Fearless Schools*. Doug is the founder of Creative Leadership Solutions, with the mission to improve educational opportunities for students throughout the world using creative solutions for leadership, policy, teaching, and learning. Through this he has worked across more than 40 countries.

Dr. Janet M. Clinton is the Deputy Dean of the Melbourne Graduate School of Education (MGSE), Director of the Teacher and Teaching Effectiveness Research Hub, and Professor in Evaluation at MGSE. She has wide international experience as an evaluator and educator and has an extensive publication record. She has led over 120 international evaluation projects across multiple disciplines, in particular education and health. Her major interest in program evaluation is the development of evaluation theory, mixed methodologies, and data analytics. Janet's current evaluation work focuses on development of evaluation frameworks and implementation protocols, as well as using evaluation as a vehicle for change and building capacity through extensive stakeholder engagement.

Dr. John Hattie is Emeritus Laureate Professor at the Melbourne Graduate School of Education at the University of Melbourne, Co-Director of the Hattie Family Foundation, and Chair of the Board of the Australian Institute for Teaching and School Leadership. His areas of interest are measurement models and their applications to education's problems as well as models of teaching and learning. John has published and presented over 1,600 papers, supervised 200 thesis students, and published 60 books, including 28 on understanding and applying the Visible Learning research.

Introduction

In research institutes across the planet, scientists are grappling with various mind-bending conundrums. Some are trying to take the notion of a *Star Trek* "warp drive" from fantasy to reality (Lentz, 2021); others are seeking to untangle the mysteries of consciousness (Hawkins, 2021); and yet others are attempting to discover whether beneath the atom is another level of near-invisible vibrating strings (Kiritsis, 2019). These researchers are largely feeling their way in the dark—developing new hypotheses, creating new tools, and conducting new research to move human knowledge forward, a few millimeters at a time. Often, their search takes wrong turns and leads them down long and winding cul-de-sacs that they must quickly reverse back out of. Once ground-breaking discoveries are made, then come further challenges: convincing the nonbelievers, finding practical applications, and rolling out innovations at scale.

We, by contrast, have a much easier time of it. Our "experiments" with education have been long-running. The "pilot studies" took place in 1760s Prussia and from this, a global model of schooling was tested, iterated, and then scaled across the planet (Vincent, 2019). The data on *what works best* have also grown at an exponential rate. By our count, there are now more than 1.5 million research articles and books on how to teach, how to learn, how to run schools, and how to improve learner outcomes. Visible Learning Meta[x] (2021) plots a course through these data—cataloging and aggregating the findings of more than 1,800 meta-analyses of over 100,000 quantitative studies, involving more than 300 million students (https://www.visiblelearningmetax.com).

Compared to the scientists tinkering with their (theoretical) warp drives and models of particle physics, our business of education arguably sits on firmer foundations. From decades of cognitive psychology lab studies, we know a great deal about memory, attention, forgetting, motivation, transfer, habit formation, and the stages of child development. We also have an Everest-sized mountain of research that evaluates school-based programs built from these cognitive psychology principles. And we have the (thousands of) programs themselves—a rich toolset to select from and implement in local educational contexts.

In fact, by the early 1970s, our collective wisdom on *what works best* was already in such good shape—with over 200 years of trial-and-error experience under our belts—that it had been codified into teacher training and licensing programs, standards, curricula, and school management systems. Coincidentally, 1970 was also the year when nations implemented the first international student assessments (i.e., the early precursors to the Programme for International Student Assessment [PISA], Trends in International Mathematics and Science Study [TIMSS], and Progress in International Reading Literacy Study [PIRLS]), with the tests then being readministered every 3–5 years. So, we should expect that with all the tried and tested tools at our collective disposal that student achievement on these international assessments would be on the up and up.

To be fair, when we look at the proportion of students achieving at the *minimum threshold* (i.e., not outright failing the test), nations have got markedly better, with an average of 93% of learners now reaching this level in the predominantly English-speaking countries. However, much of this gap closure occurred before 2000 and the needle has not moved much further in the last 20 or so years. Figure 0.1 provides an illustration.

FIGURE 0.1 ● Percentage of Students Achieving the Minimum Threshold on International Assessments, 1970–2015

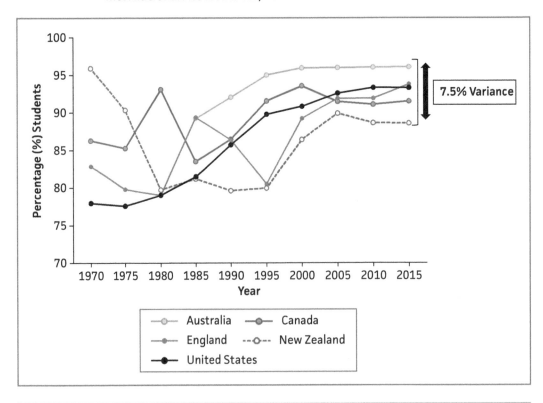

Source: Altinok et al. (2018). This dataset pools data on student achievement on international standardized student assessments for 168 countries between 1970 and 2015. Tests have been harmonized and aggregated across subject area (i.e., science, reading, mathematics) and levels (primary and secondary schooling).

When we look, however, at the translation of research evidence into action at the *advanced threshold* (i.e., students getting an "A grade" equivalent on the tests), the picture is much less impressive. As Figure 0.2 highlights, over 45 years, Australia and Canada have inched up only a few percentage points and New Zealand has (ever-so-slightly) declined. The United States and England have done better, with nearly 30% of students achieving at the *advanced threshold*, albeit with snakes and ladders along the way. However, this is still at less than half the level achieved by the likes of Singapore, South Korea, or Japan. Oh dear.

Of course, there are obvious caveats with the use of this dataset and our interpretation, which we highlight in "The Caveats" textbox.

FIGURE 0.2 ● Percentage of Students Achieving the Advanced Threshold on International Assessments, 1970–2015

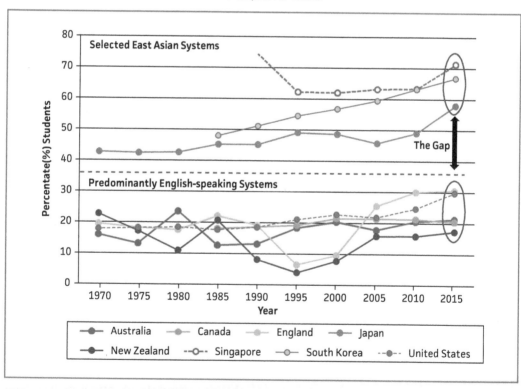

Source: Altinok et al. (2018). This dataset pools data on student achievement on international standardized student assessments for 168 countries between 1970 and 2015. Tests have been harmonized and aggregated across subject area (i.e., science, reading, mathematics) and levels (primary and secondary schooling).

THE CAVEATS

- First, we have to assume that these international assessments tell us something useful and valid about the quality of teaching and learning within each education system (not everyone agrees; e.g., see Zhao, 2020).

- Second, to compare countries on a single metric over time, student scores on different types of tests, for different subject areas, and different ages have been blended and averaged. So, we should treat this as a very rough picture rather than an ultra-precise description of the standing of each national education system.

- Third, the coverage is only to 2015. However, our own separate analysis of the most recent PISA, TIMSS, and PIRLS data does not (unfortunately) suggest a sudden radical improvement (Mullis et al., 2017, 2020; Organization for Economic Cooperation and Development, 2019).

- Fourth, even though there are *major* disparities in the performance of East Asian vs. the predominantly English-speaking systems, we can't be sure that it's the quality of schooling (and not, for example, national culture, family factors, or the prevalence of private tutoring) that explains those differences.

Despite these caveats, we still see that Singapore, Japan, and South Korea can get a high proportion of their students to *consistently* perform at the advanced threshold (and the same for Taiwan, Hong Kong, and to a lesser extent Russia and Northern Ireland, which we excluded from the graph to reduce the clutter). **This tells us that it is *theoretically* possible for the majority (and not a minority) of children in the United States, United Kingdom, Canada, Australia, and New Zealand—and indeed everywhere—to achieve at the very highest levels, too.**

There is also no shortage of research on high-impact strategies that enable children to achieve at the said highest of levels. Visible Learning Meta[x] showcases a large number of approaches that, when properly implemented, have *significantly* enhanced student achievement. A handful of these generate an effect size of over $d = 1.0$ and several handfuls consistently achieve effect sizes of over $d = 0.60$. This is powerful stuff. And it's all the more powerful because most of the research was conducted in predominantly English-speaking countries (mainly the United States, United Kingdom, Canada, and Australia) and written in English. So, it *should* be both more accessible and more directly relevant to those contexts.

Therefore, to us, it seems that there is a profound gap between the empirical wisdom locked in the global research and the subsequent translation of those pearls into impact in schools and classrooms at scale. Houston, maybe we have an implementation problem?

By *implementation problem*, we don't "just" mean the challenge of sticking to an evidence-based program and seeing it through, although this is undoubtedly an important part of it. There are, in addition, a whole host of *preceding* and *proceeding* steps, including discovery or identification of an appropriate education challenge to respond to, the design or adaptation of suitable evidence-informed interventions, and delivery to the design. Then comes the doubling-back through the prior chain of actions (a) to monitor whether you did the things you set out to and (b) to evaluate whether those actions led to (sufficient) impact. Then comes doubling-up: iteratively enhancing, sustaining, and perhaps also scaling the success to other schools. **Implementation** is considerably bigger than just implementation.

Implementation is considerably bigger than just implementation.

WE ARE NOT ALONE

We should, however, take heart that education is not the only sector confronting this global evidence vs. local impact conundrum. Our cousins in health care face the exact same challenge. By some estimates, it takes an average of 17 years for new medical advances to become widely adopted, and with considerable attrition along the way (Grant et al., 2003; Morris et al., 2011). Then, after adoption, health care practitioners frequently skip steps in these now-accepted protocols because they are not practical, and/or they localize processes to better fit their individual clinic or hospital but with crucial aspects being so watered down they are washed away (Gawande, 2010).

Take, for example, the insertion of an intravenous (IV) line, which is a common medical procedure for administering medicines and fluid drips. Medical science already tells us the optimum procedure for insertion, **monitoring**, and management. But each year more than 250,000 people still get bloodstream infections because steps in the process have not been implemented with fidelity (Haddadin et al., 2021). Some steps get plain missed. Others get adapted to fit the local context, but the adaptation reduces efficacy and bacteria creep in. Adaptation can (literally) be a killer.

Some of the common implementation barriers that medical treatment designers confront include the *Critical Nine* listed next. You might be tempted to skip over this and rejoin the conversation when we get back to education-speak, but it's worth you investing mental energy into processing these Critical Nine now. You will find out why later on!

THE CRITICAL NINE BARRIERS TO IMPLEMENTATION IN HEALTH CARE

1. **Dissemination:** making health care practitioners *aware* of the research findings and making them understand why they should care and/or how it is relevant to their work (a.k.a. *marketing*).

2. **Uptake:** clinicians being motivated to overcome the opportunity-cost and adopt the new approach rather than maintaining the status quo (a.k.a. *desire*).

3. **Productization:** turning the findings into a standardized (and easy to follow) set of protocols that can be used in the field by hospitals, clinics, and health care practitioners in different local contexts (a.k.a. *professional codes*).

4. **Need:** the new protocols actually being relevant to goals or problems in the local health care setting (a.k.a. *contextual fit*).

5. **Beliefs:** health care professionals may see what they do as an art or a craft that is *informed* by science rather than as a set of (robotic) rules-based protocols that need to be followed to the letter (a.k.a. *professional creed*).

6. **Training:** the need to support clinicians in effective implementation of the new evidence-based protocols through workshops, coaching, on-the-job training, and so on (a.k.a. *professional learning and development*).

7. **Maintenance and fidelity:** recognizing that over time, adopting clinicians may skip steps, mix and match with their previous way of doing things, or completely revert to their prior practice (a.k.a. *grit*).

8. **Scaling:** when a treatment designer works closely with a single hospital, they can support effective implementation by health care professionals. But when new treatments are implemented across hundreds of hospitals, they cannot provide the same level of support and undesirable adaptations and backsliding gradually creep in (a.k.a. *pushing water up a mountain*).

9. **De-implementation:** to adopt something new, health care practitioners need to free up space in their days to address all the above and make it stick. This requires the identification of existing value-subtracting activities and the dropping of them like hot potatoes to make room for impact (a.k.a. *there just aren't 36 hours in a day*).

And many of the above may be difficult to address without wider system change.

Health care researchers have become so concerned about the implementation gap that they have established a whole new sub-field called *implementation science* (Bauer et al., 2015). Its purpose is to systematize the effective rollout of high-impact approaches across hospitals and clinics that often operate under different and decentralized management, with different local community demographics and health care needs and with different organizational resources, skill levels, interests, willingness, and capability to implement. Most of the best-available research and practical tools for implementation now come from this health care subdiscipline!

BUT WHAT HAS ANY OF THIS GOT TO DO WITH EDUCATION?

The quick answer: quite a lot.

Before reading on, we want you to double-back to the Critical Nine in the previous subsection, but this time we want you to mentally find and replace some words.

FIND	REPLACE WITH
Health care practitioner	Educator
Clinician	Teacher
Hospital	School district
Clinic	School
Health care setting	Education setting
Treatment designer	Educational program developer

And if this is too long a list for you to remember, here's a simpler rule: just replace any medical-sounding term with a similar education-related term.

How was it for you?

We think you will see and agree that the education sector faces *exactly* the same sort of implementation challenge as health care. We hope you will also see that we, therefore, need our own version of health care's implementation science. And this is where we think *Building to Impact 5D* can help.

WHAT EXACTLY IS BUILDING TO IMPACT 5D?

It's a carefully designed **implementation** methodology for use by schools and systems to *discover* goals worth pursuing and/or problems worth addressing and then for the **design** of instruments, tools, and/or processes that are up to the task of generating that impact.

With the design work complete, next comes **delivery**, which is about bringing the designs to life. Then **double-back**, which is the act of retracing your steps to monitor progress and evaluate impact. And, finally, **double-up** to learn from the retracing to iterate, sustain, and scale. You might have noticed that all the highlighted words began with D and that there were five of them: hence, 5D!

What about the first three words, *Building to Impact*? We systematically crawled the design space in search of these special words and their specific ordering. The first word, *Building*, implies careful design. House builders, for example, do not usually arrive at a parcel of land with some diggers and make it up as they go along. They generally turn up with a carefully architected plan that is responsive to the contours of the land, meets the zoning regulations, and ensures the finished structure fits into the environment and is fit for purpose.

Of course, if you have watched TV programs like *Love It or List It* or *Grand Designs*, you'll notice that oftentimes when construction gets going there are unforeseen events that have architects and builders doubling-back to the designs in order to iterate and adapt. Sometimes an industry-standard practice just won't fit this specific context, other times something important was accidentally overlooked, and yet other times the sponsor has changed their mind: they now want a subterranean swimming pool. Ergo, the word *Building* implies that before you get implementing, you need a well-thought-out design that responds to a discovered need; but you also need to be (systematically) responsive and reactive to the changing circumstances as you deliver on that design.

The third word, *Impact*, signals a clear purpose to the enterprise. That purpose is wider than getting the initiative finished and ticking off all the items on your to-do list. You are, instead, embarking on a quest, a crusade, a compelling cause, a noble mission. It's not over until you have generated (sufficient) impact and the only thing on your mind is that impact. The design you are building is a means to your noble end. If your design doesn't deliver that end, you have no compunction in tearing the whole edifice down and starting again. Obviously, you would prefer to iterate and to adapt—as would we. But always you are driven by the impact. You don't fetishize the means.

Finally, the second word, *to*, signals that this is a work in progress. It's a building project that is underway now and that in some sense might always need to be underway. Certainly, once you have the main structure watertight and functional, the intensity of effort diminishes. But there are always going to be ongoing maintenance and repair activities to sustain the brilliance you have nurtured and stop it all from turning to dust.

WHO IS BUILDING TO IMPACT 5D FOR?

If you are looking to implement **school system–level**, **school district–level**, **schoolwide**, or **within-school improvement** at scale, we think you will find this book and its methodology extremely useful. You can use these processes, tools, and approaches to establish a backbone organization for systematic impact.

If you are part of a **professional learning community** that is looking to work together to pursue a common learning and implementation agenda, there is also a lot in here for you. You might not need to follow the processes from A to Z (you might not have the time to be able to), but you will still find approaches and ways of thinking that will significantly enhance your impact.

HOW DID WE DEVELOP *BUILDING TO IMPACT 5D* AND WHAT ARE THE PROCESSES?

To develop *Building to Impact 5D*, we undertook the following:

1. **Analyzed 50 different implementation methodologies** and processes, spanning education, business management, strategic consulting, health care, manufacturing, construction, international development, software engineering, and human resources. As a result, we identified more than 100 subprocesses and tools. See Appendices 1 and 2 for a high-level overview.

2. Identified **23 (fairly) common implementation processes** across the 50 methodologies, spanning goal selection, tool identification, implementation, monitoring and evaluation, iteration/adaptation, and maintenance and scaling (Hamilton & Hattie, 2022; Meyers et al., 2012). See Appendix 3.

3. Drew on existing **meta-analyses** and **systematic reviews** on implementation (e.g., Dunst & Trivette, 2012; Durlak & DuPre, 2008; Fixsen et al., 2005; Greenhalgh et al., 2004; Meyers et al., 2012; O'Donnell, 2008; Stith et al., 2006) to help whittle down the processes, subprocesses, and tools to a more manageable level because we know that there aren't enough hours in a

lifetime to put all these different processes and tools into practice! See Appendix 4.

4. Combined this with our hands-on experience of supporting system, district, and school-level implementation initiatives across more than 50 countries, with more than 100,000 educators—supported by our wider teams. And we also drew on our prior publications on this thorny question of implementation (e.g., Hamilton & Hattie, 2021, 2022; Hattie et al., 2020; Reeves, 2009, 2021a).

We then slotted these processes and tools into the *Building to Impact* 5D methodology. As already highlighted, the five stages of this are all D words (i.e., **5D** for short):

- **D1: Discover**—identifying goals that are worth pursuing above all else, building a theory of the present, and agreeing on what success looks like.

- **D2: Design**—systematically examining the different options in the design space, selecting/designing a high-probability intervention, stress testing before launch, and developing your monitoring and evaluation plan. It's also about identifying things you will simultaneously STOP to make room for impact.

- **D3: Deliver**—putting your agreed interventions into action and collecting monitoring and evaluation data.

- **D4: Double-Back**—monitoring and evaluating your delivery chain to decide where to next. This might take you back to Stages D1 and D2 and/or forward to Stage D5, or it might result in your stopping altogether (e.g., either because it's not working or it's already working well enough).

- **D5: Double-Up**—either implementing and maintaining enhanced versions of an intervention in the same local setting and/or working to imbed it across multiple schools (i.e., this is all about sustainability and/or scaling).

As you scan the diagrammatic representation of *Building to Impact* 5D in Figures 0.3 and 0.4, you will notice that double-back (i.e., **evaluation**) explicitly seeps into all the other stages. This is because there are evaluative foundations that need to be laid in Stages D1, D2, and D3 to make sure you can properly evaluate in Stage D4. If you miss these steps, you cannot properly evaluate your impact and you are therefore not actually implementing 5D; sadly, it is highly likely that your initiative will (horribly) die! But this doubling-back isn't just about having systems in place to evaluate after delivery has commenced. It's also about having mini-double-back cycles embedded within each stage, so that you pre-evaluate or stress test all the key links in the (hypothetical) chain prior to confirming that the goals are sound and the designs sound before calling the diggers in.

As you cycle through 5D, one of the key challenges you will face is what mathematicians call *optimal stopping*. In other words, this is the decision about how long you spend searching, gathering data, and reviewing options before you just get on and do something, anything. The mathematicians suggest that the optimum proportion of time spent on searching and exploring is 37% (Christian & Griffiths, 2017), leaving 63% of your time for implementation, evaluation, and beyond. If you are seeking to implement an initiative at a great scale, at great cost, and across multiple schools, then this seems about right to us. However, if you are working at the level of a single school or a professional learning community, we accept the case for greater speed. Otherwise, you might find that a semester or term has gone by and you are still talking/exploring and analyzing, without any doing in the works.

FIGURE 0.3 ● *Building to Impact 5D*

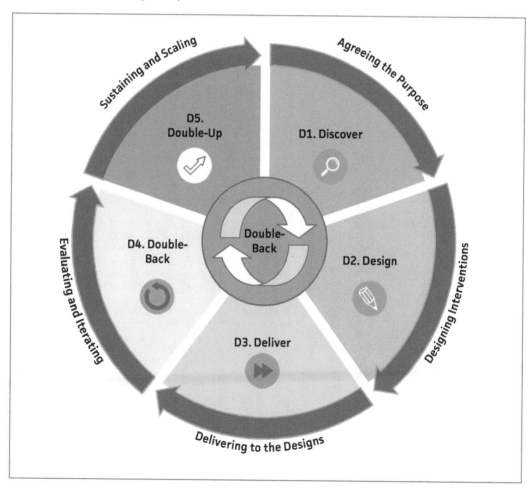

FIGURE 0.4 Unpacking the *Building to Impact 5D* Stages

D1 DISCOVER	D2 DESIGN	D3 DELIVER	D4 DOUBLE-BACK	D5 DOUBLE-UP
Agree on ONE Education challenge that's worth progressing above ALL else	Systematically search and agree on high-probability interventions to START and to STOP	Implement and de-implement AGREED designs	Monitor and evaluate your delivery chain and agree on PRIORITY actions	Maintain and grow your IMPACT
1.1 Establish a Backbone Organization 1.2 Decide the Education Challenge 1.3 Explain the Education Challenge 1.4 Agree on What Better Looks Like	2.1 Explore Options in the Design Space 2.2 Build Program Logic Model(s) 2.3 Stress Test Logic Model(s) 2.4 Agree on What to STOP 2.5 Establish a Monitoring and Evaluation Plan	3.1 Lock the Delivery Approach and Plan 3.2 Undertake Delivery 3.3 Collect Monitoring and Evaluation Data	4.1 Monitor your Evaluation 4.2 Monitor your Delivery 4.3 Evaluate Your Delivery and Agree on Next Steps Using the Step 2.1–2.4 Tools 4.4 Evaluate your Evaluation!	5.1 Sustainability Considerations 5.2 Scaling Considerations

To reiterate, *double-back* (i.e., evaluative checking) is explicitly embedded throughout the 5D framework. This is a deliberate response to the fact that too frequently evaluative actions and checking are missing at all levels of implementation. We never just turn up with educational diggers and cement mixers and make it up as we go along. We have a design, but we adjust it based on the feedback from delivery, to grow our impact.

In Figure 0.5 we provide a process map that illustrates the stages and activities you will undertake to implement the 5D process. Start at the bottom of this figure and follow the arrows up to the top and back down again! You will also see that the process map clearly delineates the Double-Back–oriented activities.

However, a clear implication of all this double-back being baked into each of the other Ds is that what looks on the surface like a highly linear implementation model is anything but. Out in the real world, actual implementation *could* look something like what is illustrated in Figure 0.6.

You circle round and round. Thinking, testing, trialing, and iterating. You can think of those double-back processes as continually flipping between *divergent thinking* (i.e., getting creative) and *convergent thinking* (i.e., getting critical) in order to *agree* on what you will do. We illustrate this in Figure 0.7.

SURELY, YOU CAN'T BE SERIOUS?

Here is one of the common reactions that we get when we share these processes: "It's way too difficult to follow this. We need something simpler." However, the case we want to make is that implementation is difficult. And that's why so much school and system improvement activity ends up failing. Yes, you can vary the quantity of time that you spend on each of these processes: either *thinking slow*, digging deep, and carefully analyzing each micropararameter before implementing; or *thinking fast*, spending a few hours on each step in brainstorming workshops before pivoting to quick implementation and review cycles. This is back to that question of optimal stopping. And our guidance is that it all depends on the scale of what you are trying to accomplish. The bigger the goal, the larger the number of people, and the more difficult it is to reverse, the more likely that you will benefit from *thinking slow*.

It helps considerably if the investigators and/or implementors are steeped in the kinds of causal reasoning, empirical cross-checking, and evaluative questioning that we outline in this book. And we know that this bit is hard. So, we want to make a play: We think that there is potentially a missing role at the school and district levels—the *implementation specialist* or even the *implementation scientist*—for this is a science-based approach. This person has been

FIGURE 0.5 A Walk-Through of *Building to Impact 5D*

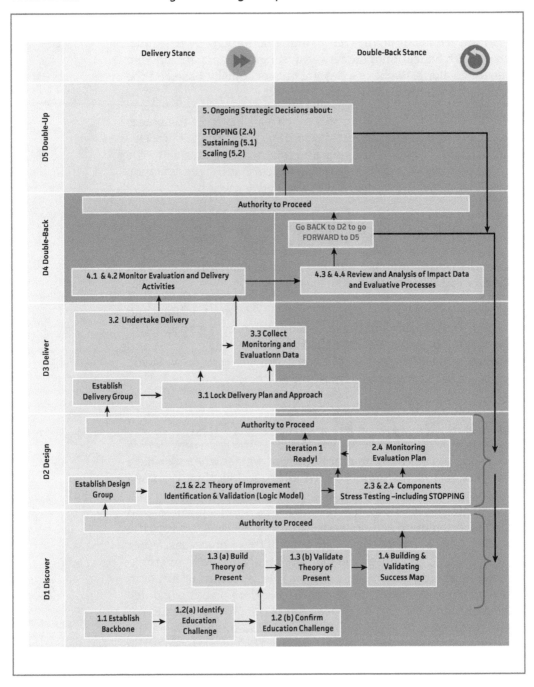

FIGURE 0.6 Iterative Implementation

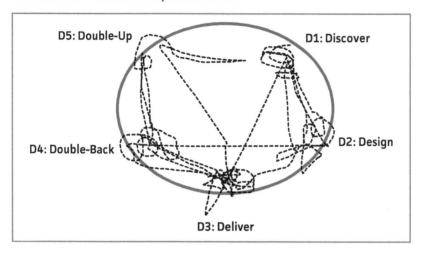

FIGURE 0.7 The Double-Back Mind Frame

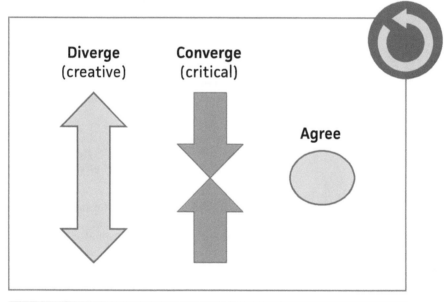

Source: Copyright © Cognition Education Group (2022). All rights reserved.

trained in the ways of thinking and acting that we unpack within the *Building to Impact 5D* framework. They know the tools, they know where to find external sources of data, and they know how to systematically evaluate the collective impact, for the purpose of growing it. They are also a source of continuity as school leaders come and go. And (ideally) they are interchangeable because they use these tools, this language, and these processes. So, when one goes and another one comes, they support stakeholders to stay true to the data, the evidence, and the impact. They don't come with anecdotal inference and suggest that everyone immediately change course because of some shiny fad that was popular at their last school or district. They see pre-existing initiatives through, and they caution new school leaders from throwing the baby out with the bathwater.

We know that such a role and activity is important because a range of studies have explicitly explored what happens when you attend to these implementation features vs. when you don't. Some of the key data points include those listed in Figure 0.8, although a longer list is provided in Appendix 4.

FIGURE 0.8 Systematic Reviews on Implementation

RESEARCH	DESCRIPTION AND FINDINGS
Daniels et al. (2021)	• Reviewed 74 studies on implementation of workplace health and well-being programs. Identified the following key implementation variables: plan continuation, learning/evaluation, and effective governance.
Derzon et al. (2005)	• Concluded that programs with **robust implementation and monitoring processes generate impact effect sizes an average of 2 times higher and sometimes up to 12 times higher**.
DuBois et al. (2002)	• Reviewed 59 mentoring studies, finding that **the single step of monitoring the level of implementation resulted in significantly higher impact effect sizes (0.18 vs. 0.06)**.
Micheli et al. (2018)	• Reviewed 104 studies on key features for successful use of design thinking–based approaches. These include abductive reasoning, design-oriented tools, interdisciplinary collaboration, and welcoming ambiguity in the design process.
Smith et al. (2004)	• Reviewed 14 whole-school antibullying initiatives. While finding that none of the programs were highly effective, they identified that **the settings that rigorously monitored implementation generated 2 times the effect size**.
Tobler (1986)	• Reviewed 143 adolescent drug-prevention interventions, finding that **well-implemented programs generated an effect size 0.36 MORE than less well-implemented programs**.
Wilson et al. (2003)	• Reviewed 221 programs, involving 56,000 participants, focused on reducing aggressive behaviors in schools, concluding that **implementation processes were the most important variable that influenced outcomes**.

Of course, the absence of an implementation specialist role is not a license for you to do nothing. Until systems come to recognize the gap, you need to take action yourselves, drawing on these tools, processes, and ways of thinking and acting to get serious and scientific about implementing.

POSTSCRIPT

Finally, a word on the structure of the book. Each of the following chapters vectors in on one of the 5Ds. These "D" chapters all start with an introduction that provides context. They then each follow the relevant part of the process map introduced in Figure 0.4, with sections devoted to unpacking and explaining each process. Implementation is a fiendishly complex topic, but we have tried to keep our language informal and to pack the book with practical tools that you can directly apply in your context. The Conclusion recaps the key messages, and (for the geeks) we include four appendices that catalog our key findings and learnings from the global implementation research. The key takeaway is that this isn't just another high-level process that pours old (implementation) wine into new bottles. It has been carefully researched and field tested, and it blends the liquids into a better drink: We hope you can leverage it to build your own impact.

With that preamble out the way, it's time to Discover!

CHAPTER 1

D1: Discover

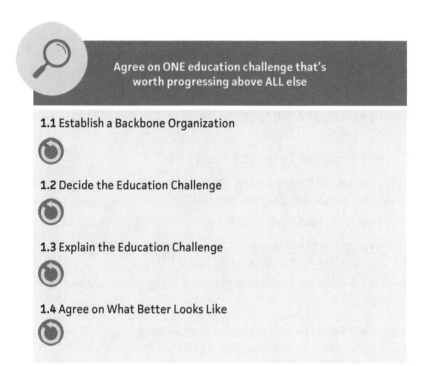

Agree on ONE education challenge that's worth progressing above ALL else

1.1 Establish a Backbone Organization

1.2 Decide the Education Challenge

1.3 Explain the Education Challenge

1.4 Agree on What Better Looks Like

INTRODUCTION

Human history is resplendent with brilliant acts of accomplishment. These include the crafting of the Pyramids, Stonehenge, and the Great Wall of China to more modern feats like carving out the Panama Canal, putting astronauts on the moon, and (more controversially) undertaking the Manhattan Project to unleash nuclear capabilities. We have become deeply skilled at bringing complex goals to life.

None of our greatest feats emerged through osmosis. They each started with a clear goal or challenge. They each leveraged the collective knowledge, capabilities, and technology available at the time. They each involved the mobilization of vast legions of people, often for long durations. Sometimes for centuries. They were each singular in focus. And none of them got it right the first time. In fact, the path to success was often littered with failure, after failure, after failure. With brilliance then (eventually) emerging from the rubble.

Take the 1969 moon landings. Humanity would never have made it if the goal was a passing whim, if there was no backbone organization to drive learning and implementation (NASA), if the goal wildly exceeded the available technology (i.e., before the invention of rocketry), or if it was one of many competing priorities of the backbone agency (Brinkley, 2019). Imagine what would have happened if alongside the quest to put people on the moon, NASA were also charged with curing cancer, inventing the internet, and building flying cars. Likely nothing, because NASA's success in the 1960s was arguably the result of its single, publicly proclaimed, and unambiguous goal: getting astronauts onto the surface of the moon (and back again) before the end of the decade.

The clear lessons from humanities' greatest past successes are as follows (Kotter, 2012):

1. Have goals that are widely agreed on.
2. Set goals with deep rather than wide ambitions (i.e., trying to push ONE dream rather than multiple dreams).
3. Establish a backbone organization to bring the goals to life.
4. Assume that success won't be achieved easily and possibly not through the means originally intended.
5. Have a rigorous implementation process (e.g., *Building to Impact 5D*).

Before you get moving, you need to ensure that you have identified the right priorities.

If you are reading these words, it is likely because you have an intuition, hunch, or inkling that there is something that could and should be improved in your school or district. Most improvement initiatives start this way. After all, unless you already have a *feeling* that something needs to be done to improve on the status quo, why would you *want* to embark on any form of crusade? However, before you get moving, you need to ensure that you have identified the *right* priorities:

*   That the area you have identified is *uniquely* important to improve vs. all the other things you could be doing with your time—including doing nothing at all;
*   That it is actually *amenable* to change; and
*   That you haven't bitten off *more* than you can ever hope to chew.

In other words, you need to make sure that you have identified the right priority, that it is something that you have the resources and expertise to meaningfully enhance, and that you are not attempting to pursue too many such agendas simultaneously (i.e., the road to nothing). This is where **Stage D1: Discover** comes into play, which is where you establish your **backbone organization** (1.1.), decide and explain your **education challenge** (1.2 and 1.3), and agree on what better looks like (1.4).

1.1 ESTABLISH A BACKBONE ORGANIZATION

Once you have an *inkling* that you want to accomplish something, you need to establish a backbone organization (Kania & Kramer, 2011) to explore the local landscape to identify and confirm a suitable goal, or what we call the education challenge. There is something a bit chicken and egg about this. On the one hand, you are unlikely to set up a formal structure unless you already have a good idea about what you want to use it for. But on the other hand—if after setting it up, you dive straight into the implementation of plans, programs, and activities—how can you be sure that you are actually spending your time on worthwhile education challenges? The danger is that you end up implementing ill-thought-out initiatives that generate not one iota of meaningful impact.

The backbone team is often a temporary organization. Its sole purpose is to (1) drive the search for appropriate meaty/challenging goals, (2) design initiatives to achieve the goals, and (3) then implement, evaluate, iterate/sustain/scale, or stop. It acts as the central nervous system of your initiative.

If you are working at the district, state, or national level, your backbone team is more likely to comprise full-time/seconded members—who live and breathe the process for 100% of their working hours. However, if you are working at the school or departmental level, it is more likely that your backbone team will be made up of people who are already wearing multiple hats; thus, you are less likely to have the luxury to enable the team to shed all their existing business-as-usual tasks. However, your quest is more likely to be effective if at least one (but ideally more) of your backbone team members has their load significantly lightened so that they can focus their thinking and implementation energies on generating big, deep impact. It also helps if at least one of the members has been explicitly trained as an implementation specialist.

Here are some of the core roles that you will want to have on your backbone team:

1. **Sponsor(s).** The sponsor or sponsorship group is the ultimate owner and endorser of the activity. They are likely to be very senior stakeholders within the organization (e.g., the school leadership team or cluster/district/system leadership), with

the authority and budget to authorize the inquiry, establish the backbone team, and communicate to other parts of the organization that *this is important, you should take it seriously,* and *you need to engage.* They should also meet with the backbone team regularly to check on progress, provide encouragement, iterate collective thinking, and agree on how they can best use their leverage, authority, and expertise to maintain collective momentum throughout the wider system or the school.

2. **Team leader(s).** The team leader is responsible for leading and coaching the backbone team to identify goals worthy of everyone's time and energy and then to design and implement initiatives with a high probability of generating impact. You might have one team leader or co-leaders. Ideal team leaders can walk the tightrope between being analytic and agile, and it helps if they have a runway of several years remaining with the organization so that they can see things through.

3. **Investigators.** In partnership with the team leader(s), the investigators are going to undertake and/or facilitate the search, design, delivery, and double-back activities. The investigators are the backbone of your backbone organization! They get into schools and classrooms and engage with teachers, students, parents, and the community—gathering data, testing ideas, supporting implementation, and doubling-back on everything.

4. **External facilitator (optional).** An implementation specialist/scientist who has a deep understanding of these processes and wider methodologies is one example of an external facilitator. Their role is to coach and support, to warn you that you are getting into the weeds, and to help you get back out again.

In living organisms, backbones are crucial. In mammals, all the important wiring and information passes through them. But they are part of a wider architecture that co-opts other resources in to do the thinking, moving, lifting, sensing, and feeling. Your backbone team will likely operate in the same way—connecting with and drawing on expertise within and outside your organization to support that thinking, moving, and lifting. And some of your membership might change to reflect the types of expertise needed at different stages of inquiry—adding different types of flesh to the bone. For example, during the Discover (D1) and Design (D2) stages of *Building to Impact 5D,* you will likely need access to more analytic and inquiry-oriented team members to help you search the options in the design space. Think of this as like an (educational) management consulting skill-set. During Stage D3 (Deliver), you also need people with a project management mindset—people who can get things done.

If you are leveraging *Building to Impact 5D* as an inquiry process within the department of a school or more informally within teaching teams, you probably won't need to get as hung up on the explicit notion of a backbone organization structure and formal role descriptors. You might, for example, already have a well-functioning professional learning community model in place, and you might decide that you want to focus on using the methodology and tools in this book *within* that existing organizational structure. That's perfectly fine.

However, if you are working at the whole school, district, or system level, then explicitly having a backbone organization and giving the members a label and *articles of incorporation* (i.e., license to operate) significantly increases the probability that they and the wider system will take the investigation seriously. These articles outline the purpose of the entity and the rights and duties of the members.

Your articles of incorporation likely include the following:

- A statement of purpose,
- A term limit,
- Membership,
- Roles and responsibilities,
- What it is that people are committing to do,
- How meetings will be organized and chaired,
- How decisions will be made (e.g., voting/consensus, power of veto, etc.),
- Delegated authorities (i.e., what decisions they can make directly and what needs to be agreed on by the sponsors),
- Resources that will be made available, and
- The process for amending the articles of incorporation.

We deliberately provide no template for you to do this because (for your community) the process is likely to feel more considered, important, and legit if it is crafted locally, rather than with a cookie-cutter template for you to fill in the blanks.

You might also go so far as codifying a responsibilities and accountabilities matrix so that everyone is clear what their specific role is within the backbone organization. If your backbone team is relatively small, you may not need to do this. But the larger it becomes, the more likely you are to suffer from the **Ringelmann effect**. This is the tendency for groups to become less effective the bigger they get (Forsyth, 2014; Ringelmann, 1913). There are two aspects to this. First is a loss of motivation (i.e., social loafing) as you assume someone else will do the work, and they do too! Second is a lack of coordination between the various players who all trip over one another. Maximilien Ringelmann first noticed this phenomenon when measuring the amount of effort that participants made during tug-of-war rope-pulling contests. The more players, the less coordination and (even) less pulling.

We illustrate how you could set out a responsibilities and accountabilities matrix for your backbone team in Figure 1.1. Here is a

FIGURE 1.1 ● Example Responsibilities and Accountabilities Matrix

CODE	STANDS FOR	THIS PERSON IS
R	Responsible	Responsible for performing the task or creating the product and/or output
A	Accountable	Accountable for and has sign-off authority for the task (e.g., the project manager, sponsor, or technical lead)
S	Supports	Provides expertise, advice, and support to the person responsible for the task or document and others
I	Informed	Informed of task progress or results, usually by the person responsible

TASK	PERSON 1 TEAM LEADER	PERSON 2 INVESTIGATOR	PERSON 3 INVESTIGATOR	PERSON 4 SPONSOR
Developing discovery methodology	**R**	S	S	**A**
Leading discovery workshops	I	**R**	S	**A**
Developing a long list of potential education challenges	S	**R**	S	**A**
Shortlisting education challenges	S	**R**	S	**A**
Validating shortlisted challenges	**R**	S	S	**A**
Identifying interested stakeholders	I	S	**R**	**A**
Gathering insights from interested stakeholders	I	S	**R**	**A**
Reporting findings of the discovery team back to interested stakeholders	**R**	S	S	**A**

quick rule of thumb: make sure everyone is responsible for at least one thing.

Finally, so that the wider community is aware that the backbone organization has been established, you will also want to think about how its purpose and proposed activities are communicated. Depending on your organizational culture, this might need to include reassurances that the purpose and processes are absolutely not a witch hunt—that the focus is not on deficit theorizing or individual fault-finding, but on unleashing deep, positive impact.

BACKBONE ORGANIZATION DOUBLE-BACK

You also need to explicitly double-back during the activity of establishing your backbone organization. Here are some of the evaluative questions that you can consider:

1. Have we identified the right people for the right roles?

2. Does the team currently have the capabilities to undertake the investigation, or would they benefit from external support?

3. Have we established clear governance and operating structures?

4. Does everyone understand their roles and responsibilities?

5. Do people actually have the time to undertake the actions they have signed up for? How will we make time? (*Hint*: Look at the processes in Step 2.4.)

6. Are we setting up a new bureaucracy that is going to get bogged down in paperwork and busywork or have we got the parameters right for agile and meaningful inquiry that generates impact?

7. Who do we need to communicate the purpose and activities of the backbone organization to? Why are we communicating? What are the messages? Is the plan in place and what happens if we don't implement it?

8. What are the double-back actions that we need to imbed within our backbone organization plans before moving to Step 1.2? Have we incorporated these sufficiently?

1.2 DECIDE THE EDUCATION CHALLENGE

With your backbone team in place, the last thing you want to do is get busy implementing random and ill-thought-out initiatives that address needs that you may (or may not) have. Instead, you need to take time to carefully explore your environment to identify an agenda that you agree is worthy of concerted and sustained collective action. We call this your *education challenge*. It's the big and meaty goal, crusade, mission, quest, or just cause that you have decided you want to progress above all else.

To avoid the bear trap of doing lots but accomplishing little, your backbone team needs to carefully explore the existing environment to *decide the education challenge* (Step 1.2). So, how do you do this?

There are three key considerations you need to have in mind at the start:

- **Your philosophy** (i.e., whether you are looking for *problems*, *opportunities*, or a current level of adherence to an "ideal standard")
- **Your values** (i.e., the ethical principles that guide your inquiry)
- **Your methodology** (i.e., when and how you collect data and how you use them)

YOUR PHILOSOPHY

Here are three of the philosophical stances that you can adopt at the very start:

1. **Problem-driven inquiry.** This stance involves looking critically for things that are broken or need fixing, oiling, or upscaling (Pritchett et al., 2013). Here are some examples: "Our school is the worst performing in the district," "We have too much variability in the quality of impact across all our classes and students," "Student dropout rates are getting worse," or "We have a problem with our literacy results"

2. **Opportunity-driven inquiry.** This stance involves being appreciative of all the brilliant things you have already accomplished in your local context, while looking for the next important thing to achieve to make things even greater (Cooperrider et al., 2014). Here are a few examples: "We get good academic results but if we introduce a 'playful' learning ethos, we might further increase student engagement and outcomes" or "It's brilliant that most of our students opt to attend school regularly but maybe we could enhance their achievement levels."

3. **Standards-driven inquiry.** This involves using explicit success criteria like teaching standards, leadership competencies, and student achievement levels that have been developed for your system as a benchmark to measure against. Here are some examples: "Our lesson observations suggest that our teachers are not uniformly using the state-mandated high-impact

teaching strategies" or "Our kids are—on average—exceeding the state numeracy learning standards."

When the various Chinese dynasties embarked on the Great Wall project, this was to address a major *problem* (i.e., continuous incursions by heavily armed nomadic bands across long and difficult-to-defend territorial borders; Barfield, 1989). Ditto for the Pyramids, where, by some accounts, the problem was death, to which the "solution" was a resurrection machine that magically launched pharaohs to the spirit world. Of course, this raises wider questions about whether the problem is genuinely fixable and, if it is, whether the proposed solution is the best mechanism. This is why thoroughly testing your thoughts, beliefs, and assumptions prior to implementation is at the beating heart of the *Building to Impact 5D* methodology.

NASA's quest to get to the moon, by contrast, was arguably *opportunity driven*. There was no specific problem that walking on the moon was directly going to solve. It was "just" a brilliant application of human ingenuity from which all sorts of other technological advances and opportunities unexpectedly emerged, including more than 2,000 NASA spinoff technologies (NASA, 2021). However, an obvious question is whether moon walking really *needed* to be done or whether it might have been better to focus energies on solving the big problems of the era, like high smoking rates and lung cancer deaths, hyperinflation, and rampant poverty. If you decide to adopt an opportunities-driven approach, you will need to be ultra-sensitive to the possibility that you might be pursuing—moon walk-style—brilliant grand plans at the expense of ignoring pressing problems and/or needs that are still on the table.

In contrast, when Olympic divers jump off the high board, their success is judged against *standards-driven* criteria. They don't receive medals for the speed of their dive but for the technical competency, as assessed by a judging panel who award a score. The high-diving community has established global success criteria for what constitutes "exemplary" execution—from arm and leg position, the amount of twist, and the level of the splash on entry—for each type of "officially recognized" dive (see FINA, 2019). The divers are scored on the degree to which their performance meets (or diverges from) this "ideal." And the divers themselves watch (and rewatch) videos of their performances to understand the points of divergence and to identify their needed improvements. However, the obvious question is who sets these standards and why should they be taken seriously? They are but an opinion and they are scoring an opinion of an opinion. So if you decide to adopt a standards-driven inquiry, you also need to look at the standards themselves. Here, we have more confidence in the value of student achievement benchmarking, and we have more skepticism (or at least curiosity) about teaching/leadership standards and the degree to which their opinions on "best practice" genuinely correlate with student outcomes.

You start with an opportunities-driven appreciative stance; and you do this because it's much more motivational for everyone to celebrate the power of their prior achievements and to reflect on and be grateful for what they already have.

Given the benefits and challenges of each of these three perspectives, we suggest a *hybrid approach*. That is, you start with an opportunities-driven appreciative stance; and you do this because it's much more motivational for everyone to celebrate the power of their prior achievements and to reflect on and be grateful for what they already have than to immediately be self- and collectively critical. Once you have framed the positives, you can then pivot to a problem-driven inquiry: "We've achieved so much but what issues are still on the table that if we can address them will result in a much better tomorrow?" And concurrently, you can move to a standards-driven approach: "Which standards represent more than just someone's opinion and how are we tracking against them?"

YOUR VALUES

Some of the values that are important to us include the following:

- Privileging evidence over beliefs and opinions
- Deliberately putting our pet beliefs and opinions to the test
- Not misinterpreting the data to make the facts fit our sacred ideas
- Accepting when we are wrong, even when it's emotionally painful
- Respectfully engaging with others
- Being gleeful evaluators of our own impact
- Remembering that it's *all* about growing student learning outcomes
- Embracing the fact that education is fundamentally transformative to lives and life chances. What we do comes with a *major* responsibility.

We think that these values are likely to be equally applicable to you. Most of the above are bound up in the Enlightenment values of reason, rationality, and empiricism that propelled humanity from astrology, flat-Earth theorizing, and human sacrifice to the brilliance of the modern age (Pinker, 2019). But there will also be other values that are especially relevant to you and your local context.

Once agreed on, these values become the test by which all your decisions are made. It's worth you taking some time to tease this out, to include those values in your articles of incorporation, and to regularly swing back to them as you undertake your inquiry. Then when someone in your backbone organization says, "I think we should introduce [*insert shiny program name*]. My friend in the neighboring school swears by it," you can have a collective response like this: "Are we sure we are privileging evidence over beliefs? Let's look at the impact data."

Almost as bad as not searching for data is limiting the search to evidence that supports the assumed hypothesis and deliberately *not* looking for disconfirming data. This is pseudo-science, or what Richard Feynman (1974) calls "cargo cult science." Here is another way of putting it: "I think X is true and I will now search for research that supports X. I will not look for anything that disconfirms X and if I accidentally find it, I definitely won't read it" (see Hattie & Hamilton, 2020a).

YOUR METHODOLOGY

Once you have decided your philosophy and deliberated your values, you then need to consider how you will explore your environment to identify and validate appropriate goals. One non-negotiable thing is that this *always* involves collecting, reviewing, and analyzing data. Without data, you are operating entirely on hunch, instinct, or intuition, and you have no way of knowing whether you have selected an appropriate education challenge or whether you are wasting your energy on low-priority (or even unattainable) initiatives. You're just another person with an opinion, possibly even a "crazy uncle."

Here are three of the ways that you can undertake your exploration:

1. **Ideas-driven approach (a.k.a. the deductive method).** Here, you begin by unpacking your collective *inklings* or *beliefs* about what the important improvement agendas *could* be, and you then collect and review data about each of these hunches to test whether the facts or on-the-ground realities correspond with your beliefs. For example, "We think that migrant children in our school are being short-changed. Is this the case?" or "We want to make learning more fun. Is it true that learning isn't fun for our kids, and does it actually need to be? Or is 'real' learning generally painful and challenging?"

2. **Data-driven approach (a.k.a. the inductive method).** Here, you keep your preconceived ideas firmly locked away and instead collect and analyze all the data you can get your hands on and search for patterns, needs, and opportunities in the data. Some examples are as follows: "The data are telling us that student achievement in standardized assessments has declined over the last 5 years. Should we be concerned about this?" or "The data are telling us that our teacher retention rates have increased significantly. Should we be pleased?"

3. **Reason-driven approach (a.k.a. the abductive for parallelism method).** This starts from your seeing some problem, surprising details, or some event that cannot be readily explained. Abduction invites the educator to choose the "best" explanation among alternatives to explain this

conundrum. And if it does not convince, then move to the next "best" explanation. Here's an example:

> I note the brightest students seem to be cruising. My explanation is that they need gifted classes. But upon trying them they are still cruising, so I ask teachers in regular classes about their concept and implementation of "challenge." I find their view is that challenge is coverage more of the curricula with these students, but the students want more challenge in the depth and not merely move coverage at a surface level.

During Step 1.2, it is not *yet* necessary for you to use the reason-driven approach to explain the root causes of each potential education challenge. You may have identified quite a long list of potential problems and/or goals. It is more efficient to wait and then to apply abductive reasoning *only* to the challenge(s) you have subsequently decided to prioritize. The whole of Step 1.3 leverages this abductive method—because in order to improve, we need to understand what we are building on top of.

If you have the resources, you could undertake your exploration in all three ways. First, have a mini-search party that starts with their hunches, and looks for confirming and/or disconfirming data. Then another search party tries their best to keep their hunches firmly locked away and instead looks for the signal in the (data) noise. Finally, develop another list of possible explanations to then rule out if the evidence does not support them (but again, it is not essential that you build explanations for the identified education challenges until Step 1.3). You can then compare what each party comes up with and see whether they vector in on common agendas.

Whichever way you choose, some of the sources of data that you will want to explore include those identified in Figure 1.2.

Depending on your national context, there may also be data available from external reviews or school inspections.

THE MANY, THE FEW, THE ONE

In our work, we have had the privilege of working directly with and learning from thousands of schools and more than 50 system-level agencies. Most of the schools and systems we have collaborated with were skilled at analyzing their present situation and identifying (very) long lists of potential goals and problems as well as improvements and initiatives. However, what many were less good at was whittling these down to an achievable number of priorities.

FIGURE 1.2 ● Sources of Data

	NATIONAL/ STANDARDIZED ASSESSMENTS	INTERNAL ASSESSMENTS	LESSON OBSERVATIONS	INTERVIEWS AND SURVEYS	ELECTRONIC MANAGEMENT INFORMATION SYSTEM (EMIS) DATA

Benefits	• Usually reliable; centrally/professionally designed, assessed, and moderated
	• Provides comparative data across years and decades
	• No extra effort required to collect
		• Usually more valid/ connected to the local learning context
		• More amenable to item-level analysis (i.e., can unpack the areas where students performed well or need additional support)
			• Direct insights into classroom activity
			• Also has developmental value as part of professional inquiry
				• Ability to gather perceptions from students, teachers, and/or community members
				• Can tailor to specific inquiry areas
					• Provides wider data on topics such as these:
					  ○ Student attendance
					  ○ Teacher retention
					  ○ Teacher sickness
					  ○ Health and safety
					  ○ Financial management
					  ○ Student characteristics and needs

Challenges	• Only available for exam years • Often reports holistically (i.e., cannot always access item/question-level data)	• May not be as reliable as national assessments • Extra time/effort/cost to design, administer, and assess • May not provide comparable data across years	• May not be representative of day-to-day activity in the classroom • Presence of an observer may influence behavior of teacher and learners • Difficult to "see" student learning with your eyes/open to different interpretations by different observers	• Extra workload to design, administer, and interpret • Willingness of stakeholders to engage in the process • Provides insight into perceptions and/or beliefs rather than impact and outcomes	• Often difficult to benchmark your school's data against other schools, as these data are often not in the public domain
Best for	Big-picture longitudinal analysis	Vector analysis of specific cohorts, classes, curriculum areas, and topics	Holistic understanding of what is happening in individual classes	Understanding stakeholder perceptions and for gathering ideas	Understanding input drivers that might impact teaching and learning in classrooms

Source: Adapted from Sharples et al. (2018).

They often really struggled to take things *off* the table and wanted to progress *all* of their identified education challenges. But being highly selective is extremely important. In our own school and system improvement work, we have consistently found that the smaller the number of priorities, the higher the probability of impact. To repeat, *the smaller the number of priorities, the higher the probability of impact.* You need to be extremely ambitious about a very small number of things, or in the words of Viviane Robinson (2018) in her book of the same name: "Reduce change to increase improvement."

Previous research based on an analysis of more than 2,000 school plans, along with 3 years of student achievement data for those schools, suggests that the optimal number of initiatives is no more than six (Reeves, 2013). Some of the world's premier organizational consultations from Booz Allen and PwC (Leinwand & Mainardi, 2011) came to similar conclusions. In a survey of more than 1,800 organizations, the researchers found that the majority said that they had too many initiatives, including some that were conflicting, and more than 80% said that initiative overload was wasting time. They concluded that the optimal number of initiatives was three to six. That represents a confluence of evidence between the worlds of education and other organizations. Thus, when we see the common occurrence of dozens of priorities in school and district improvement plans, we are dismayed at yet another example of how prevailing and consistent evidence in favor of focus is ignored.

Where schools and systems have long lists of priorities for improvement, the *less* likely it is that stakeholders

- understand the big picture, let alone agree with it;
- understand how the various initiatives that are being implemented contribute to making things better within the frame of that big picture;
- can carve out time to make meaningful progress in leading or contributing to these multiple agendas;
- can systematically measure and reflect on their progress; and
- can identify where to next.

You need to focus on less to achieve more. This means that you need to find a way to progress from a universe of near-infinite education challenges or goals that all seem worthy of your time and energy to a shortlist of viable challenges and to then boil this down to ONE agreed priority. In other words, from the many, to the few, to the ONE. We illustrate this in Figure 1.3.

You need to focus on less to achieve more.

If you are thinking that one priority is too restrictive, you're right—it's deliberately so. For you to be able to agree on one thing, it normally ends up being a big all-encompassing sort of challenge that

FIGURE 1.3 ● The Education Challenge Funnel

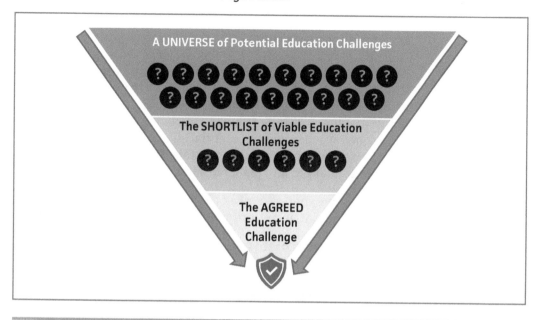

Note: Copyright © Cognition Education (2022). All rights reserved.

requires the design and implementation of several work strands, initiatives, or programs to tackle different aspects of the improvement area. So while Doug Reeves originally advocated the *rule of six* in some of his earlier writings, we now collectively propose *the rule that one priority will probably end up sprouting into six contributing initiatives*. So, it's better to start with one priority because 1 education challenge × 6 initiatives is more realistic to manage than 6 education challenges × 6 initiatives.

But how do you home in on the ONE? For every education challenge you identify, you almost need to be looking for reasons not to do anything at all. You might find it useful to ask questions like these:

- What's the absolute worst that could happen if we did absolutely nothing?
- What's the likelihood this worse-case outcome will actually happen?
- Does it really matter if it does happen and/or continues to happen?
- Why should we or anyone care?

We completely get that it seems shockingly cruel to try and conjure up reasons not to address burning platforms or not to embrace big audacious goals. But there is method in our madness. We just want you to select among your competing priorities with great care—to increase the probability that the one you progress actually matters most and ultimately gets done.

The idea is that you whittle and winnow down until you get to the (hopefully) small handful that stakeholders are extremely reluctant to take off the table. When you ask, for example, whether it really matters whether one-third of children are leaving your school or school system without functional literacy and the collective reaction is complete horror, anger, or incredulity, then you just might have identified a potential education challenge that sufficiently rouses sentiments for all stakeholders to be prepared to make great changes and personal sacrifices to act on.

In Figure 1.4 we share a worked example of this potentially heated and cognitively jarring priority review process.

One of the benefits of this approach is that it encourages you to take a long-term perspective and think beyond test grades to long-term life chances. We know from research on the **Matthew effect** that children not achieving a year's learning growth for a year's teaching input often spiral into a doom loop that is more likely—in adulthood—to translate into higher periods of unemployment, higher incidences of clinical depression and substance abuse, higher incidences of incarceration, and lower life expectancy (Hamilton & Hattie, 2022). So, it is important to keep sight of the fact that today's low-test scores are not a "1-year problem" but a compounding multidecade problem. *That* vision, as awful as it is, should be front of mind as you decide which education challenges are worth your collective effort.

If you are still struggling to vector in on the ONE, it might help you to undertake head-to-head matched pairs comparisons. We illustrate this approach in Figure 1.5.

This process involves your backbone team and potentially also wider stakeholders coming together to review each of the competing priorities to decide which is more important. The idea is that the process is repeated until every potential focus area is compared against every other. You might do this comparison through group discussion and by coming to a group consensus, or you may choose to literally vote individually on each priority and tally up the collective wisdom of the crowd.

One of the interesting things that often emerges from this process is that stakeholders usually begin to express thoughts like, "Maybe the shortage of qualified teachers *could* be one of the reasons why such a high proportion of our kids are functionally illiterate?" These discussions about whether some potential challenges could actually be *causes* and others *symptoms* or *effects* are really important—in terms of both deciding what the real priority should be and also in understanding what factors could be contributing to the existence of any identified problems.

FIGURE 1.4 ● Education Challenge Hunting ↻

POTENTIAL EDUCATION CHALLENGES	DOES IT REALLY MATTER? (I.E., THE *SO WHAT?* PROVOCATION)	WHAT'S THE WORST THAT COULD HAPPEN IF WE DID NOTHING? (I.E., WHERE IS THE EVIDENCE? HOW STRONG IS THE EVIDENCE?)	SHOULD WE CARE? (I.E., IS THIS OUR MOST IMPORTANT MEGA-CHALLENGE?)
Our school buildings are shabby and overcrowded	*Is there a strong relationship between the quality of infrastructure and class size and student attendance/ achievement?*	No statistically significant difference in learning outcomes or attendance between "shiny" and "shabby" schools in Visible Learning Meta^X. Reducing class size also seems to have only a modest impact on student achievement but at relatively high cost.	Not right now. But we might need to explain to community stakeholders why they should worry less, too.
Difficulty in recruiting qualified mathematics and science teachers—76% do not have an advanced qualification in the subject they teach	*Do teachers really need to have an advanced qualification in the subject they teach?*	Mathematics and science teachers with an advanced qualification are an average effect size $d = 0.10$ more effective.	No. This is probably not big enough to warrant the investment right now.
33% of our 13-year-olds are functionally illiterate	*Is it essential that everyone is literate? Can we live with 66%?*	Illiterate adults in our context are • 4 times more likely to be in low-paying jobs • 2.7 times more likely to be convicted of a criminal offense • 3 times more likely to die before age 60	This feels pretty bad. But maybe they will catch up?

FIGURE 1.5 ● Matched Pairs Comparison

Difficulty in recruiting qualified mathematics and science teachers	**vs.**	33% of our 13-year-olds are functionally illiterate

Another potential approach to education challenge identification is what we call *So What and So Prove It*, which we illustrate in Figure 1.6.

As you undertake your whittling and winnowing, you are also going to want to gather and rank the quality of the evidence that you are using to help you make decisions. Do you have

- **High confidence** that the backbone team has unearthed a significant trove of quantitative and qualitative data from local and global sources, which all pull in the same direction;
- **Medium confidence** as above but with some gaps, or that data seem to pull in different directions; or
- **Low confidence** because judgments are being made based on anecdotes, hearsay, and intuition?

For example, if you look carefully at Figure 1.6, you will see that the quality evidence for the *So Prove It* statements varies considerably. Many are just assertions or opinions without underlying data in their support.

If at the end of your whittling and winnowing, you cannot identify a single priority that the majority of stakeholders strongly agree is worth collective action (and collective pain) to resolve, then you might want to consider disbanding your backbone team. You are very unlikely to make progress on goals that are either non-systemic or where sentiments are not sufficiently aroused to drive and sustain the hard graft of implementation.

FIGURE 1.6 ● So What and So Prove It

EDUCATION CHALLENGE: 33% OF OUR 13-YEAR-OLDS ARE FUNCTIONALLY ILLITERATE	
So What 1: They can't read!	**So Prove It 1:** Internal assessment data demonstrate that 33% of our students are not achieving the expected literacy standards.
So What 2: They will fall further behind.	**So Prove It 2:** If they can't read, they can't engage with the curriculum sufficiently.
So What 3: They are more likely to drop out of school.	**So Prove It 3:** We ran the numbers across the district. Children who did not meet the functional literacy standards are five times more likely to drop out.
So What 4: They are less likely to get good jobs.	**So Prove It 4:** National employment data correlate illiteracy with a significantly higher probability of unemployment and lower lifetime earnings.
So What 5: They are more likely to have a lower life expectancy.	**So Prove It 5:** Correlational data show an association between lower literacy levels and earlier onset of comorbidities.

Source: Copyright © Cognition Education. (2022). All Rights Reserved.

You also want to think deeply about whether your selected challenge is genuinely amenable to change. For example, if NASA had been established in 1860, it would have made much less progress with its Moonshot goals and would likely have quickly given up because the supporting rocketry and computer technology were a long way from being developed sufficiently.

However, if you have identified a worthy and amenable challenge, the next key step is to define it and explain the causal elements. This is also known as *building a theory of the present*, because you cannot improve or enhance the future without properly understanding the present from which it builds.

1.3 EXPLAIN THE EDUCATION CHALLENGE

Imagine waking up in the night with searing back pain and hobbling to the doctor the next day. It is extremely unlikely that your chosen physician will pull out a random treatment option without a diagnosis. Instead, they have been trained to do two key things before even *thinking* about potential options (Wilson, 2012):

1. **Understand and define your problem or need as clearly as possible.** The doctor might ask questions like these: What is the severity of the back pain? How much does it interfere with your daily life? Does it affect the whole back or just a specific part? Which part? Are there certain times of day, temperature conditions, or types of activities that are more painful? Is it muscle or joint pain? Has it gotten progressively worse over time? Have you ever had it before? Does it run in the family?

2. **Build a hypothesis about the causes.** Painful symptoms do not usually emerge on their own. They generally present at the end of a causal chain that starts in some other bodily system and then ricochets through different cells and organs to manifest as "back pain." The cause *might* be arthritis, a kidney infection, bad posture, pregnancy, a sports injury, or tens of other possibilities. Your doctor might order X-rays or imaging scans to find out more. But even if the scans identify, say, arthritis, the causal chain does not stop here. Arthritis *might* have been caused by environmental factors, like a lifetime of picking up boxes resulting in joint damage; by a genetically primed immune response; by being overweight; or by many, many other influences. Without having a plausible working model of the causes, your doctor cannot prescribe the right sorts of treatment.

This type of medical reasoning is called **abduction**, which is the third sister to **induction** and **deduction** (Hattie & Larsen, 2020). The same abductive principles apply to education improvement. If we have not defined the target area (i.e., the education challenge) and if we have not built a working model of the causes, we are flying blind. We would be like doctors randomly prescribing muscle relaxants when a more careful diagnosis might show that what's really needed is weight loss and dietary change, or even surgery.

Given that whatever changes we make in schools and systems incur an opportunity cost (time, money, buy-in, good will, etc.), we need to be as sure as we can be that the treatments, interventions, programs, activities, or designs that we propose will actually push *our* needle—as opposed to pushing needles on agendas we do not currently have. This means that we need to employ the same abductive diagnostic protocols as good doctors.

DEFINE THE EDUCATION CHALLENGE

Let's assume that during your whittling and winnowing process, you selected *33% of our 13-year-olds are functionally illiterate* as your education challenge. This is a bit like going to the doctor and saying you have a nondescript type of back pain. So, like the doctor, you need to interrogate and expand your definition. Here are some of the questions you might find it useful to ask:

1. What is our **definition** of the challenge?

2. What **data** have we used to inform our definition?

3. How **valid and reliable** are the data?

4. What is the **span** of our challenge? That is, does it relate to all, many, some, or a few stakeholder groups?

5. What are the **stakeholder characteristics** of those that the challenge most relates to (e.g., males or females, younger or older, teachers or students, resource rich or resource poor, etc.)?

6. What is the **severity of impact** on the different stakeholder groups?

We call this the **breakdown structure**, and we illustrate what the outcomes of this process might look like in Figure 1.7.

What do you notice as you scan Figure 1.7? Take time to reflect and then compare your thoughts with our observations as follows.

First, it's clear that the challenge *might* be under-recorded, because the measuring tool *could* be letting some false positives slip through the net. Equally, it might also be over-reported because the school currently assumes that children who have not taken the literacy assessment would also have failed it. Both these observations suggest the need for more digging and possibly also for more robust student assessment and reporting mechanisms to be put in place.

FIGURE 1.7 ● Education Challenge Breakdown Structure

EDUCATION CHALLENGE	
33% OF OUR 13-YEAR-OLDS ARE FUNCTIONALLY ILLITERATE	
DEFINING CHARACTERISTICS	**COMMENTARY**
1. *Functionally literate* is defined as achieving 75%+ on our school's internal literacy assessment. Functional *illiteracy* = scoring less than 75%	External consultants have recently benchmarked our internal assessment and suggested it is of low validity and reliability. The challenge could actually be much bigger (!!!).
2. In our school, 15% of 13-year-olds not meeting the standard have not actually taken the assessment.	Can we assume that all those who have not taken the assessment would have failed to achieve the 75% threshold?
3. Students who have not taken the assessment are ○ Disproportionately boys (68%) ○ Disproportionately in rural areas (74%) ○ Disproportionately from low socioeconomic status (SES) backgrounds (83%)	Is this a consequence of teaching quality in our rural districts or of lower levels of community engagement and/or aspiration?
4. Of the students who took the assessment and did not achieve the 75% threshold, they were: ○ Disproportionately boys (57%) ○ Disproportionately from low SES backgrounds (83%)	Can we find any data on teacher demographics? For example, are these students more likely to be taught by less experienced teachers or are their teachers more frequently absent?
5. There is a wide dispersal in the degree to which students missed the 75% threshold: ○ 32% missed it by 5% or less ○ 41% missed it by 5–15% ○ 27% missed it by more than 25%	Putting to one side that our assessments may not be as valid or reliable as external assessments, the data suggest that there are varying degrees of student support required. For example, for 32% of students, it might be the case that they only require light-touch additional support.

Second, there do *seem* to be some patterns among the students who have not met the assessment threshold. It seems to affect boys and children from lower socioeconomic status (SES) backgrounds, so we need to start building a theory about why this is. Do all these children share the same teacher? If so, it could be a characteristic of the teaching. If they have different teachers, it could be related to out-of-school factors. Or it could be that while the teaching approach connects with other learners, there is something about it that's off-putting for these particular learners.

Third, there is variability in how affected students are: 32% of the children who did not meet the literacy standards were actually within a hair's breadth. They might only require a little additional support and guidance to get them over the line. Yet the type of support required for the 27% of students who missed the target by 25% or more is likely to be more intensive.

So, we already have three lines of inquiry: (1) review the testing instruments and reporting assumptions, (2) consider whether and why children from specific backgrounds are more likely to have support needs, and (3) consider whether the package of support can be varied depending on the severity of need.

BUILD A HYPOTHESIS ABOUT THE CAUSES (A THEORY OF THE PRESENT)

By defining your education challenge with clarity, you have already taken the first step toward building a **theory of the present** and thinking about viable interventions. But we recommend you go deeper. By exploring intensely, you will better know whether your "backache" is caused by bad posture, arthritis, or a bone tumor. You can then select the right treatment pathway (e.g., posture correction, anti-inflammatory medicines, or radiotherapy). And if it is caused by multiple things, you can then mix and match your intervention options.

In addition, there are often multiple layers even within a single causal chain. For example, (1) engrained habits lead to (2) slouching, that leads to (3) a slipped disk, that causes (4) a pinched nerve, and results in (5) excruciating pain. And it may be that the selected interventions tackle many of these links in the causal web, such as paracetamol for the pain, physical manipulation or even surgery for the slipped disk, and cognitive behavioral therapy to adjust your deportment.

By moving beyond folk theorizing and toward building a robust understanding of our present, we are far more likely to be able to reach for the right interventions that support improvement across the whole causal chain.

The exact same causal thinking processes can be applied to education improvement. By moving beyond folk theorizing and toward building a robust understanding of our present, we are far more likely to be able to reach for the right interventions that support improvement across the whole causal chain.

One excellent tool for doing this is called the *Five Whys*. It was developed by Sakichi Toyoda and used within the Toyota Motor Corporation (Ohno, 1988). *It involves continually asking "Why X is the case?" We provide an illustration in Figure 1.8.*

The idea is that you ask these *why* questions over and over and that you use the outputs to build a causal theory. Depending on your inquiry topic, your team composition, and stakeholder beliefs, it is extremely likely you will build many different *Five Whys*, each telling a different story or pointing to a different causal chain. Some of these narratives might be about children's home backgrounds. Others might be about the language or

FIGURE 1.8 ● The *Five Whys* Approach

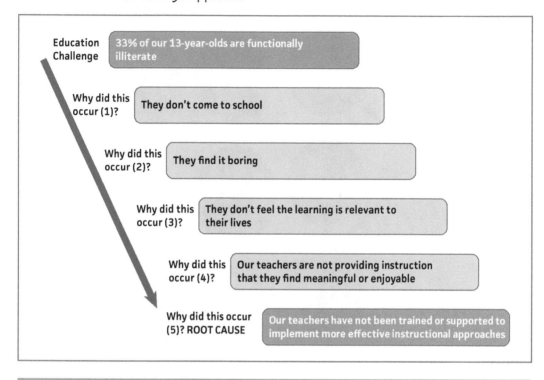

Education Challenge: 33% of our 13-year-olds are functionally illiterate

Why did this occur (1)? They don't come to school

Why did this occur (2)? They find it boring

Why did this occur (3)? They don't feel the learning is relevant to their lives

Why did this occur (4)? Our teachers are not providing instruction that they find meaningful or enjoyable

Why did this occur (5)? ROOT CAUSE: Our teachers have not been trained or supported to implement more effective instructional approaches

Source: Copyright © Cognition Education. (2022). All rights reserved.

medium of instruction, yet others about instructional approaches (i.e., pedagogy), and others still about classroom relationships, trust, empathy, and well-being. Some might also be about short-term variables like COVID-19 school closures, where the original issue has (hopefully) ceased to exist but where there could still be long-lingering legacy effects.

In Figure 1.9 we illustrate how these different stories can be woven together into a **path analysis** (i.e., theory of the present). This is not a full map, but it gives you an idea of how you might start to blend your many *Five Whys* into a deep and rich explanation of your present. Note that this example is presented from the perspective of an external consultant. If you undertake this type of mapping internally, you may wish to be considerably more appreciative (i.e., sugar coated) in how you label the *influence bubbles*—particularly when you engage with target improvement groups. No teacher wants to hear that they employ "poor-quality instructional approaches" or that they "deficit theorize." Talking in such language is the pathway to defensiveness, mutual blaming, and people barricading themselves in their minds and classrooms.

One of the benefits of path analysis is its freeform nature. A second benefit is that you can easily build it with sticky notes on

FIGURE 1.9 ● Path Analysis

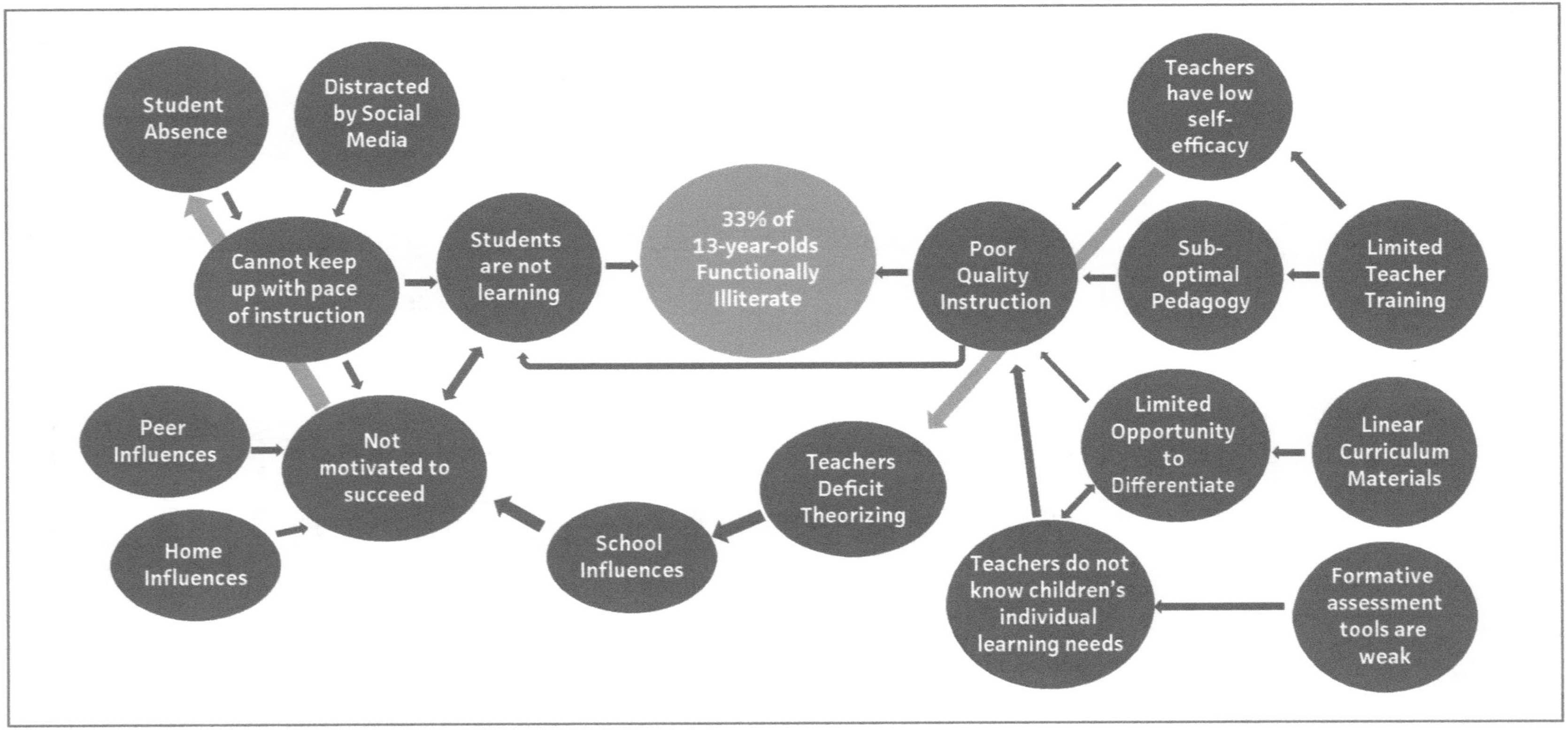

Source: Copyright © Cognition Education (2022). All Rights Reserved.

a whiteboard and draw the connector arrows with a marker pen. However, if you need more structure, other tools you can leverage include *Fishbone* and *Issues Tree* mapping (see Figure 1.10).

However, a disadvantage of both the Fishbone and Issues Trees approaches is that they tend to encourage linear thinking. The arrows only move in one direction—from cause to effect. However, some causes might also impact other causes (this is known as mediating and moderating in the technical jargon), and some might have greater influence or power of effect than others. This is why we prefer path analysis, which was first developed by Sewall Wright (1921) and is vigorously championed today by Judea Pearl and Dana Mackenzie (2020). You can move the arrows in any direction and even have them going to multiple places. And you can also vary the size of your "bubbles" to reflect your hypothesis about how important each is in the overall scheme of impact.

This process is also a form of *abductive reasoning* and is a lot like the way a police detective undertakes a criminal investigation. Often the detectives wheel out a large whiteboard: at the center is the crime or the victim. In orbit around the "vic" are an array of potential suspects (or "perps") and their respective means, motives, and opportunities. Each of these chains tells a different story. Maybe the crime was perpetrated by Colonel Mustard in the library with the dagger because of a longstanding grudge? Or by Professor Plum in the ballroom with the candlestick because his scandal was about to become exposed?

The detective builds a range of such theories and then searches for evidence that either confirms the suspect as a person of interest or eliminates them from the inquiry. That search for evidence involves the collection of witness statements, review of surveillance video, confirmation of alibis, and so on. When Professor Plum presents flight tickets showing he was out of town the day of the crime and this is corroborated by airport camera footage, his picture is removed from the whiteboard.

During this stage of the inquiry, you are *exactly* like an educational data detective. With your "crime" (or education challenge) at the center of the board and your hunches about different causal chains, you are gathering data to validate (or dismiss) your theory of the present. You are *doubling-back* to test the evidence chain. However, one thing makes this a little more complex than the world of the police detective: we can rarely explain an "educational crime" with a single causal chain such as "Mustard, library, and dagger." More often, there is a range of interconnected influences—each applying force to varying degrees and contributing to the outcome.

We get that, yes, you may be rolling your eyes at the prospect of undertaking this data detection and that instead you might be itching to just get on with implementing something, anything—because

FIGURE 1.10 ● Fishbone and Issues Tree Mapping

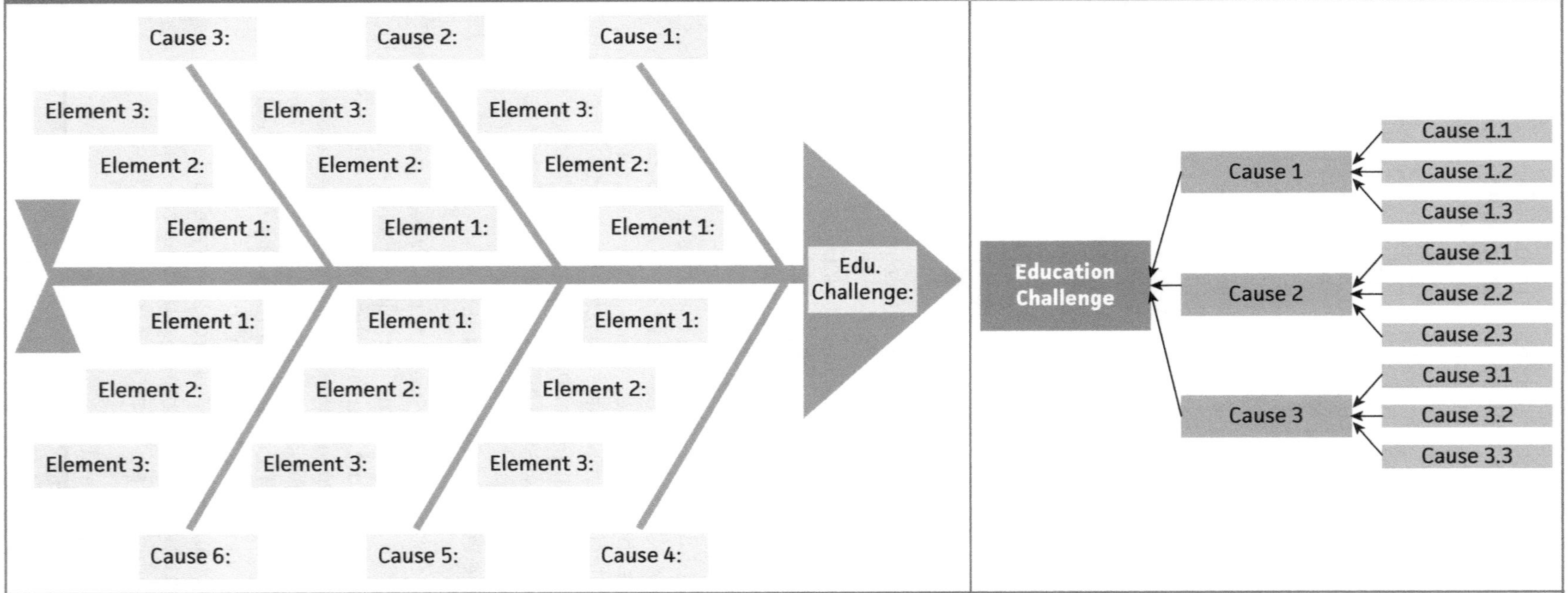

	FISHBONE	ISSUES TREE

The education challenge is in the "head" of the fish. Each "bone" represents a potential causal factor. Under each bone are contributing elements or "sub-bones." See Ishikawa (1968).

Similar reasoning model to the Fishbone but without the fishy graphics! See Chevallier (2016).

Source: Copyright © Cognition Education. (2022). All rights reserved.

you think the causes of your "education crime" are, well, obvious. But if you don't have a robust (and tested) theory of the present, you are likely to select completely the wrong activities or interventions. You will not then push the needle one iota and you may as well have done nothing. Wild-goose chase galore.

In Figure 1.11, we illustrate how you can collate and review each variable in your path analysis, leveraging a range of data including eMIS, learning walks, student voice, lesson observations, and surveys. This is the built-in double-back.

The idea is that as you explore the supporting data for each link in your causal map, you

- remove influences that have *not* been verified,
- add *new* influences that emerge from your action research, and
- adjust the position of the arrows as you reconsider which variables push energy and in which direction.

Your finalized map is *crucial* to the design activity that you will undertake in Stage D2 (Design), where you will be crafting activities and initiatives that are explicitly designed to interact with and impact the key causal variables. This means that you can then block, weaken, and/or ideally reverse their impact.

If you are working at an individual school level, a single path analysis should do it. However, if you are operating at the district level

FIGURE 1.11 • Validating the Causal Drivers ↻

CAUSAL VARIABLE	CAUSAL HYPOTHESIS	SOURCES OF VERIFICATION DATA	OUTCOME OF VERIFICATION	VARIABLE REMAINS?
Student absence	Because they are missing from class, they fall behind and cannot catch up	• Student attendance data	**Not verified.** The level of student absence for our target group is no different from the high-performing students.	**Removed**
Cannot keep up with pass of instruction	Students do not have sufficient prior knowledge to scaffold and bridge to new curriculum content	• Formative assessment data • Student voice	**Verified.** Both the assessment data and student interviews suggest 70%+ of the target group does not have appropriate prior knowledge.	**Remains**

(Continued)

FIGURE 1.11 ● (Continued)

CAUSAL VARIABLE	CAUSAL HYPOTHESIS	SOURCES OF VERIFICATION DATA	OUTCOME OF VERIFICATION	VARIABLE REMAINS?
Poor-quality instruction	Students are not making progress because they do not enjoy their classes and do not believe what they study is relevant	• Student voice • Lesson observations • Curriculum review	**Verified.** Students consistently reported that they found lessons unengaging. Lesson observations also suggested disengagement.	**Remains**
Limited opportunity to differentiate	Teaching is linear and does not cater to differences in children's prior knowledge	• Lesson observations • Curriculum review • Student voice	**Verified.** Limited use of grouping/differentiation strategies or assessment data to inform teaching.	**Remains**

or higher, you may find you need more than one map, reflecting the fact that similar symptoms across your schools might have quite different root causes.

1.4 AGREE ON WHAT BETTER LOOKS LIKE

The good news is that we are now (almost) at the end of the Discover Stage (D1). You have identified an education challenge worth progressing and now also have a (pretty) good idea about why it exists. The final thing we recommend you do before moving to the Design Stage (D2) is to start thinking about what success looks like.

By visualizing and articulating what success means in your context, you are more likely to stay focused and motivated to bring it to life. The further piece of good news is that (at this stage) you don't need to go overboard on identifying measures and setting targets. You will swing back to this bit in Stage D2. However, you can discuss and provisionally agree on the following:

- **An empowering aspirational statement** (e.g., *ALL children at this school will attend regularly, will enjoy their classes, and will achieve the district literacy standards*)

- **Provisional metrics** (like those listed in Figure 1.12)

Things that get visualized remain important and get done!

FIGURE 1.12 ● Establishing Provisional Success Criteria

CURRENT SITUATION	"TO BE" SITUATION	BY WHEN	MEASURED HOW
33% of our 13-year-olds are functionally illiterate	88% of 13-year-olds are functionally literate	December 2025	Percentage of total school-age population that achieves Level 3 threshold in national literacy assessment
JUSTIFICATION OF SELECTION OF "TO BE" VALUES			
A review of regional comparator data suggests that an average of 90% of students achieve functional literacy in those other contexts.			

D1: Discover Summary

You have now reached the end of the Stage D1: Discover processes. During this stage of your inquiry:

You will have agreed on ONE education challenge that's worth progressing above ALL else

You will have done this by:

1.1 Establishing a Backbone Organization

1.2 Deciding the Education Challenge

1.3 Explaining the Education Challenge

1.4 Agreeing on what better looks like

In the next chapter we shift our focus to D2: Design.

CHAPTER 2

D2: Design

Systematically search and agree on high-probability interventions to START and to STOP

2.1 Explore Options in the Design Space

2.2 Build Program Logic Model(s)

2.3 Stress Test Logic Model(s)

2.4 Agree on What to STOP

2.5 Establish a Monitoring and Evaluation Plan

INTRODUCTION

When COVID-19 emerged in late 2019, the first question for governments was whether the virus was a *genuine* risk. The second question was about the *severity* of the impact. If you cast your mind back to those early days before COVID-19 was declared a pandemic, many of us dismissed the news of a new virus from a distant part of the world. It ended up taking a few months before policymakers across most parts of the globe accepted that it was, indeed, a *genuine* risk. And it still is a risk for many citizens and is likely to be with us well into the future.

A common feature in those early closed-door government sessions was that someone (almost) always asked whether COVID-19 was something that required a response or whether it would simply be better to allow the virus to wash over us and quickly generate herd immunity. In most countries, after the numbers were crunched, the consensus was that the *severity* of risk was extremely high, that (on average) 1–2% of the population could die, and that many more would be left with what we now call long COVID (i.e., lingering health difficulties for the long haul). The consequence of this assessment was that most countries decided to act and protect their populations from these harrowing consequences.

The diagnostic processes that governments went through to assess whether COVID was *genuine* and to calculate the *severity* of impact are not dissimilar to those we outlined in Stage D1 (Discover). Governments explored data to answer the question, "What's the worst that could happen if we do absolutely nothing?" And their scientists then began to define and map the key features of the virus (i.e., the breakdown structure). They also undertook their own version of path analysis, exploring

- **transmission pathways** (i.e., how quickly and under what conditions the virus passes from one person to another) and
- **biological interactions** (i.e., how it enters the body, what it does, and how the immune system responds to this).

Armed with this information, the next step was to investigate and agree on interventions to slow, block, or reverse the different nodes or bubbles on that path analysis map. Ultimately, this bit was a design activity that culminated in the identification of a range of high-probability options. With virus transmission, for example, the identified interventions included face mask wearing, handwashing, social distancing, and lockdowns. These interventions were not randomly selected. Scientists looked carefully at successful strategies that had been used to curb the transmission of other similar viruses in the past (for an early account of public policy responses to COVID-19, see Murphy, 2020).

But it didn't stop there. The next level down was to agree on the **design features and setting levels** for each selected intervention. For example, did face masks need to be worn outside and indoors? Was it okay to reuse masks? Were standard surgical masks sufficient, or was double-masking or even the use of more robust N95 masks required? How would people be encouraged to wear them? Would there be any sanctions if they refused? Would the sanctions be enforced and by whom?

The same questions were asked about the optimal design features and setting levels for social distancing, for lockdown protocols (including whether schools needed to close), and for the design and distribution of both vaccines and treatments for individuals infected with the virus. And each of these "work packages" was built out into a carefully designed plan, which was then implemented and iteratively evaluated, to decide *where to next*.

The processes and tools that we will outline in **Stage D2: Design** of the *Building to Impact* 5D framework are remarkably similar to those used by the scientists and policymakers to investigate and agree on how they would respond to COVID-19. This is not by chance. Remember that in developing this framework, we explored the successful tools used in a range of settings, including health care and even the business sector.

Rather than selecting random approaches and hoping for the best, the idea is that through the use of these systematic design approaches, you will significantly increase the probability that you push the impact needle on your priority education challenge.

2.1 EXPLORE THE OPTIONS IN THE DESIGN SPACE

During Stage D1 (Discover), you established your backbone organization (1.1), decided your ONE education challenge (1.2), undertook a path analysis to explain the education challenge (1.3), and then set provisional improvement goals to agree on what better looks like (1.4).

The activity that you undertook in Step 1.3 is especially crucial and directly linked to what you are going to do now. During that specific activity, you mapped the key causal dimensions of your education challenge and then doubled-back to validate these. The outcome of this process is a checked and cross-checked path analysis with arrows and **influence bubbles**, like the one we presented in Figure 1.9, which we recap again in Figure 2.1.

What you are now going to do in Step 2.1 is systematically explore the options in the design space that could potentially be leveraged to block, reverse, or weaken each of the identified influence bubbles on your path analysis. In the example map recapped in Figure 2.1, there are 17 influence bubbles, all contributing to the education challenge at the center. This means that you (ideally) need to search for a range of options or **opportunity sketches** for *each* of those 17. And for clarity, by opportunity sketches, we mean initiatives, programs, actions, interventions, and so on—things that you can implement that bring you ever closer to your success criteria.

As you undertake this search, you might identify opportunity sketches that could impact multiple influence bubbles. For example, you might identify a specific type of teacher coaching program that potentially addresses the "limited teacher training" + "suboptimal pedagogy" + "teachers have low self-efficacy" influence

Through the use of these systematic design approaches, you will significantly increase the probability that you push the impact needle on your priority education challenge.

FIGURE 2.1 ● Recapping the Path Analysis

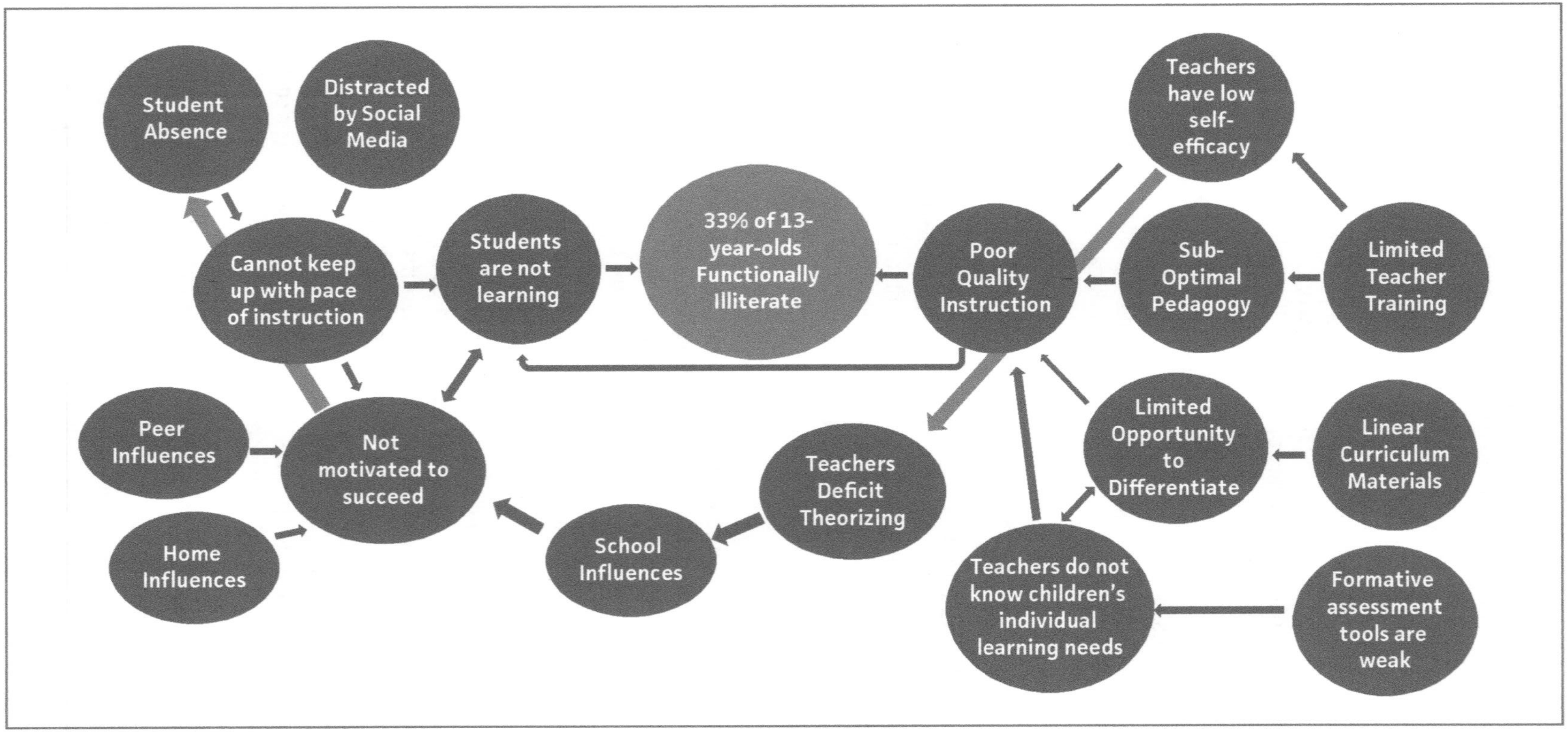

bubbles, at the same time. This is good and actively encouraged because the less complex your designs, the less likely that the wheels will fall off during delivery (Stage D3).

However, the key question is *how* should you go about that search through design space to identify potentially viable opportunity sketches? In our work with schools, sadly it is all too often done informally and unsystematically. Someone went to a conference and heard a "guru" talking about the X-Program, saw a blog post, or got a testimonial from a friend who works at another school. And these signals get treated as "evidence" that the X-Program works and that it works for *your* specific education challenge. Daniel Willingham's (2012) excellent book *When Can You Trust the Experts?* highlights the marketing puffery and questionable claims that are all too often made by commercial education products and program developers. What we need, of course, is a "Crap Detector" or "Crap Avoidance protocol", so that we vector in on the highest-probability opportunity sketches.

The first step to avoiding junk is to stick closely to your *actual* needs. You have your path analysis with influence bubbles, and you are proactively searching the design space for opportunities that are directly connected to these. We repeat with additional emphasis, you are searching for opportunities that are *directly* connected to these. By contrast, you are *not* engaging in a cognitive bias that's commonly called *The Law of the Instrument* (and sometimes *Maslow's Hammer*). This is where you have this pet thing called the X-Program that, for example, teaches children how to ride bicycles in 10 easy steps, when your identified education challenge is cyberbullying and suicide prevention. Yes, you can make a causal leap that exercise increases endorphins, which makes people happy, and that cycling is a form of exercise. But it's a bit of a stretch.

Therefore, the first step is to systematically search the options in the design space to address *your* actual education challenge. In Figure 2.2, we illustrate three key sources of data that you can leverage, and we then go on to explore each in more detail.

These are the three key informational levers:

A. **Existing practice.** This is what you currently do and what you have learned from it.

B. **Positive outliers.** These are the behaviors and actions of local stakeholders that significantly buck the current trend, in a good way.

C. **Theoretical best practice.** This is what you can glean from research about how other schools and systems have generated impact on the same or similar goals.

The idea is that by mining and triangulating these three sources of information, you are then able to identify:

FIGURE 2.2 ● Identification of Options in the Design Space

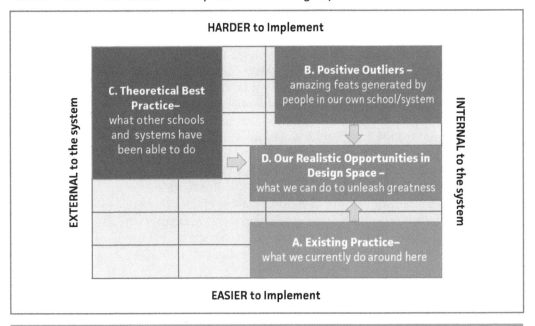

HARDER to Implement

EXTERNAL to the system

INTERNAL to the system

C. Theoretical Best Practice– what other schools and systems have been able to do

B. Positive Outliers – amazing feats generated by people in our own school/system

D. Our Realistic Opportunities in Design Space – what we can do to unleash greatness

A. Existing Practice– what we currently do around here

EASIER to Implement

Source: Adapted from Andrews et al. (2017).

D. **Realistic opportunities in the design space.** These are the locally feasible activities, based on your current capabilities and resourcing and that, importantly, also have a strong probability of progressing your education challenge. And to have that strong probability, they need both strong evidence of impact and a strong connection to one or more of your influence bubbles (i.e., they address a need that you actually have).

Let's now explore each of these in turn.

EXISTING PRACTICE

The good news is that you will likely have already made good progress toward mapping what you currently do. During Stage D1 (Discover), you undertook a *challenge breakdown structure* activity to better define your area of inquiry and you also developed a *path analysis* to better understand your challenge context. However, if you feel that you still need to collect more information on your challenge area, you can supplement this with the following:

- Lesson observations, including a collection of video or even audio transcriptions
- Interviews with teachers and students
- The development of process maps, where you can use sticky notes to plot out end to end how existing activities are undertaken

POSITIVE OUTLIERS

No matter what your area of inquiry, there will always be some stakeholders in your school or system who do significantly better than average. If, for example, you are trying to significantly enhance literacy outcomes, you might find that certain teachers consistently generate above-average outcomes or that certain cohorts of students do phenomenally well irrespective of the teachers.

You need to know why this is and what it is they are doing differently, so that you can evaluate whether it is something that could easily be scaled and replicated by others. If you discover that the students who do well irrespective of the teacher tend to come from higher socioeconomic backgrounds and that their parents tend to pay extra for tuition or additional tutoring support, you might conclude that this would be extremely difficult to replicate. Whereas if you uncovered that the successful students had established a study group and a range of codified study-skills practices for how this operated, there is significantly more replication potential.

The same goes for teachers. In some of Arran's work, he has explored how to increase student attendance at schools in low- and middle-income countries. Some remote schools have done extremely well at this, even with indigenous students whose parents are sometimes initially reluctant to enroll their children. But some mechanisms are easier to replicate than others. In one school, the success seemed to be down to an inspiring and passionate teacher who perpetually sang in the indigenous language while skillfully strumming his guitar. This was beautiful and brilliant but difficult to replicate. Where do we find 500 guitar-wielding teachers? Whereas in other settings, success had been achieved (1) through structured parental outreach sessions to inform them of the benefits of educating their children and (2) by supplementing this with conditional cash transfers to reduce the economic burdens to these parents of sending their children to school. These approaches are much easier to map, codify, and replicate than the guitar-playing teacher, albeit they are less fun.

Figure 2.3 draws on the rich practice-based research into **positive outliers** (LeMahieu et al., 2017; Pascale et al., 2010). It provides you with a framework to map and record the positive outliers in your context.

FIGURE 2.3 ● Identification of Positive Outliers

OUTLIER STAKEHOLDER	OUTLIER OUTCOME	OUTLIER BEHAVIORS	REPLICATION POTENTIAL
Who are they?	**How** do their outcomes buck the general trend?	**What** do they seem to be doing differently?	**How easy** would it be for other stakeholders to replicate the outlier behaviors?

This is all about the identification of *positive* variance, the explanation of that variance, and the ease with which others could do the same. Areas that have high replication potential represent high-potential opportunity sketches.

THEORETICAL BEST PRACTICES

The third place you should look for high-probability bets is **theoretical best practices** identified in the global *what works best* literature. As we explained in the Introduction to this book, there are now more than 1.5 million research articles on the whole gamut of education interventions. Admittedly, it would take you several lifetimes to explore, map, and catalog these—but the good news is that this has (largely) been done already. There are several places you can go to find high-quality **systematic reviews** that synthesize the findings of multiple studies to come to an overall conclusion and that make recommendations, as shown in Figure 2.4.

The reason that we *strongly* advocate explicitly mining high-quality systematic reviews is that they get out of the swampland of *what works* and into the Goldilocks zone of *what works best*. Indeed, one of the unfortunate features of the more than 1.5 million research articles on effective practices is that if you look hard enough, you will be able to find "proof" of anything. You can find "evidence" that homework is ineffective (Kohn, 2006), effective (Roschelle et al., 2016), or sometimes effective (Heffernan, 2019). You will also see many variations in the quality of the research design. The danger, therefore, is that you begin with an idea firmly lodged in your mind about the opportunity sketches that have the most potential for impact (i.e., your pet ideas). And you then only search for data that conform with that view. After enough searching, you will surely find "evidence" that homework works/does not work/sometimes works [*delete as appropriate] or even that the moon landings were faked and that the Earth is flat.

The beauty, however, of going to the systematic reviews is that professional researchers have already done the heavy lifting of mining and aggregating the more than 1.5 million studies to give you an overall probability of impact. This means that you can make a decision based on *all* the relevant studies rather than just your own initial search.

From these and other sources, you will be able to identify high-impact strategies that have worked in other contexts to progress *similar* education challenges. They could *potentially* work in your context, too.

You are especially interested in productized and codified programs that have impact. The beauty of such interventions is that someone else has already done the heavy lifting and had tested, iterated, and refined the protocols in a range of contexts. For better programs, this also includes activation, implementation, and maintenance

FIGURE 2.4 ● Global Education Research Repositories

REPOSITORY	CONTENTS
Visible Learning Meta[x] Global	Catalogs 1,800+ meta-analyses of 100,000+ studies, involving 300 million+ students. Findings are segmented into 300+ influences on student achievement across nine domains, including school, classroom, teacher, teaching strategies, and curricula https://www.visiblelearningmetax.com/
Education Resources Information Center (ERIC) Global	Catalogs (Google-style) 1 million+ research articles, some of which are behind publisher paywalls (although most of these are individual studies rather than systematic reviews) https://eric.ed.gov/
What Works Clearinghouse (WWC) United States	Catalogs a range of evidence-based interventions and/or programs across a range of areas, including literacy, mathematics, science, behavior, and teacher excellence https://ies.ed.gov/ncee/wwc/
Best Evidence Encyclopedia (BEE) United States	Synthesizes findings on effective programs for mathematics, reading, science, and early childhood education. https://bestevidence.org/
Education Endowment Foundation (EEF) United Kingdom	Catalogs 30+ common educational interventions, scoring them based on the cost of implementation vs. impact of implementation https://educationendowmentfoundation.org.uk/
Campbell Collaboration Global **Campbell-UNICEF MegaMap on Child Well-being Interventions** Global	Provides systematic reviews in a range of areas, including education, health, crime, and social justice https://www.campbellcollaboration.org/ https://www.unicef-irc.org/megamap/
Iterative Best Evidence Synthesis (BES) New Zealand	Offers narrative-style systematic reviews on 8+ common education improvement categories, including teacher professional development and high-impact instructional approaches https://www.educationcounts.govt.nz/topics/bes
Australia Education Research Organisation (AERO) Australia	Provides evidence guides on a range of "tried and tested" approaches, including formative assessment, mastery learning, and explicit instruction https://www.edresearch.edu.au/
Ontario Education Research Exchange (OERE) Canada	Catalogs evidence, exemplar resources, and frameworks for effective implementation https://oere.oise.utoronto.ca/

tasks. Why reinvent the wheel? It's better to find the type of wheel that best fits your terrain.

However, as we illustrate in Figure 2.5, the quality of the evidence is key. You can have much higher confidence if you start with the large-scale systematic reviews that bring together the research findings from hundreds, thousands, or tens of thousands of different deployments.

FIGURE 2.5 ● Not All Evidence Is the Same

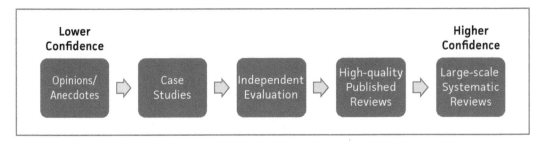

You can also undertake the search the other way around and collect opinions on suitable interventions or programs from colleagues within your wider system. You then look for the research data on each specific recommendation, keeping in view the programs and initiatives that have stronger supporting data from similar contexts to your own and discarding the rest.

In Figure 2.6, we illustrate these two different approaches. Strategy 1 starts with the wider systematic reviews, leveraging these to identify warm leads for programs and then crosschecking program-specific evaluation data in order to decide. Strategy 2 starts with the programs themselves, which may have been brought to your attention as warm leads from the practice-based insights of colleagues and collaborators in the wider system. You then check the program-specific evaluation data for each of these warm leads and, finally, cross-check them against the findings of large-scale systematic reviews to confirm alignment. Then you decide.

FIGURE 2.6 ● Evidence to Programs vs. Programs to Evidence

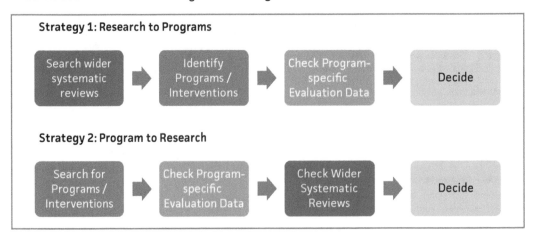

Both of these strategies are perfectly acceptable, as long as you implement them properly—that is, you search for disconfirming as well as confirming data.

However, here is one final look-for as you explore program-specific data. Many education program developers use language like "research-based" or "based on proven research" in the marketing of their wares. What they are basically saying is this:

> Someone, somewhere, [not us] developed something a bit like what we have built, and they gathered evaluation data that demonstrated impact. Therefore, you can be assured that our thing works just the same—even though it's not actually the same.

While it is understandable that product developers should engage in this kind of puffery before they have robust impact data about their specific program, these kinds of statements are still at the opinion/anecdote end of the claim spectrum. If their design and implementation protocols are extremely similar to the programs they are emulating and if those other programs have high-quality published reviews or large-scale systematic reviews supporting their efficacy, then yes, you can have higher confidence. But why not just go to the original program?

YOUR REALISTIC OPPORTUNITIES IN THE DESIGN SPACE

As you explore your existing practice, positive outliers, and the theoretical best practices, the idea is that you "longlist" the ones that have the potential to significantly improve your local context. In Figure 2.7, we illustrate one way that you can do this. At the far right, your education challenge is listed. In the middle column, you transcribe each of the influence bubbles from the path analysis that you undertook in Step 1.3. Then in the far-left column, you list your opportunity sketches—that is, the interventions or actions that *could*

FIGURE 2.7 ● Opportunity Sketch Mapping

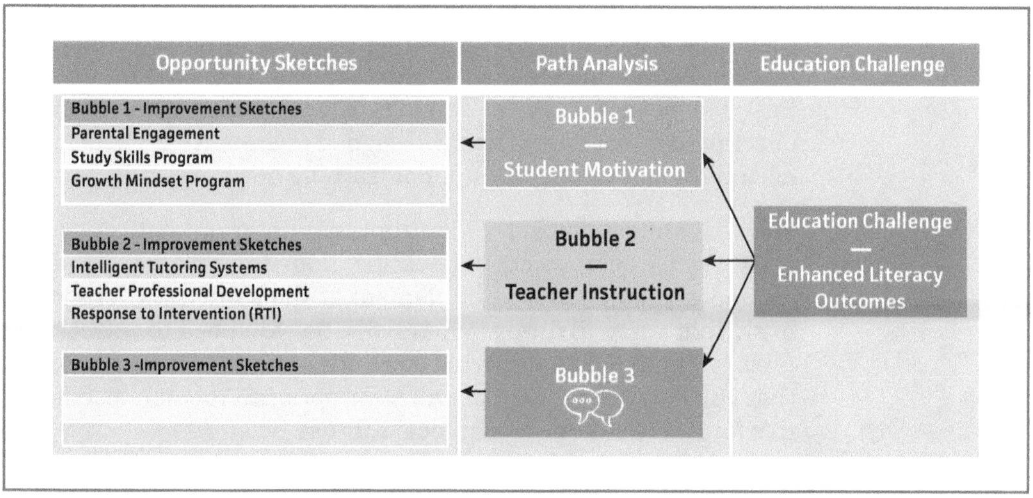

Source: Copyright © Cognition Education. (2022). All rights reserved.

interact with specific bubbles to improve outcomes. You may find that some of these improvement sketches are relevant and can contribute to more than one bubble or your path analysis. This is even better: remember the adage about one stone and multiple birds?

In the opportunity sketch map in Figure 2.7, we have only listed three potential sketches per **influence bubble**. Depending on how long and carefully you search, you could identify hundreds of potential opportunities. Of course, it all comes back to optimal stopping—that decision about how long you should search before moving on.

Each of your opportunity sketches will likely contribute to enhancing outcomes in a different way, with a different theory of improvement and a different causal pathway. For example, sticking with our student literacy example, let's say two of your influence bubbles were (1) students lacking motivation and (2) misaligned instructional approaches. You might identify a range of potential opportunities for each:

- **Student motivation:** parental engagement, growth mindset programs, study-skills programs, behavior management programs, and so on
- **Misaligned instructional approaches:** intelligent tutoring systems, teacher professional development, Response to Intervention (RTI), scripted direct instruction, and so on

Each of these interacts with its respective influence bubble in a different way. Parental engagement initiatives focus on co-opting parents as partners in the learning, whereas growth mindset programs focus on directly enhancing students' self-efficacy and thereby their motivation and approach. Intelligent tutoring systems bypass teacher instruction, providing an overlay of remediation. In contrast, teacher professional development combined with either RTI or scripted direct instruction is designed to enhance what teachers do and thereby accelerate student learning outcomes.

You will almost certainly identify more potential options in the design space than you could possibly hope to implement. Indeed, the more you attempt to implement at the same time, the more likely that you will drop all your balls. So, you need to select carefully. In Figure 2.8, we provide you with a rubric and scoring sheet that you can use to evaluate all your options. You can also adapt this for a better fit with your local context.

In Figure 2.9, we provide an example of how you might collect and record preliminary information on each opportunity sketch in order to undertake the scoring and ranking just described. As

FIGURE 2.8 ● Ranking Your Options in the Design Space

FACTOR	CRITERIA
Evidence of impact	• Outcomes achieved in other contexts (e.g., effect size data) • Number of studies and population of studies (e.g., in Visible Learning Meta[x], we include a confidence ranking for each influence) • Quality of the research (i.e., opinions/anecdotes → **systematic review**) • Similarities between the context of the studies and your local environment
Ease of Replicability	• Is the intervention "productized" or do you need to build it yourself? • Are the steps easy to follow or open to wildly different interpretations? • Was it developed for your cultural/linguistic context and/or has it already been localized?
Local Capacity to Implement	• Do you have access to high-quality internal or third-party technical assistance to support implementation? • Is there buy-in from stakeholders? Does the intervention model conform with local stakeholder beliefs/theory of action? • Do stakeholders have sufficient time to engage/participate at the levels required for success? • Do local stakeholders have the skills to implement the new approach? How easy will it be to upskill them?
Cost of Implementation	• Total cost ÷ Total number of *Direct Beneficiaries* ***Note:* You also need to factor in reoccurring costs, not just the initial setup.**

 OPPORTUNITY SKETCHES	EVIDENCE OF IMPACT 1–5 (5=STRONG EVIDENCE)	EASE OF REPLICABILITY 1–5 (5=HIGH EASE)	LOCAL CAPACITY TO IMPLEMENT 1–5 (5=HIGH CAPACITY)	COST OF IMPLEMENTATION 1–5 (5=LOW COST)	TOTAL
Intelligent tutoring systems	5	3.5	2	3	13.5/25
Scripted direct instruction	5	2.5	1	4	12.5/25

Source: Hamilton and Hattie (2022).

you undertake this analysis, a subset of the opportunity sketches you identified will probably stand out as being much better bets for impact. These are the ones you will carry forward to the next stage of Design.

OTHER APPROACHES TO OPPORTUNITY SKETCHING

In addition to the systematic search processes that we outlined earlier, here are other approaches you could consider to triangulate and test your thinking.

1. **Worst possible idea.** This is where you literally and deliberately come up with as many bad ideas as you can think of for "improvement" in your content. Then you identify all the similarities in those bad ideas, and then search for activities or programs that do the opposite of these bad idea features. You can also attempt to combine different features of the bad ideas together to see if it results in a good idea. One of the potential benefits of the deliberate search for bad ideas is that it's less stressful and inclusive than asking stakeholders to generate good ideas. Everyone can think of bad ideas!

2. **Analogy.** Make comparisons to other situations to test the logic of your thinking. You may have noticed that we have used analogy a lot throughout this book (getting to the moon, the Pyramids, high diving, COVID-19, etc.). We consistently find that making our thinking generic and applying this to new contexts helps us to quickly unpack the flaws in our logic. There is also a great deal of research on the benefits of analogy in transferable skills and critical thinking (e.g., Aubusson et al., 2006; Holyoak, 2012).

3. **Bodystorming.** Here you use roleplay to literally act out the steps of implementing your identified opportunity sketches in order to explore what the practical barriers to delivery might be from the perspective of different stakeholder groups (e.g., teachers, leaders, students, parents) and even personas of different subcategories of each, such as newly qualified teachers vs. experienced teachers. This is very useful for stress testing, which we explore in Step 2.3.

4. **Creative pause.** If the ideas are not flowing, just stop. Take a break, even for a few days. And start again.

5. **Get a second opinion.** Speak to colleagues in other schools, districts, and/or systems that have progressed similar education challenges. Draw particularly on their lessons learned and wrong turns. However, be careful not to take their claims at face value. Always be driven by the evidence of impact and form a third opinion on their second opinion.

6. **Subtract.** Systematically explore whether your education challenge might exist because you are doing too much, rather than too little. Could you make more progress by subtracting activities, programs, and initiatives? Sometimes less is more. However, by some accounts, we are cognitively primed to add rather than subtract (Adams et al., 2021).

All six of these approaches just provide you with *opinions*. You still need to cross-check these warm leads against high-quality evidence of impact—for example, by using the "Ranking Your Options in the Design Space" criteria outlined in Figure 2.8—even if this is locally adapted.

FIGURE 2.9 ● Example Opportunity Sketch Analysis Framework ↻

OPPORTUNITY SKETCH	TARGET GROUP	ASSUMED CAUSAL MECHANISMS	RESEARCH EVIDENCE	MODIFICATIONS	EXISTING PROGRAMS	COST	EASE OF IMPLEMENTATION	PROBABILITY OF IMPACT
What is it?	*Who will we engage with?*	*What is the theorized path from A, to B, C, to Impact?*	*What evidence is available that supports this opportunity sketch?*	*Based on our review of the research, what tweaks would make it more effective?*	*Are there any pre-existing programs that we can buy/ adapt? Do those programs have strong evidence of impact?*	*How much will it cost per school, per student, and per target student?*	*Can this be done quickly and with little effort or will it require protracted effort and buy-in?*	*How do we rate the chances of it working?*
AI-driven early warning system to pre-identify at-risk learners	Students and teachers	Assumes that there are student data patterns that can be used to provide early warning of future absenteeism Assumes that educators can do something with these data and that this *will* reduce absenteeism in the targeted group	Correlational data from a range of US deployments where back tests show that their systems successfully predicted "challenging" students 18 months prior to emergence of absenteeism and behavioral challenges	The system alone will not bring about change. Requires structured intervention with the identified students	There is a range of off-the-shelf software systems, including: System "1" System "2" System "3"	$1500 per school per annum/ average of $2.50 per student per annum	**Medium.** Key issues: • Data-system integration • Actual use of the system by educators to reduce absenteeism	**Moderate.** It will provide data to enable educators to target support to at-risk learners but will not on its own solve the absenteeism challenge
Intelligent tutoring system to provide personalized instruction to students and actionable dashboard data to teachers	Students and teachers	Assumes that children's individual learning needs can be identified through standardized online assessment and that an AI algorithm can select appropriate learning content to enhance each learner's progress in their area of need	6 meta-analyses of 357 studies, involving 22,000+ students, generating an effect size of $d = 0.51$	These systems are "black boxes" (i.e., we cannot vary how they work). However, we can vary: • Which students have access • Duration of access • Where they access • How we link to classroom instruction	There is a range of off-the-shelf software systems, including: System "A" System "B" System "C"	The average cost is $2.5 per student per week	**Medium.** Key issues: • Making time for students to use • Access to devices for all students • Selling the benefits to students, parents, and teachers	**High.** The systematic reviews are from our country. However, we need to make sure the selected system has high-quality independent evaluation data, rather than just being "based in the evidence"

2.2 BUILD PROGRAM LOGIC MODELS

Now that you have identified and agreed on your higher-probability opportunity sketches, the next step is to decide how you will bundle and sequence them together into a coherent and integrated program design that addresses the various influence bubbles on your path analysis.

Back in the 1920s, American cartoonist Rube Goldberg became famous for a genre of cartoons, as illustrated in Figure 2.10.

This is a **Rube Goldberg machine**. It shows a man sitting in a chair, who we will call Dave, and his goal is to switch on the television. There are many ways Dave can go about it. First, he could stand up and walk across the room. Second, he could buy a long stick to poke the buttons on the front of his TV from the comfort of his chair. Third, he could buy a new TV that comes with a shiny remote control. Or fourth, he could build a complex contraption with many moving parts to do his bidding. These are each **theories of improvement**, or high-level ideas about broad types of intervention that *could* be effective. This is akin to an opportunity sketch. The next level down from this is a **theory of action**. This is significantly more detailed and spells out the end-to-end inputs, activities, outputs, and outcomes that will bring the theory of improvement or opportunity sketch to life.

In Dave's case, he has opted for the "complex contraption" theory of improvement. And the cartoon spells out step by step the specific theory of action. In this case, he flicks a seesaw with his foot (A),

FIGURE 2.10 ● A Rube Goldberg Machine

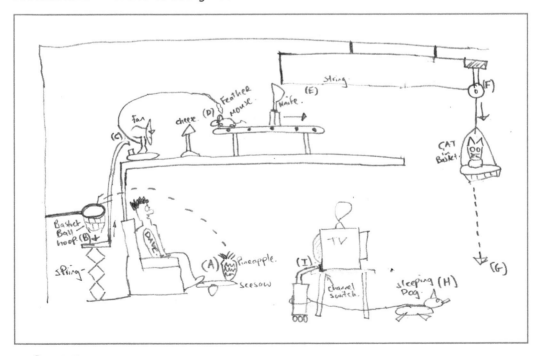

which fires a pineapple through a basketball hoop that then activates a spring-loaded platform (B). This activates a fan that shunts a mouse into action on a conveyor belt (C and D), which in turn pushes a knife through a piece of string (E), thus dropping a cat in a basket (F and G), propelling a dog forward (H), and, abracadabra, changing the TV channel (I)!

Of course, for something as simple as changing a TV channel, this theory of action seems a tad too elaborate. There are too many moving parts—all prone to failure. What if the mouse wanders off or the dog falls asleep? The TV stays stuck on the same channel. Indeed, the sheer beauty of Rube Goldberg machines rests in the fact that we all know they simply won't work; and the joy (and giggling) comes from visualizing all the places where theory and practice are bound to diverge.

However, your selected education challenge is probably a lot more complicated than changing a TV channel. You wouldn't have set up a backbone organization to progress something *that* simple. Instead, it is likely that your implementation requires many complex moving parts—some of which might be prone to failure or at least not do quite what you intended, when you intended. Therefore, it helps considerably if you map out your version of the Rube Goldberg machine end to end to see whether it makes sense and what the potential points of failure could be.

If you want to draw this out like a cartoon, you can. If you want to use sticky notes, you also can. However, one tool that we have found useful in our work is the **program logic model**. This was first formalized by the United States Agency for International Development (USAID) in the late 1960s, based on the thinking tools used at NASA for the moon landings (World Bank, 2000). However, it has taken more than five decades for this approach to catch on to education, and it is still early days for use and adoption.

The program logic model template gives you a structured framework to explore and address the following questions:

1. **What is our education challenge** (i.e., the "problem" we are trying to fix or the moonshot goal we are seeking to progress)?

   For Dave: changing the TV channel, without getting out of the chair

   For you: whatever it was that you agreed on during the D1 Discover Stage

2. **What activities will be undertaken** with this resource to generate improvement in the education challenge area and with what stakeholders?

   For Dave: actions A–I in Figure 2-10. Dave will need to STOP doing some things: to build the machine, to keep it oiled, and to train and feed the animals. In this case, he's decided to forgo playing within his model railway set for 2 weeks.

For you: again, those you identified in your opportunity sketches (i.e., the specific programs, interventions, actions, etc.)

3. **What resources do we need to deploy** to implement our identified opportunity sketches (i.e., the people, time, budget, etc.)?

   For Dave: mouse, cat, dog, and some metal parts and foodstuffs to make the contraptions

   For you: those you identified in your opportunity sketches

4. **What assumptions are we making** about how and why this will work?

   For Dave: that the mouse will be obedient; that the dog "likes" cats; and that all the springs, levers, and belts will interact perfectly

   For you: that the interventions you selected are robust, relevant to your context, and will generate impact

5. **What will the outputs of the activity be** (e.g., the "products" created, the number of people engaged with, etc.)?

   For Dave: the device for changing TV channels is successfully built and installed

   For you: it could be curriculum materials developed, people coached, training events that have taken place, etc.

6. **What measurable outcomes** do we expect to see from implementing the intervention over the short, medium, and longer term?

   For Dave: being able to switch over from *The Simpsons* to *MacGyver* at 7 p.m. daily, without getting out of the chair

   For you: an increase in student literacy outcomes or whatever your specific education challenge areas happen to be

7. **How will we collect data and measure** for monitoring and evaluation purposes? And what types of data will we collect?

   For Dave: maintain a logbook detailing whether the device successfully switched the channel at 7 p.m. each day. He will also commission an independent evaluator to explore each point of linkage in his machine and identify areas of efficiency (Dave likes to overengineer everything!).

   For You: data on teacher participation in your literacy training program and on enhanced student achievement, or in the specific education challenge you have decided to progress.

THEORY OF THE PRESENT VS. THEORY OF IMPROVEMENT VS. THEORY OF ACTION

THEORY TYPE	DESCRIPTION
1. Theory of the present	• Your validated explanation about why your education challenge exists (i.e., what drives it, what is the root cause, and what is the path analysis?) • Dave cannot change the TV channel easily because the TV does not have a remote control
2. Theory of improvement (i.e., high-level)	• Your high-level theory of what you will do to improve the situation • Dave will build a mechanical contraption to change the channel
3. Theory of action (i.e., detailed)	Your more detailed explanation of the key design features and setting levels Dave's contraption will be made out of steel and contain nine linking elements (pineapple, cheese, mouse, knife, cat, dog, etc.)

All of the previous steps in the *Building to Impact 5D* framework have been explicitly designed to support you to answer these questions and to then build your answers out into an integrated and coherent program logic model.

Let's recap some of the key steps that support your readiness to develop that logic model, after you decided and defined your education challenge. See Figure 2.11.

With this thinking and these outputs, you are now ready to start completing *some* of the dimensions in the program logic model template, as introduced in Figure 2.12.

What you insert at this stage might look something like what we present in Figure 2.13.

If you think back to the very start of the book, we introduced the notion of *optimal stopping*. Basically, this is about whether you will luck out and select the "best" option the first time you view a new house, go on a first date, or search for a new car. Most of us do not buy the first house we view, marry the first person we meet, or buy

FIGURE 2.11 ● Recapping Key Prior Steps

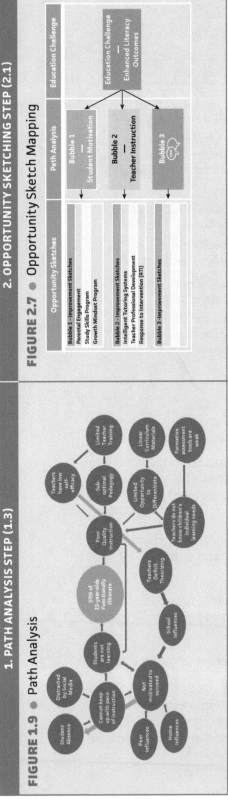

1. PATH ANALYSIS STEP (1.3)

FIGURE 1.9 ● Path Analysis

You built a causal model of the present to explain the key dimensions of your education challenge. This contains a number of influence bubbles.

2. OPPORTUNITY SKETCHING STEP (2.1)

FIGURE 2.7 ● Opportunity Sketch Mapping

Opportunity Sketches	Path Analysis	Education Challenge
Bubble 1 – Improvement Sketches Parental Engagement Study Skills Program Growth Mindset Program	**Bubble 1** — **Student Motivation**	
Bubble 2 – Improvement Sketches Intelligent Tutoring Systems Teacher Professional Development Response to Intervention (RTI)	**Bubble 2** — **Teacher Instruction**	**Education Challenge** — **Enhanced Literacy Outcomes**
Bubble 3 – Improvement Sketches	**Bubble 3**	

You then developed a longlist of *ALL* the potential opportunity sketches that could interact with the various Influence Bubbles to negate or reverse their impact.

3. RANKING OPPORTUNITY SKETCHES STEP (2.1)

OPPORTUNITIES SKETCHES	EVIDENCE OF IMPACT 1-5 [5=STRONG EVIDENCE]	EASE OF REPLICABILITY 1-5 [5=HIGH EASE]	LOCAL CAPACITY TO IMPLEMENT 1-5 [5=HIGH CAPACITY]	COST OF IMPLEMENTATION 1-5 [5= LOW COST]	TOTAL
Intelligent Tutoring Systems	5	3.5	2	3	13.5/25
Scripted Direct Instruction	5		1	4	12.5/25

You then scored and ranked the opportunity sketches using criteria to identify those with the most potential for impact across the widest range of influence bubbles. The highest-potential opportunity sketches are now what gets translated into your **Activities and Stakeholders, Resources, Assumptions,** and **Outputs** in your program logic model.

FIGURE 2.12 ● Program Logic Model Template

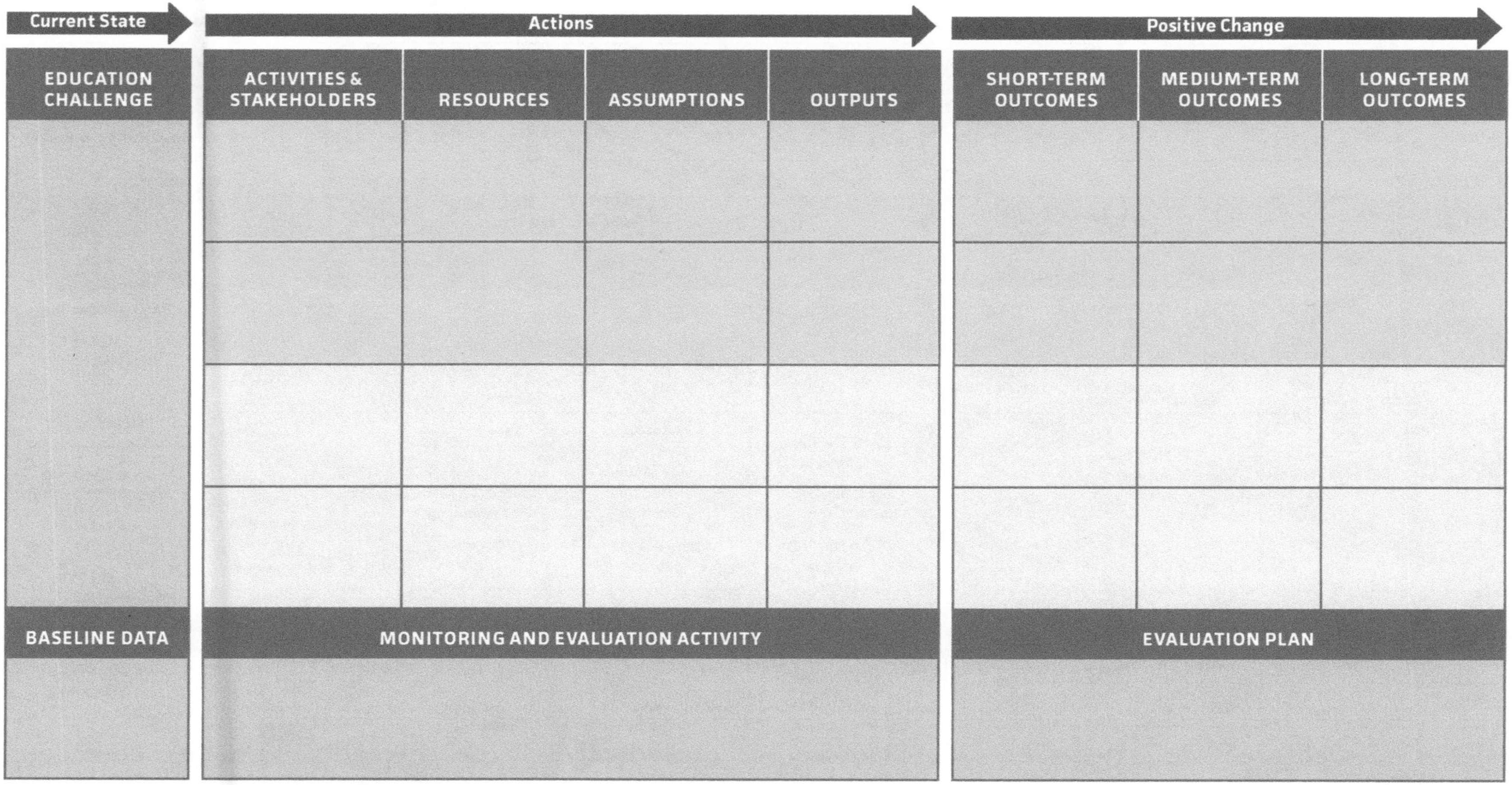

Current State	Actions				Positive Change		
EDUCATION CHALLENGE	ACTIVITIES & STAKEHOLDERS	RESOURCES	ASSUMPTIONS	OUTPUTS	SHORT-TERM OUTCOMES	MEDIUM-TERM OUTCOMES	LONG-TERM OUTCOMES
BASELINE DATA	MONITORING AND EVALUATION ACTIVITY				EVALUATION PLAN		

Source: Copyright © Cognition Education. (2022). All rights reserved.

FIGURE 2.13 ● Partially Completed Program Logic Model

Current State → Actions → Positive Change

EDUCATION CHALLENGE	ACTIVITIES & STAKEHOLDERS	RESOURCES	ASSUMPTIONS	OUTPUTS	SHORT-TERM OUTCOMES	MEDIUM-TERM OUTCOMES	LONG-TERM OUTCOMES
Our student literacy rates are significantly below national averages. Disproportionately boys (68%) Disproportionately rural (74%) Disproportionately low SES (83%) 32% missed target by 5% or less — 41% missed it by 5-15% 27% missed it by more than 25%	Response to Intervention Program that provides triaged and targeted support to priority students	• RTI Program Materials • External Trainer $XX	1. Program will transfer to our context 2. Teachers will be able to implement	1. Teacher training completed			
	Intelligent Tutoring System that provides AI-driven personalized learning to all students	• Software Platform $XX • 90 minutes per week of access on the timetable	1. All students will use the platform 2. The use will generate improved literacy outcomes	1. Platform procured 2. Student logins distributed 3. Student inductions			
BASELINE DATA 33% of our 13-year-olds are functionally illiterate	MONITORING AND EVALUATION ACTIVITY				EVALUATION PLAN		

Source: Copyright © Cognition Education. (2022). All rights reserved.

the first car we see. And, equally, home builders and car manufacturers do not put their first ideas straight into production. They build multiple prototypes—some just on paper, others in physical form. They do this to double-check and to mitigate the risk that they launch a lemon when they go to market.

The same principle applies to *your* program logic modeling activity. Yes, you *might* hit the jackpot the first time. But it's just as likely that you will land on the lemon. Therefore, we strongly advise that you work up a few different logic models. Going back to our literacy example, some logic models might be simple with only one core work package or opportunity sketch—such as the introduction of an intelligent tutoring system, which children access at home once a week and for one period a week in school. Others might be more complex and involve the introduction of major packages of teacher professional development and perhaps even a whole new instructional approach, like RTI. Obviously, more moving parts = more risk that the dog doesn't play ball. Conversely, fewer moving parts might mean that what you are doing is too simple and that it does not properly interact with the various "bubbles" in your path analysis.

You can now either pick your best design(s) and quickly get to implementation *or* you can spend a little more time **stress testing** before lift-off. If you are working at the district level (or higher), we recommend that you use the tools and processes in Step 2.3 to pre-test your proposed logic models. You will likely be seeking to progress an education challenge across multiple schools, at scale. Therefore, it's profoundly important that you explore your selected activities or interventions from *all* angles before you inadvertently waste the time of stakeholders on ineffective initiatives. If you are working at the school, department, or professional learning community level, we encourage you to understand these tools and perspectives, although they are not mandated. We completely get that sooner (rather) than later you need to get on with implementing *something* and that you can collaboratively adjust it as you go. The longer you procrastinate, the more likely you'll just stop altogether. In which case, draw on Step 2.3 for inspiration and additional considerations and then move on to Step 2.4.

> *It's profoundly important that you explore your selected activities or interventions from* all *angles before you inadvertently waste the time of stakeholders on ineffective initiatives.*

2.3 STRESS TEST AND IMPROVE ON STEP 2.2

These processes are mandated if you are working at the whole-school or district level. They are highly recommended if you are working as part of a teaching team or professional learning community, but you might undertake them more quickly (i.e., reach optimal stopping sooner).

GOING DOWN THE RABBIT HOLE

While program logic models help you to build a high-level map of how the mouse *should* interact with the feather, cheese, string, and cat, there's a second tier of detail. This might also significantly impact whether your Rube Goldberg machine is effective. This includes the type of mouse, whether it has been trained, how frequently it is fed, whether it actually likes cheese, and therefore whether fruit or seeds would be better bait. And, of course, we can ask the same types of questions about every other link in the machine: the weight and size of the pineapple, the length and sharpness of the knife, the size and color of the cat, and so on.

In our work, we have found that leaving these considerations to chance, just assuming that "any old cheese or mouse" will be just as effective, and also not considering which should come first (the mouse or the pineapple) creates too much risk that you fail to convert your initial energy into a drive that positively impacts all the other links and connectors in your program logic model.

Every potential activity or intervention that you decided to include in your logic model can be varied. Here are some of the generic sources of variation (Hamilton & Hattie, 2022):

- **Dosage** (How much "medicine" do we give?)

- **Duration** (How long do we give it for and at what spacing between "doses"?)

- **Target group** (Who is selected for "treatment"?)

- **Delivery group** (Who implements the initiative?)

- **Fidelity** (How much variation is allowed in how the treatment is delivered locally?)

Other opportunities for variation will be dependent on the specific activity/intervention you plan on implementing (i.e., they are *regimen specific*). For example, if you are opting for an intelligent tutoring system to remediate children's literacy, other considerations will include these:

- Which of the many available systems is selected for use?

- Is use mandatory or optional?

- Is it only for struggling students or for all learners?

- Are parents going to be briefed or even co-opted as activators?

- Is it used at home and/or at school?

- Is it standalone or is the system also used in class for group teaching?

- Will teachers use the formative assessment data to enhance their classroom teaching?

- Will the school leadership use the baseline assessment data as an accountability tool to (secretly or even openly) evaluate teacher performance?

- Will children be allowed to access it on their phones or only on tablets and desktops?

- Will children's use be monitored?

- Will there be any rewards or sanctions for students that under or over-use the platform?

We call these considerations **design features**. For each design feature, there are multiple **setting levels**. Some design features can be switched off entirely or set to zero. And for all the active features, there are several different positions (i.e., setting levels) that the dial can be set to. In our work, we have found it useful to explicitly map *all* the potential design features and setting levels and to use this information to select the optimum ones with great care. Not to do so risks random pineapples, cats, and feathers getting thrown into the mix without much thought for how they can be selected and sequenced with greater care and deeper impact.

In Figure 2.14, we illustrate how you can map the design features and setting levels for each of your opportunity sketches.

The mapping table in Figure 2.14 is only a worked example. For the average activity or intervention, it is possible that there will be 25 or more design features that are worth thinking about. Once you have identified them, initial questions are whether to switch them on or off, whether to leave them to local discretion, or whether to pick and lock a specific setting level.

There is a second level of complexity. For each design feature that you decide to activate and lock, there might be 10 or more setting levels for you to choose from. This means that there are likely 250 or more different settings that you can move the various dials through (i.e., 25+ dials × 10+ setting positions on each dial). And this is just for one intervention! If you decide to combine intelligent tutoring with a growth mindset program, RTI, *and* teacher professional development, there are equally many design features and setting levels for each of these too!

FIGURE 2.14 ● Design Features and Setting Levels ↻

	DESIGN FEATURE 1: WHICH SYSTEM DO WE SELECT?	DESIGN FEATURE 2: IS IT MANDATORY?	DESIGN FEATURE 3: HARDWARE	DESIGN FEATURE 4: PARENTAL ENGAGEMENT	DESIGN FEATURE 5: DOSAGE LEVEL
ACTIVITY: INTELLIGENT TUTORING SYSTEM					
Setting Level 1	Tutoring Platform A	Mandatory for all students	Students' own devices (any)	None (all done in school)	Left to personal choice
Setting Level 2	Tutoring Platform B	Optional for all students	Students' own devices (non-smartphone only)	None (but used at home and school)	Minimum 60 minutes per week
Setting Level 3	Tutoring Platform C	Mandatory for students who have fallen behind. Optional for all others	School tablets	Parent newsletter	Maximum of 90 minutes per week and minimum of 60
Setting Level 4	Tutoring Platform D		Hybrid	Parent briefing session	
Setting Level 5	Tutoring Platform E			Telephone call to parents	
ANALYSIS	Platform E has been used in other schools locally. Staff very positive. Also, strong independent evaluation data	If it's optional, no one will take it seriously. If it's mandatory only for students that have fallen behind, this creates stigma	We are not sure it will make much difference. Let's start with hybrid and see what happens	It would probably be helpful to inform parents!! Let's start by putting it in the newsletter and see if any request more information	The global research suggests that 90 minutes a week spread over 3 × 30-minute sessions is about optimal
CONCLUSION	**Platform E**	**Mandatory for all**	**Hybrid**	**Parent newsletter**	**90 minutes, split between three sessions**

Source: Adapted from Hamilton and Hattie (2022).

One day soon, we will hopefully be able to run all these options through a software engine like IBM Watson or WolframAlpha to help us identify and select between a seemingly infinite number of design options and setting levels. Until this happens, it's important that you give the selection and interaction of design features as much thought as you can. Even seemingly minor details like letting students access intelligent tutoring systems from their personal smartphone devices can have unanticipated implications—with the screens being too small to view the content or to type their responses, plus the feed of K-pop videos on TikTok acting as a constant distractor.

It's important that you give the selection and interaction of design features as much thought as you can.

In our work, we find those initiative designers often only work down as far as the high-level program logic model—that is, agreeing that there will be mice, cats, cheese , and industrial-looking machinery connecting them. They never quite get to the detail of whether all these features are needed, whether they are connected in the right order, and whether it should actually be a kitten rather than cat. Our message to you is that one of the key reasons that implementation often fails is that each of these microfeatures is left to chance, being considered as an unimportant detail. Of course, another source of failure is spending so long on this that you end up in analysis-paralysis! This is why **optimal stopping considerations** are so important. At some point you need to make a judgment call about *when* it's time to follow Elvis's sage dictum: *A little less conversation, a little more action, please.*

However, even if you spend a relatively small amount of time going down the rabbit hole, one of the benefits of mapping (at least some of) the various design features and setting levels is that if during implementation and evaluation you are dissatisfied with the degree of impact, you can go back to your mapping and identify aspects of your design that could be iterated to enhance the overall efficacy. It may be that you subsequently decide to activate or deactivate specific design features or to incrementally adjust the setting levels on those that are activated.

We also find it helpful to think about design features and setting levels as being a little like the graphic equalizer deck that you used to find on old-fashioned HiFi music centers and that you still see in sound studios. Figure 2.15 illustrates what we mean by this. The idea is that you carefully consider the "best" position for each of the sliders and you explicitly lock those setting levels before you start Stage D3 (Deliver).

FIGURE 2.15 ● The Graphic Equalizer

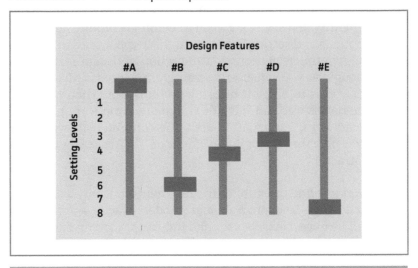

Source: Copyright © Cognition Education. (2022). All rights reserved.

THINK (A LITTLE BIT) LIKE EEYORE

Many things look good on paper. In fact, the process of typing them up in pretty fonts and colors and inserting icons and infographics can often give hair-brained notions a self of authority or legitimacy that they don't deserve. There's a risk that as you undertake the 5D processes in this book—potentially using our templated tools—you (initially) become seduced by the words on the page and (much later) surprised when your initiative comes apart at the seams.

You probably know or have heard of the *Winnie-the-Pooh* books by A. A. Milne. One of the characters is a gray overstuffed donkey called Eeyore, who is renowned for his pessimism. He always expects bad things to happen and imagines them in advance. Unfortunately, he also stoically accepts what happens and never (usually) tries to prevent what happens.

We now want you to think (a little bit) like Eeyore. Before you get busy implementing your dashing design(s), it helps if you take the time to explore all the ways what you are about to do could go hideously wrong. Unlike Eeyore, you are not going to stoically accept and embrace these impending visions of doom. You are doing this so you can preempt and build mitigations and contingencies into your program logic model—to reduce or even to "design out" the risk.

To get your Eeyore-like mental juices flowing, here are *some* of the different types of implementation risks you could consider.

EEYORE 1: STAKEHOLDER BELIEFS

From research across a range of sectors, we know that people's existing beliefs are a key determinant of whether their collective future actions will generate impact (Knoster, 1991; Robinson, 2018; Robinson et al., 2009). There are two dimensions to this:

- **Self- and collective efficacy.** Where you believe that you have the individual and collective power to make a difference, generally you do! This positive belief drives positive action. Of course, you are more likely to hold those beliefs where you have confidence that (1) what you are about to embark on is within your existing wheelhouse or capability set and (2) it builds on and stretches your existing "superpowers" rather than requiring you to, say, learn Arabic overnight.

  Implication: You need to make sure that your program logic model is predicated on "desirable difficulty" (Bjork, 1994), that it builds on existing capabilities in your team, and that you factor in time, support, and love for people to fall into a few bear traps and learn from this along the way.

- **Worldview.** We all have an implicit theory about human nature, what is important in life, and what being a good educator is all about. Even if we can't consciously articulate those beliefs, they implicitly drive our actions. For example, in some of our work we have engaged with school leaderships that want to implement scripted instructional approaches. While there is a strong evidence base for some of these types of intervention (depending of course on what it is exactly that you are trying to achieve), experienced teachers often do not see themselves as actors reading a script. So, their worldview about teaching and the execution of their professional competency is implicitly misaligned with the philosophy of the intervention. And all of us, when asked to do something that we don't believe in, either go along grudgingly or (perhaps) even attempt to drill holes in the side of the boat while everyone else is rowing away.

  Implication: You either need to select actions that are strongly aligned with your team's existing mind frames, to avoid the jarring dissonance, or to build in time to positively engage, build bridges, and shared understanding (i.e., thesis – antithesis – synthesis).

Note that there are two contrasting perspectives on how we confront the misalignment of people's existing beliefs with the actions we are asking them to carry out, which we illustrate in Figure 2.16. Theory 1 suggests that we need to spend a significant period of

FIGURE 2.16 ● Theory 1 vs. Theory 2

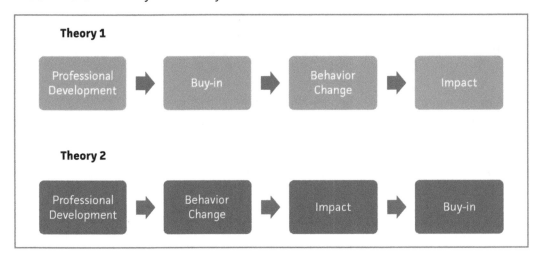

Source: Copyright © Cognition Education. (2022). All rights reserved.

time engaging with those prior beliefs, convincing stakeholders that they are wrong (or coming to some compromise perspective) and getting their buy-in *before* they will go on to adopt and implement. It is a common perspective in generic business improvement texts; and the Japanese call it *Nemawashi*, which roughly translates as 'laying the groundwork'. Theory 2 is championed by Thomas Guskey (2020) and Doug Reeves (2021a). It suggests that *seeing is believing*—that most of us are only weakly convinced by dialogue and data; and that by shining a light on the difference of perspective, we might inadvertently encourage people to hunker down further into their pre-existing mind frames (i.e., the Backfire Effect). Theory 2 suggests that we are only strongly convinced/converted *after* we have put something new into practice and seen the positive impact with our own eyes. In other words, behavior change and impact come first, and belief changes a lagging second.

Behavior change and impact come first, and belief changes a lagging second.

The research on these two different theories on the relationship between beliefs and action is still a work in progress. However, recent research involving students suggests that initial task success (i.e., impact) often precedes and primes the motivation to continue to invest more time and energy (Sinha & Kapur, 2021). This offers support for Theory 2.

In the context of *Building to Impact 5D*, we offer the following guidance. If there is a low buy-in for what you are seeking to implement but there is (a) extremely strong evidence that it has been effective in similar contexts to yours and (b) the new approaches can be learned and/or acquired to a satisfactory level with relatively low investments in training, then you could opt for the Theory 2 approach. You ignore the noise, push on with mandated implementation, and you wait (with bated breath) for people to report back that "it works!" and to ask for more.

EEYORE 2: MOTIVATION

From the research on deliberate practice and elite performance (Ericsson & Harwell, 2019; Ericsson et al., 1993), we know that across the full range of sectors and professions, becoming highly proficient in technically complex fields like teaching takes 10 years or around 10,000 hours of *effortful* practice. We also know that educators are often more motivated to do this early in their careers and more prone to plateau later (Papay & Kraft, 2015; Rice, 2013). Therefore, you may find that if you expect stakeholders to do something radically different to their current repertoire, those who are earlier in their careers might be more open to it. In contrast, more established teachers might require additional support and motivation to encourage them to make the leap. Or you might need to design features into your intervention that enable it to be effective even without that leap.

EEYORE 3: FRICTION

This is about the quantity of change and the level of (personal) time and effort required to achieve it. If you are introducing a new step to an existing process (i.e., juggle *one* extra ball), the implementation friction is likely to be lower. Whereas if you expect stakeholders to quickly learn to juggle five extra balls or to shift from juggling to "cake decorating," the level of friction is likely to be significantly higher.

EEYORE 4: MAINTENANCE

Many of us make New Year's resolutions to lose weight or increase our fitness. However, how many times have you heard someone else making such a resolution and then inwardly thought to yourself "by February all that gym equipment will be in the cupboard collecting dust"? And how many resolutions have you made yourself and subsequently failed to keep or maintain? Maintenance is *really* hard. In the domain of weight loss alone, the research tells us that around 80% of successful dieters rebound to their previous weight (or more) within 5 years (Wing & Phelan, 2005). If something as simple as watching what we eat is so darned hard, you need to consider whether what you are asking or expecting stakeholders to do will be easy or difficult to maintain. And you may also need to consider what ongoing support measures you could build into your program logic model to keep everyone on the up-and-up. We come back to this in Stage D5 (Double-Up).

EEYORE 5: MUTATION

Dylan Wiliam (2018) argues that through professional development it's relatively easy to get teachers to adopt new ideas: the hard part is getting them to stop what they were doing before. To us, this is profound. Often, "new ways" are designed to be implemented with fidelity—much like the insertion of a medical intravenous line, as we discussed in the Introduction. There are highly effective ways to do this that significantly reduce the probability of a bacterial infection. However, many, many line infections still occur; and the reason is that medical practitioners do not always follow the training or the protocols to the letter. They sometimes adapt, cutting corners to enhance the efficiency or blend bits and pieces of their new training with their prior practice.

We often see the same kind of challenge in the implementation of new education initiatives. Larry Cuban (1984, 1990), in his analysis of the transition from "traditional" to "progressive" pedagogies, concluded that very few teachers made a genuine transition from one "way" to the other. It was more common that educators cherry-picked the bits that they liked and blended these with their existing repertoire.

In stress testing your program logic model, you need to consider whether fidelity of implementation is important and/or the level of mutation that you can live with and accept. If fidelity is critical, you will need to build in a support infrastructure to ensure that in implementation, what happens at the chalk face does not end up becoming a grainy imitation that bears a passing resemblance to the original (i.e., a photocopy of a photocopy of a photocopy) (Elmore, 1996).

EEYORE 6: VOLTAGE DROP

When the great industrialists of the 19th century laid cables across the lands to transport electricity, they quickly discovered that the voltage dropped or dissipated over greater distances. Hence, distribution is required at much higher voltages than are needed in domestic settings and for substations to dilute the juice, so that it doesn't blow up your TV.

A common challenge when implementing new initiatives at scale (e.g., across multiple schools) is that, metaphorically, the initial "voltage" is too low. That is, it's strong enough to "power" one or two schools but when you try and hook up 50 to the same "grid," the power that is transmitted is too low (e.g., see Kilbourne et al., 2007).

So, if you are planning on implementing at scale, you will need to consider how you boost the juice or whether you can accept lower levels of current as you support more and more settings with adoption. The same thinking also applies *within* a single school. Perhaps your program logic model envisages training a small group of path-finder teachers and you then *assume* they will "pass it on" without voltage drop to their colleagues.

EEYORE 7: SIDE EFFECTS

When you buy medicine from the pharmacy, there is usually a leaf-let inside the packet that contains the small print. A key element of that text is usually a list of all the known side effects that *could* materialize if you take the pills and what you should subsequently do if they occur. It is well known and accepted in medicine that occasionally the cure can be worse than the disease.

Yong Zhao (2017, 2018) has applied the same notion of side effects to education interventions, noting that every opportunity comes with a potential cost. For example, problem-based learning *might* increase student creativity, engagement, and attendance but with a side effect that the overall speed of learning is slower, that misconceptions may be inadvertently reinforced, and that students may not be exposed to key bridging concepts that they required to develop advanced subject matter knowledge. Ditto for direct instruction. This *might* increase the efficiency of learning and ensure content is appropriately sequenced and staged. But it *might* also come with the side effect of inducing boredom and stifling creativity.

You need to consider what the potential side effects of your interventions could be. Whether those are acceptable or whether they require countermeasures. In medicine, doctors often respond by either (a) identifying a different treatment whose side effects are more acceptable or (b) by prescribing an additional intervention that is *for* the side effects (e.g., *medicine A makes me nauseous, so I also take antinausea meds*).

HOW DOES THIS EEYORE THINKING HELP?

The idea is that you use this Eeyore thinking (1) to identify all the things that could go wrong in the implementation of your pro-gram logic model and (2) to map out mitigations. You can also use the bodystorming technique we introduced in Step 2.2 to roleplay the implementation steps of your logic model, particularly from the perspective of stakeholder reaction. With this tech-nique, you can literally act out the revulsion, misunderstandings, and horde of villagers descending with their burning pitchforks. Of course, your reason for doing this is to develop mitigations and countermeasures and then to consider whether these will be strong enough to hold the Eeyores at bay.

You can use Figure 2.17 to map all these Eeyores. In the first col-umn, you describe the risk. In the second and third columns, you rank the probability of the risk occurring and the severity

FIGURE 2.17 ● Program Logic Model Risk Mitigation Planning ↻

NO.	RISK DESCRIPTION (OR "EEYORE")	STAKEHOLDERS	LIKELIHOOD (L) 1–5	SEVERITY (S) 1–5	IMPACT L × S	MITIGATION
1	Project design includes a requirement for teachers recording and sharing videos of their lessons. They may be extremely uncomfortable doing this and/or interpret it as accountability rather than an improvement initiative	Teachers	4	3	12	● Use a specialist video capture platform, so that teachers can control when and to whom they share their videos ● Lead by example. The SLT will film an exemplar lesson and share video for review at a film club event
2	We will be providing teacher professional development in RTI via a third-party training program. Our educators may not engage with it because they did not build it and it was developed overseas	Teachers	5	5	20	● Have the identified teachers [opinion leaders] conduct a study visit to other schools nearby that are using the program. They will then report back to the whole teaching body on their findings ● Consider the option of localizing the materials (i.e., running workshops with our teachers to make modifications to materials, particularly key terms and linkage to organizational vision)
3	Project design involves the use of an intelligent tutoring system by all students. They may not want to participate	Students	4	3	12	● Make it optional at first to fully test the system and generate buzz and buy-in via trail-blazers ● Make it recommended and then publish league tables of top users and give them school house-points ● Include each student's usage ranking in their parental report card

Note: SLT, senior leadership team.

Source: Adapted from Hamilton and Hattie (2021).

of impact. Then in the final column, you outline your mitigation strategy.

Assuming that you stress test your preferred program logic models carefully (and we really think you should), you will likely identify many bear traps you could have stepped into and many improvements that reduce your probability of ankle pain. The idea is that you circle back around, and you adjust your initial logic model to incorporate all this learning.

2.4 AGREE ON WHAT YOU ARE GOING TO STOP

As we are sure you have noticed, there are 24 hours in a day. Not 26 or 37. You will also have noticed that not all those hours are amenable to being leveraged to progress your education challenge. For a start, you need to ringfence 8 hours of shut-eye. You probably also want to have a life outside your work. And within your working day, there are undoubtedly a myriad of business-as-usual activities, pre-existing special projects, and the occasional bit of ad hoc firefighting filling up your time. We have yet to meet an educator who has an hour or two allocated each day for navel gazing or with flex time waiting to be filled. In fact, when we look at the comparative Teaching and Learning International Survey (TALIS) data, it's pretty clear that no matter where you are in the world, you are likely to be working long, grueling hours already (Organization for Economic Cooperation and Development, 2020).

Therefore, before you start progressing your new education challenge, you really, really, really need to take stock of all the other special projects you are already progressing. And you need to do this to find some to STOP, so that you can reallocate the time to this new and more pressing agenda. In Figure 2.18, we present a four-column tool that you can use to support this audit.

You may think this process extreme and, yes, it is. The whole point is to get you to think about all your competing priorities and the level of data you have on hand that demonstrates they are worth continuing rather than deep-sixing. If you take a hard-core approach to this, you will only continue to progress the projects in column 4 of your table and you will drop everything else. However, as an absolute minimum, we propose the RULE of TWO-for-ONE. In other words, for every ONE change initiative that you propose to start, find TWO initiatives of similar *time commitment* that you are going to stop.

FIGURE 2.18 ● The STOP Audit ↻

ALL OUR CURRENT PROJECTS	PROJECTS WITH SYSTEMATIC EVALUATION DATA	PROJECTS WITH REALLY POSITIVE EVALUATION DATA	POSITIVE PROJECTS THAT STILL NEED PUMP-PRIMING
In this column, you list all your active special projects.	Here, you narrow down to those that you have bothered to systematically collect evaluation data for. If you have not set up evaluation protocols, your initiative is more likely to be busywork that's not worth your time; and we recommend that you **assume that anything you are NOT evaluating is having no impact.**	Now you narrow down even further to the projects you are systematically evaluating and where the data show extremely strong returns. Elsewhere we have suggested the use of effect size statistics. If your pre/post-assessments don't show a gain of at least $d = 0.40$, then consider carefully whether they are worth continuing.	Of the positive projects that are generating profound impact, how many still need centralized support to keep them going? It may be that many of the changes have already become engrained and sustained, or that the original need no longer exists. Put the projects that *still* need continuing/backbone team oversight here.

FIGURE 2.19 ● The Cognitive Bias Codex

COGNITIVE BIAS	DESCRIPTION	KEY REFERENCE
Optimism bias	The tendency to be overoptimistic about the probability of success and not to develop contingency plans/mitigations (e.g., "I'm sure it's working and that we need to continue with it. Otherwise, why would we have even started it, right?")	Sharot (2011)
Plan continuation bias	Failure to recognize that the original plan/design is no longer relevant and to adapt to the changing situation (e.g., "I know the building is on fire, but we still need to hold the parent–teacher conference")	Heath (1995)
Sunk cost fallacy	Continuing to implement even where data show lack of impact: because so much time, effort, and money have already been invested and it is too emotionally distressing to conclude it has all been in vain: the show must go on!	Arkes and Blumer (1985)
Anecdotal fallacy	Treating anecdotal evidence as being of equivalent value to more rigorous evaluation protocols (e.g., "Everyone likes it, so we should carry on")	Gibson and Zillman (1994)

COGNITIVE BIAS	DESCRIPTION	KEY REFERENCE
Continued influence effect **Conservativism bias** **Confirmation bias**	Holding on to prior beliefs about the efficacy of an intervention, even when systematically collected data contradict the misinformed prior belief (e.g., "I don't care what the data say. I know what I can see and feel. I believe it's working!")	Nickerson (1998)
Expectation bias **Observer expectancy effect**	Tendency for evaluators to believe, collect, and publish data that conform with their prior expectations and to treat contrary data with disbelief/skepticism (e.g., "The data aren't looking so rosy. They must be wrong. I'll delete them and focus on the two positive anecdotes")	Rosenthal (1966)
Ostrich effect	Avoidance of monitoring/collecting data that might cause psychological discomfort. Originally identified in the financial sector, where investors stop monitoring their investment portfolios during market downturns (e.g., "This isn't looking so good. Let's just stop collecting data. It's too painful to look. We'll keep going with the initiative though. People will be upset if we stop")	Galai and Sade (2006)

Source: Adapted from Hattie and Hamilton (2020a).

Of course, we recognize that stopping is extremely hard. There is a range of cognitive biases that seem to prime us to continue with things that really should be stopped. These are biases that make it hard for us to just say, *No! Enough is enough!* We list some in Figure 2.19 (for more details, see Hattie & Hamilton, 2020a, 2020b).

Obviously, de-implementing is just as hard as implementing. People become emotionally attached to the work they have engaged in— and to the effort and the long hours. No one wants to admit that it has all been pointless. So, you actually need a strategy for de-implementation and this also needs to confront the seven Eeyores that we unpacked in Step 2.3.

Therefore, we recommend that you divide your program logic model in half and that 50% of the rows or work packages are about implementing your new agenda and 50% are focused on the initiatives you are concurrently dismantling. This is why half the program logic model template that we already introduced was in a different color: half for starting and half for stopping! We illustrate this in Figures 2.20 and 2.21.

FIGURE 2.20 ● Program Logic Model—STOPPING AND STARTING

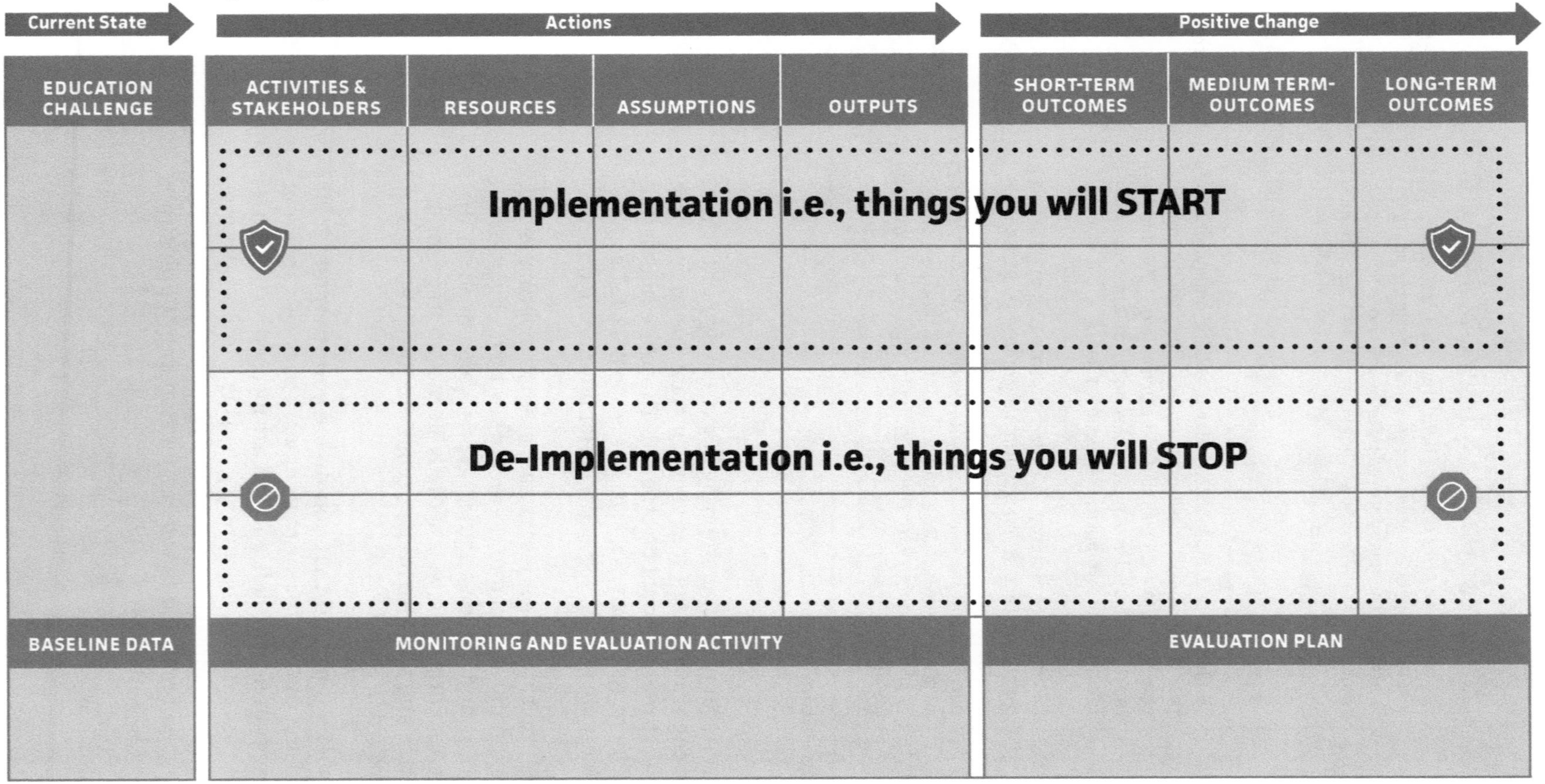

Source: Copyright © Cognition Education. (2022). All rights reserved.

FIGURE 2.21 ● Program Logic Model—Example of Stopping and Starting

Current State | Actions | Positive Change

EDUCATION CHALLENGE	ACTIVITIES & STAKEHOLDERS	RESOURCES	ASSUMPTIONS	OUTPUTS	SHORT-TERM OUTCOMES	MEDIUM TERM-OUTCOMES	LONG-TERM OUTCOMES
Our student literacy rates are significantly below national averages. **Disproportionately boys (68%)** **Disproportionately rural (74%)** **Disproportionately low SES (83%)** — **32% missed target by 5% or less** **41% missed it by 5–15%** **27% missed it by more than 25%**	Response to Intervention Program that provides triaged and targeted support to priority students	• RTI Program Materials • External Trainer $XX	1. Program will transfer to our context 2. Teachers will be able to implement	1. Teacher training completed			
	Intelligent Tutoring System that provides AI-driven personalized learning to all students	• Software Platform $XX • 90 minutes per week of access on the timetable	1. All students will use the platform 2. The use will generate improved literacy outcomes	1. Platform procured 2. Student logins distributed 3. Student inductions			
	STOP: **Learning Styles** Teacher Professional Development Program	• Briefing sessions on why we are stopping and what we are starting	1. Program is ineffective 2. Time better spent on RTI	1. Teachers have additional 2 hours per week 2. Time transferred to RTI			
	STOP: **Student Co-curricular Project**	• Vice Principal time for communications sessions with students and parents	1. A 'happy program' without evidence of impact 2. Stakeholders will accept cancellation.	1. Students have additional 3 hours a week 2. 1 hour saving for teachers			
BASELINE DATA	MONITORING AND EVALUATION ACTIVITY				EVALUATION PLAN		
33% of our 13-year-olds are functionally illiterate							

Source: Copyright © Cognition Education. (2022). All rights reserved.

2.5 ESTABLISH A MONITORING AND EVALUATION PLAN

> **Warning: This section is long and requires concentration. Consider taking a break before pushing on!**

> Do not skip this section. If you do, you are not implementing the 5D methodology properly.

When long-distance runners train for marathons, they have a *distance* goal in mind: to successfully run 26 miles and 385 yards. They usually also have a *time* goal—the current speed record, for example, is just over 2 hours. Generally, they don't just turn up on the day and hope to wing it. Professional runners work with a coach to prepare for the race. The coach uses a range of tools to gauge (i.e., *evaluate*) the runner's current performance, including a stopwatch, heart rate monitor, weighing scales, and even AI-driven video analytics to assess posture, technique, and gait. The coach and runner then use these data during training to decide whether the training strategy is working and what to do next. The decision could be to carry on as is or to change footwear, adjust stride length, eat more protein, or a host of other adjustments. Then, once a change is made, the measuring tools are used (yet) again for a bit more evaluation and a bit more iterative variation until the runner is (hopefully) able to complete the course in the desired time.

The same principle applies to the evaluative rules of deciding who has won the race. As a thought experiment, imagine that the starting gun has gone off while at the same time World Athletics (the global governing body for running sports) is still debating the rules and is still deciding what constitutes *success*. Imagine further that some committee members are arguing for the critical measure to be speed (i.e., who passes the finish line first), while others argue that performance should be measured against an agreed standard of technique (i.e., who has the best running gait). Yet others wade in and suggest that score points should be added or subtracted depending on the footwear of the athletes, their social background, or the length of their respective legs. While this is a good debate to have, it happens (and has happened) well *before* the starting gun has been fired. No competition organizer would contemplate having the debate *after* the race was in play. This is (literally) moving the goal posts.

However, in our work with schools, we see this thought experiment playing out for real. Some of the horrors include the following:

1. **Not evaluating at all.** Yes, this happens and all too frequently. In the mad rush to get an initiative out of the starting blocks, everyone forgets to define what success means, to agree on how they will measure it, or what they will do if the collected data aren't rosy.

   Takeaway: Unless you systematically evaluate, you will have no idea whether you have generated *meaningful* impact or how you can grow this further.

2. **Using the wrong evaluative tools.** Running coaches tend not to include water pressure gauges in their evaluative toolkit: knowing the pressure in the stadium pipes does not help to make athletes run faster. Equally, medics no longer use mercury thermometers—if they can help it. While, yes, body temperature is a useful indicator of health, the current preference is for digital devices that are more accurate and less inclined to toxic spillage.

   Takeaway: You need the right tool for the right job. Select your (evaluative) divining rods with great care and be aware of any potential side effects (like seeping mercury) or perverse incentives, particularly if they are linked to accountability systems or performance appraisals.

3. **Not implementing the agreed evaluation plan.** Here, the plan gets created and (sometimes) to a very high standard. But it gets locked in the draw. No one has the urge to measure— the fear is they won't like what they see. This is linked to a cognitive bias called the *Ostrich Effect*, which we discussed earlier: this is literally the act of burying your head in the sand to avoid looking at disconcerting data.

   Takeaway: You have to implement the plan and look at the data. Get your head out of the sand!

4. **Not measuring before, during, and after.** Weight loss 101: Get on the scales and take a baseline reading. Implement your slimming strategy. Get back on the scales. Do more implementation, with variation. Get back on the scales. Repeat, repeat…

   Takeaway: Unless you measure regularly and take an initial baseline value, you cannot gauge your success.

5. **Cherry-picking the data, if you don't like what you see.** This is possibly the worst sin of all: You've established a robust evaluation plan and you are regularly collecting data, of the *right* sort. But rather than using the data to enhance your program logic model and your impact, you keep doing the same old thing. Instead, you put your energy to work on mining the data looking for some random thing that has

gotten better—even if it isn't connected to your original education challenge (e.g., "Our girls' literacy program has had a brilliant impact in enhancing boys' numeracy").

Takeaway: You need to use evaluative data for evaluative purposes. The whole point is to get better. Your initial program logic model won't be perfect; it might even be riddled with faulty assumptions. It's far, far better for you to confront these (quickly) and to improve than to waste effort on actions that generate scant impact.

You may be wondering why we have written so much about evaluation here. You might also have flicked ahead and noticed that there are many more pages of this to come in the remainder of this chapter. Potentially, you might be confused by this, given that the Double-Back Stage (D4) is entirely focused on evaluation. But if you have fully processed the five evaluative horrors that we just unpacked, we hope you will see that the key is to confront them *now* (!!!) before you get anywhere near the Stage D3 (Deliver). To select the appropriate tools, establish a baseline, and implement your evaluation plan, you need to build that plan in the first place. And you need to do this *before* you get anywhere near delivery. If you tack evaluation on as an afterthought once your initiative is already underway, then you have a serious problem. We repeat: a serious, serious, serious problem.

Now that you understand why you need to think about evaluation at this juncture—and not delay it until later—here are some mind tools or lenses to help you with that process.

LENS 1: THE PURPOSE

Figure 2.22 compares **monitoring** and **evaluation**.

FIGURE 2.22 ● Purpose: Monitoring vs. Evaluating

MONITORING	EVALUATION
Monitoring is about checking that you have done the things you set out to do. When you think from a monitoring perspective, you are asking questions like these:	Evaluation is about whether the things you did actually improved outcomes. When you are thinking from an evaluative perspective, you are asking questions like these:
• Did we do what we set out to do? • Did we do it on time? • Did we do it within budget? Monitoring is a project management activity, focused on keeping your initiative moving	• Did our actions improve outcomes in our target area? • Is the improvement more or less than we expected? • What have we learned that we can feed forward to further enhance our impact? Evaluation is an improvement focused activity

You need to plan for and do both of these things. You monitor to check that you are doing the things you said you would do. And you evaluate to check whether those things are worth continuing with. Too many initiatives measure impact solely in terms of the former: "We were successful! We achieved all our milestones and deliverables. All the training sessions were run, and all the teachers attended." But not in terms of the latter: "Yes, we met our milestones but there has been no noticeable improvement in student literacy outcomes."

LENS 2: EVALUATIVE APPROACHES

Figure 2.23 describes the **Black-Box, Gray-Box,** and **Clear-Box evaluation** approaches.

FIGURE 2.23 ● Black-Box, Gray-Box, and Clear-Box Evaluative Approaches

APPROACH	DESCRIPTION
Black-Box Evaluation **Did it work?**	You get on the scales at the start and again at the end to measure the degree of "weight loss" or learning gain. This tells you whether your intervention generated impact, but the inner workings of the machine are literally a black box. You have no insight into *why* what you did was or wasn't effective, which makes it challenging to identify areas for improvement.
Gray-Box Evaluation **Why do we *think* it worked?**	In addition to collecting before, during, and after outcomes data, you also attempt to prize open the lid of the machine and peek inside. You conduct interviews and focus groups with stakeholders to gather their opinions or *perceptions* about why the initiative was or wasn't successful.
Clear-Box Evaluation **What worked for whom, in what context, to what extent, through what mechanisms and how can it be improved?**	This is more about the *rigor* with which you use the collected data. It includes • Segmenting outcome data by category of stakeholder (e.g., gender, age, SES, teacher, etc.) • Going back over every link in your Rube Goldberg machine and your map of design features and setting levels to identify and agree to variations that have a high probability of enhancing impact.

Source: Adapted from Hamilton and Hattie (2021).

If you are working at a district level (or higher), our suggestion is that you will want to be undertaking a Clear-Box Evaluation. If you are working at a school or professional learning community level, at the very least, you want to be working at a Gray-Box level. We admit that the Black-Box level is better than nothing. And, too often, there is nothing.

LENS 3: THE LEVELS OF EVALUATION

Donald Kirkpatrick (1993) and Thomas Guskey (2000) have done some excellent work on mapping the types of evaluation questions that are worth asking and the types of tools that are worth using. We have adapted these in Figure 2.24.

FIGURE 2.24 ● Levels of Evaluation

LEVEL	FOCUS	TIME HORIZON	EVALUATIVE TOOLS
1	**Monitoring** Did we do the things we said we were going to do? Did we do them according to the anticipated timelines and with the anticipated level of resources?	Short term	• Project plan monitoring • Budget monitoring • Time tracking • Product acceptance criteria
2	**Engagement** Did stakeholders engage positively with the improvement initiative? Did they *like it*, and did they participate at the expected level/frequency?	Short term	• Satisfaction surveys • Interviews • Focus groups
3	**Learning** Did stakeholders (usually teachers) successfully learn new skills/techniques/approaches that have the *potential* to enhance their collective performance?	Short term	• Portfolio evidence aligned (e.g., to teaching standards) • Lesson observation • Interviews and focus groups • Questionnaires
4	**Change** Was there noticeable change in stakeholders' performance behaviors? Did they (usually teachers) put the learnings into practice in their classrooms?	Medium term	• Lesson observation (e.g., with video tools) • Questionnaires • Structured interviews • Self-/collective efficacy psychometrics
5	**Impact** Did the (L2) engagement, (L3) learning, and (L4) change actually result in improvement in the targeted area? Did outcomes from the students improve?	Longer term	• Student achievement data • Student attendance data • Student voice • Structured interviews with teachers, parents, students, and leaders
6	**Improvement and Sustainability** How can we further enhance the impact, and what do we need to do to stop backsliding?	Continuously	All the above—for the purpose of reviewing and enhancing your program logic model

LENS 4: THE LEVEL OF ADOPTION

Early in your implementation, you are unlikely to be able to capture outcomes and impact-type evaluation data, simply because of the time lag between implementation and impact. However, you will be able to gather a great deal of engagement data. A basic way of doing this is simply to ask people whether they *like* what they are being exposed to. Many training providers use "happy sheets" to evaluate the level of satisfaction from those that they are supporting. However, liking something does not mean it's good for you. The four of us like cake but that doesn't make eating truckloads of it healthy. And there are many things we don't like that are profoundly good for us and that with repeated exposure we might also eventually come to like.

Therefore, we need to get beyond measuring *like* to measuring engagement in terms of level of adoption. We present a rubric for this in Figure 2.25.

FIGURE 2.25 ● Level of Adoption

LEVEL	DESCRIPTOR
Unaware	"I don't know what it is. Never even heard of it."
Aware	"I vaguely know what it is. But I don't have time to engage and am not sure it's relevant to me. I'm probably doing it already."
Considering	"I'm reading some materials on it and thinking about applying it at some future stage."
Priming	"I've done the workshops and have set aside dedicated time each week to practice implementing."
Deliberate practice	"I'm attempting to implement but it's requiring major cognitive effort to juggle all the balls. My head hurts."
Effortless execution	"It used to be hard to implement but I don't really have to think about it anymore."
Adaptation	"I've started making tweaks to the protocols to better fit my context. I couldn't really do this before now, because it was hard enough just remembering and implementing the steps." ***Note the risk that this adaptation might be mutation that reduces efficacy.****
Spread	"Some other teachers have joined the school who don't know how to use the protocols. I've been coaching them so that they understand why it's important and so they can do it." ***Note the risk that spread might also be mutation/dilution that reduces efficacy.****
On to the next thing	"I've been implementing the program for a few years now and have made several improvements, so it better fits our local context. Although I am still interested in it, I've started looking at other approaches for other more important education challenges." ***Note the risk of backsliding and see our discussion in Chapter 5 (Stage D5: Double-Up).****

Source: Adapted from Hall and Hord (2011) and Hall and Loucks (1977).

You can capture this progression via surveys, interviews, focus groups, and lesson observation. While this will not tell you whether the program you are implementing is generating impact, adoption is an important precursor to impact.

BUILDING A MONITORING AND EVALUATION PLAN

Now that we have introduced the four key lenses, the next key question is what you do to bring them alive within your improvement initiative. You need to approach this from two key dimensions:

- **Indicators** (what evaluative tools will you use for measuring?)
- **Targets** (what readings from these tools would we consider to be "good" progress?)

INDICATORS

You will, no doubt, have already noticed that everything within the *Building to Impact 5D* framework is extremely systematic. It's all about searching for options in the design space, mapping those options, and then considering which are likely to be better bets for progress and improvement. The exact same logic applies to the selection of your evaluative indicators. So rather than (randomly) selecting a couple of tools that you happen to have on hand, we want you to think *deeply* about what types of tools will help you to evaluate the *specific* program logic model that you have crafted—subject, of course, to your local constraints related to optimal stopping.

In Figure 2.26, we illustrate how you could record and analyze each potential indicator or tool, within the context where the goal is to improve children's literacy outcomes. You will see that we list the following in the figure:

- **Potential indicators.** This is your shopping list of *all* the potential measuring tools that *could* be leveraged (i.e., the educational equivalent of weighing scales, stopwatch, blood pressure monitor, etc.).
- **Linkage to education challenge.** Indicators are only useful if they indicate something that is relevant to what you are trying to improve. This column is about you spelling this out to double-check that the identified tool measures a useful thing.
- **Ease of data collection.** This is about assessing whether you need to create the tool (which requires more time and energy) or whether it is something you have on hand or even perhaps already use and already have data for.

FIGURE 2.26 ● Evaluative Indictor Selection—Worked Example

NO.	POTENTIAL INDICATOR	LINKAGE TO EDUCATION CHALLENGE	EASE OF DATA COLLECTION	VALIDITY AND RELIABILITY	PERVERSE INCENTIVES?	CONCLUSION
1	**National literacy assessment**	**Direct and strong.** Our agreed education challenge is about student achievement levels in national literacy assessment.	**Easy.** We already have a national assessment testing infrastructure.	Requires further investigation. External consultants have correlated our internal/national assessment grades to assessments and raised concerns about validity (i.e., we might not be measuring the right things). Our challenge is also with younger learners who have not yet taken the national assessment. We need to be able to screen earlier.	If the measure becomes a performance target for schools, there is risk that they may be incentivized to game outcomes.	
2	**Student attendance**	**Indirect and strong.** Students need to be regularly attending school in order to receive literacy instruction.	**Easy.** We already collect attendance data twice per day.	**High validity.** Direct measure of the education challenge. **High reliability.** Binary measure that is not open to subjective interpretation.	As above. Need to consider whether there is any incentive for any stakeholder to falsify attendance data.	
3	**Lesson observation data**	**Indirect and causal.** Our theory of change is that students are not achieving L3 literacy because they do not enjoy their lessons and are therefore neither learning nor attending school regularly. Our assumption is that as lesson observation scores increase, we should also see corresponding increases in student attendance and test scores.	**Medium.** We already undertake two lesson observations each year. However, we are not currently using a structured rubric or training observers to increase inter-rater reliability.	**Medium validity.** We are not sure whether students are not attending/not achieving because they do not enjoy their lessons. **Low reliability.** The current rubrics are open to different interpretations when used in classrooms.	Possible that educators will specially prep and deliver their "best lesson" for the observation (i.e., what is observed is not representative of daily classroom practice).	

95

- **Validity and reliability.** This asks whether the tool measures the right thing in a way that gives you *consistent* and *accurate* measurements.

- **Perverse incentives.** Is there any danger that there could be unanticipated consequences from using the tool (i.e., that stakeholders dance to its tune and this makes it look like things have been improved but that nothing has changed)?

The idea is that you weigh each of these considerations and then select appropriate tools that will give you short-term, medium-term, and longer-term insights into the effectiveness of your program logic model. You want a mixture that gives you **leading indicators** (i.e., quick data on engagement, learning, and change) and **lagging indicators** (i.e., slower data on change, impact, improvement, and sustainability).

Once you have agreed on your indicators, you can then set out the *what, why, when, where,* and *how* of your evaluation approach in an Evaluation Plan Methods Grid, as outlined in Figure 2.27.

TARGETS

Once you have selected your indicators, the next step is to baseline your take-off values and set your short-, medium-, and longer-term targets. In Figure 2.28 we outline six different methods you could adopt to set your targets, each a significant improvement on guesswork.

If you are working at the district level (or higher), you might even seek to benchmark against all six of these methods. Of course, there is still some "art" to the process of selecting your target. You also need to consider the Goldilocks principle of desirable difficulty. Your target needs to be challenging enough that it's genuinely worth doing but not so challenging that achieving it seems nearly impossible.

FIGURE 2.27 ● Evaluation Plan Methods Grid

EVALUATION DOMAIN	INDICATOR	INSTRUMENT	DATA SOURCE	FREQUENCY	RESPONSIBILITY
L1: Monitoring *L2: Engagement* *L3: Learning* *L4: Change* *L5: Impact* *L6: Sustainability and Scale* **Example:** *L4: Change*	The category of instrument you have selected to help answer each evaluation question **Example:** *student attendance*	The specific instrument that will be utilized **Example:** *student attendance register*	What type of data you will generate **Example:** *frequency of student absence*	When you are going to do it **Example:** *daily*	Who is going to do it **Example:** *all teachers, with monitoring and oversight from XX*

FIGURE 2.28 ● Six Approaches to Target Setting

NO.	METHOD	DESCRIPTION
1	**Improvement on previous year (%)**	Using the local benchmarked value to set incremental percentage increases over time
2	**Peer average**	Using the mean average performance of comparator schools that share similar features (e.g., similar size, cohort, geography, education challenge, etc.)
3	**Regional average**	Using the mean average performance of comparator schools in the same region (or whole-region average) as the long-term target
4	**National average**	As per approach 3 but based on the mean average of all institutions within a country/state
5	**International average**	As per approach 4 but based on the global average of data (e.g., World Bank EduStats Data; UNESCO Institute of Statistics; OECD PISA, etc.)
6	**Theoretical best**	Using logical reasoning to postulate what the maximum possible improvement that *could* be achieved

Note: OECD, Organization for Economic Cooperation and Development; PISA, Programme for International Student Assessment; UNESCO, United Nations Educational, Scientific and Cultural Organization.

Source: Adapted from Bryk et al. (2017).

Once you have deliberated and agreed on realistic (but stretching) targets, you can then use a column table like the one in Figure 2.29. This delineates the indicator, the instrument, the baseline value (i.e., the current status), and then successive targets over time.

LOCKING EVALUATION INTO YOUR PROGRAM LOGIC MODEL

The final step is to record your agreed evaluative actions within your program logic model. In the illustration in Figure 2.30, you can see that there are a number of "zones" within the tool that relate to this:

- **Baseline Data.** This is where you record or map to your current status (i.e., your starting point on the weighing scales).

- **Monitoring and Evaluation Activity.** Here you record or map to the tools you will use and frequency of use.

- **Evaluation Plan.** This is about the frequency (1) with which you will look at the evaluative data collected from the monitoring and evaluative activity, to make decisions about whether any of your actions need to be iterated, and (2) with which you will iterate (e.g., will you take an agile approach where you make micro-adjustments all the time, or will you let things play out for several months and collect lots or robust data, then explore the pros and cons of change carefully, before deciding what to do?).

FIGURE 2.29 ● Target Setting—Worked Example

NO.	INDICATOR	INSTRUMENT	BASELINE VALUE	TARGET VALUE T1	TARGET VALUE T2	TARGET VALUE T3	TARGET VALUE T4
1	Overall student absenteeism	Student attendance register	12% absence	9%	7%	5%	5%
2	Target group boys (13–17) absenteeism	Student attendance register	17% absence	12%	10%	8%	8%
3	Teachers' implementation of the RTI protocols	RTI lesson observation Rubric compliance (%)	TBC	50%	60%	75%	90%
4	Student usage of intelligent tutoring system	System time log	TBC	45% students 90 minutes per week	55% students 90 minutes per week	75% students 90 minutes per week	85% students 90 minutes per week
5	Student literacy rate	State screening tool	66%	68%	73%	78%	88%

Note: TBC, to be calculated.

FIGURE 2.30 ● Monitoring and Evaluation in the Program Logic Model

Current State | Actions | | | | Positive Change

EDUCATION CHALLENGE	ACTIVITIES & STAKEHOLDERS	RESOURCES	ASSUMPTIONS	OUTPUTS	SHORT-TERM OUTCOMES	MEDIUM TERM-OUTCOMES	LONG-TERM OUTCOMES
Our student literacy rates are significantly below national averages. **Disproportionately boys (68%)** **Disproportionately rural (74%)** **Disproportionately low SES (83%)** — **32% missed target by 5% or less** **41% missed it by 5-15%** **27% missed it by more than 25%**	Response to Intervention Program that provides triaged and targeted support to priority students	• RTI Program Materials • External Trainer $XX	1. Program will transfer to our context 2. Teachers will be able to implement	1. Teacher training completed	90% of teachers implementing RTI Approach	75% Student Literacy Rate	88% Student Literacy Rate
	Intelligent Tutoring System that provides AI-driven personalized learning to all students	• Software Platform $XX • 90 minutes per week of access on the timetable	1. All students will use the platform 2. The use will generate improved literacy outcomes	1. Platform procured 2. Student logins distributed 3. Student inductions	85% students using platform for 90 minutes per week	75% Student Literacy Rate	88% Student Literacy Rate
	STOP: Learning Styles Teacher Professional Development Program	• Briefing sessions on why we are stopping and what we are starting	1. Program is ineffective 2. Time better spent on RTI	1. Teachers have additional 2 hours per week 2. Time transferred to RTI	100% STOP of Learning Styles PD	75% Student Literacy Rate	88% Student Literacy Rate
	STOP: Student Co-curricular Project	• Vice Principal time for communications sessions with students and parents	1. A 'happy program' without evidence of impact 2. Stakeholders will accept cancellation	1. Students have additional 3 hours a week 2. 1 hour saving for teachers	100% STOP of Co-Co PROJECT	75% Student Literacy Rate	88% Student Literacy Rate

BASELINE DATA	MONITORING AND EVALUATION ACTIVITY	EVALUATION PLAN
33% of our 13-year-olds are functionally illiterate	1. Project Plan with milestones, completion dates and activity owners that will be reviewed by Backbone team on weekly basis 2. Student Login and usage data for the Intelligent Tutoring System 3. Teacher lesson observation and questionnaires for the RTI approach 4. Continued use of existing student literacy screeners to track medium/long-term outcomes	See detailed evaluation Plan. We will undertake 6-week review cycles. Sponsor group and backbone will review data to decide on continuation, iteration or STOP. We will not stop before month 8 but we may iterate the protocols after month 2, onwards

Source: Copyright © Cognition Education. (2022). All rights reserved.

- **Outcomes.** These are your short-, medium-, and longer-term targets. These are likely to be linked to the Lens 3 levels of the evaluation framework:
  - **Short-term targets** will more often be focused on whether you did what you said you would (i.e., monitoring whether you delivered the outputs) and whether stakeholders engaged and learned anything.
  - **Medium-term targets** are more likely to be focused on levels 2 and 3 (i.e., learning and change).
  - **Longer-term targets** take us to levels 4 and 5 (i.e., outcomes and iterative improvement).

Remember that you are setting an evaluation plan for implementation and de-implementation. Half of your program logic model will be focused on stopping activities to free up time that you can better devote to your agreed education challenge, so it is just as important that you monitor and evaluate whether you are successful with this de-implementation.

D2: Design Summary

You have now reached the end of the D2 Design processes. During this stage of your inquiry:

You will have systematically searched and agreed on high-probability interventions to START and to STOP. You will have done this by

2.1 Exploring Options in Design Space

2.2 Building Program Logic Model(s)

2.3 Stress Testing Logic Model(s)

2.4 Agreeing on What to STOP

2.5 Establishing your Monitoring and Evaluation Plan

In the next chapter, we shift our focus to D3: Deliver. The designs come to life!

CHAPTER 3

D3: DELIVER

Implement and de-implement AGREED designs

3.1 Lock the Delivery Approach and Plan

3.2 Undertake Delivery

3.3 Collect Monitoring and Evaluation Data

INTRODUCTION

Delivery is about getting the *right* things done to progress the *right* education challenge to generate a deep, deep impact. The activities that you have already undertaken during Stages D1 (Discover) and D2 (Design) will significantly increase the probability that you are indeed progressing the most important education challenge and in a manner that makes your effort worthwhile and generates powerful outcomes.

We approach delivery with a profound sense of urgency. In the previous chapters, we have deliberately used evidence from the field of public health to illustrate the essential elements of effective implementation. In fact, most of the good research on effective implementation actually comes from health; you can find it cataloged in Appendix A. Some readers may, however, find the parallels between health and education far-fetched or at least stretched, as the sense of urgency in the surgical suite may be far greater than that in the typical school. There is also a hierarchy in the operating room: the surgeon gives an instruction, and the rest of the team implements that instruction with precision. To do otherwise would place the health of the patient at grave risk. Change in education is often more voluntary, and the fear that "the staff might not like it" can be enough to stop even the most necessary changes before they start. Nevertheless, we insist that the medical analogy is not only apt but accurate.

Before the global COVID-19 pandemic, the evidence of the long-term impact of educational underperformance on children was already overwhelming (Currie & Aizer, 2016). As researchers then studied the disparate impact on students who fell behind due to school closures during the pandemic, the multidecade impact in poverty, unemployment, and health was becoming even more pronounced (Oster, 2020). These impacts fall disproportionally on children from lower socioeconomic backgrounds and those from ethnic and cultural minority groups. Even as schools have reopened, we continue to observe secondary schools with failure rates exceeding 50%—a condition that will lead to a drop-out crisis if a change is not implemented immediately and deeply. In sum, this is not a 1-year issue or even a pandemic issue, but a calamity that will last more than half a century. Fifty years from now, history books will have but a few paragraphs about the global COVID-19 pandemic that began in 2020. But 50 years from now, the students who failed because schools were unable or unwilling to *deeply improve* will still be impoverished, unemployed, and making disproportionate use of the medical care and criminal justice systems (Reeves, 2020a).

Educational success and failure need to be viewed as a (long-term) public health and safety issue.

If a school building were on fire and children were inside, you would not commission a study, conduct a focus group, or fret that taking decisive action might be unpopular. You (and we) would evacuate immediately and call the fire department. We suggest that implementing effective educational improvement must have the same sense of urgency and that educational success and failure need to be viewed as a (long-term) public health and safety issue. Each year of failure increases and compounds the probability that bad long-term life chances become irreversible. However, the solutions to thorny education challenges are not so straightforward to identify, so that sense of urgency must be accompanied with *systematic approaches* to discovery, design, and delivery and doubling-back and doubling-up. We can't just call the fire department.

In Stage D2 (Design), we also established the essential and very challenging step of de-implementation. The advocates of change in education and most other fields are often better at telling teachers and school administrators what they should be doing rather than what they should stop doing, and this inevitably leads to the common complaints of initiative fatigue (Reeves, 2021a, 2021b). The phenomenon of initiative fatigue is compounded when government funds, designed to alleviate some of the burdens of the global pandemic, are used to purchase shiny new programs and initiatives for which teachers are not trained and for which the calendar does not allow time. This is particularly true when the new initiatives are added to the formidable agenda of programs and products already in classrooms.

However, to implement, you also need to make room for impact by (ruthlessly) culling projects that have no evidence of relevance or impact. So, worthwhile delivery is always going to be about adding AND subtracting. This means that it must address the practical issue of what to stop doing so that leaders and teachers do not engage in the illusion that with just the right combination of Pangloss-type optimism and administrative commands, teachers can just "work smarter" and a miracle will ensue.

In your delivery, you will also need to keep your eyes constantly on the potential derailers that you identified and stress tested when you developed your program logic model. These include the individual, cultural, and organizational sources of friction that undermine every attempted change implementation. Finally, you need to collect monitoring and evaluation data. This is because evidence of impact from other times and places, however formidable, is not enough to guarantee successful delivery of change in *your* context. To put a fine point on it, if prior evidence alone were sufficient to guarantee successful implementation, John and Doug would have retired a decade ago and the four of us wouldn't have needed to collaborate on this book. We make the point that even the best prior evidence can only start the implementation conversation; it will take systematic gathering of internal evidence to sustain it. The whole message of *Building to Impact 5D* calls loudly for a shift from traditional evaluation, a formal process that typically happens (grudgingly) at the end of a funding cycle, to a continuous stream of feedback that allows for real-time leadership decisions, mid-course corrections, and continuous improvement.

Even the best prior evidence can only start the implementation conversation; it will take systematic gathering of internal evidence to sustain it.

With that preamble out the way, let's get to into the **D3: Deliver Stage** of 5D!

3.1 LOCK THE DELIVERY APPROACH AND PLAN

Before you embark on delivery, you need to set out your roadmap. That roadmap builds out from your program logic model (Steps 2.2–2.5) and it enables you to clearly set out the *when, where,* and *who* to the already decided *what* and *why.* Now, you might be reasonably thinking, "We've already spent a lot of time thinking about and mapping these things in Stages D1 and D2, so surely it's time to just put the pedal to the metal and drive." However, there are further decisions you still need to make before you get implementing.

To be fair, these questions and actions are actually design oriented but we felt that we had already covered so much ground in Chapter 2 that if we crammed more in without pause, it might make your eyes bleed.

QUESTION 1: THE DELIVERY APPROACH

To bring your program logic model to life, you need to decide your *delivery approach*. There are three broad option baskets for you to choose from, as we illustrate in Figure 3.1.

OPTION 1: RIGID

A *rigid* approach means that once you start delivery to the agreed design and to the agreed education challenge, you do not pivot or reverse even in light of niggling feedback. This way of thinking and acting is relatively common on construction projects, because any reversal comes at great cost. If the architect decides, after building work has commenced, to change the exterior walls from brick to glass, it creates major expense. Once the bricks are up, they need to be smashed back down and replaced. Therefore, property developers often employ the Waterfall project management methodology, which involves spending lots of time on feasibility studies, site surveys, and architectural design work *before* breaking ground or doing any site work. In other words, optimal stopping happens much later as all the potential options and scenarios are explored to the ninth degree, during the Discover and Design Stages, before the green light is given to proceed.

In education, there are fewer scenarios in which an embarked-upon change becomes immediately irreversible but these situations still exist. Many years ago, Arran developed national qualifications for school-leavers in England. Each was a package of syllabus materials and grading rubrics that were used to deliver assessments and award school-leaving certificates. Once each qualification was developed, it was submitted for approval to the government regulator; once approved, the assessment objectives and grading system were set in stone for a period of up to 5 years. Commercial

FIGURE 3.1 ● Delivery Approach Options Basket

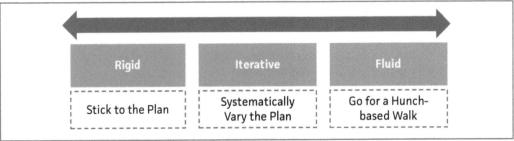

Source: Copyright © Cognition Education. (2022). All rights reserved.

publishers would then produce textbooks and teaching resources for each, with that same 5-year shelf life. Obviously, this had major implications for thousands of schools, tens of thousands of teachers, and hundreds of thousands of children. It shaped what was taught in the last 2 years of school, as children prepared for their high-stakes assessments. Understandably, a high proportion of the qualification development effort went into the Discover and Design Stages, because there was limited room for adjustment after the syllabus packages arrived at schools.

If you are operating at a system level and you are considering embarking on change that, after implementation, will be as difficult to reverse as unscrambling an egg, then you may want to think and act from the more rigid end of the spectrum. This means that your approach to implementation will be more akin to the Waterfall model used in construction and that optimal stopping will happen much later, because you are implementing something that is difficult to reverse. If you are working at the school level and your plans involve procuring support, technology, or subscriptions that have multiyear contractual implications, you may not need to be so rigid but you will still want to consider those long-term funding commitments before signing on the dotted line!

OPTION 2: FLUID

At the opposite end of the spectrum is what we call the *fluid* delivery approach. Here, you begin with an idea that you test informally, using your intuition and instinct to then decide where to next. Software developers sometimes orient to this approach, using the Agile methodology and daily Scrum meetings to "fly a thousand kites" and build out those that work best. It's easy and cheap to produce, edit, or delete a paragraph of computer code.

Many of the high-impact teaching and learning approaches that are signposted in Visible Learning Meta[x] also likely emerged through this fluid approach. The first step is almost always a teacher with a hunch who tries something new and who gradually perfects it through real-time feedback from the learners. Then come the academics who write it up and formally test the efficacy, and then come the program developers who seek to scale the new innovations with the strongest evidence of impact.

If you are operating at the individual classroom level or are collaborating informally with a small group of colleagues, you might merely be drawing on the 5D framework for ideas and inspiration and using a rule of thumb to adjust as you go. We can live with that as long as you are continually (and carefully) evaluating your own impact. However, if you are working at scale—for example, across a whole school or district—going on a fluid hunch-based learning walk is not at all recommended. Yes, you might optimally stop your searching much sooner than system-level actors, but you need to spend some time on *each* of the 5D steps.

OPTION 3: ITERATIVE

In the middle sits the *iterative* approach. It is not rigid, but it is also not fluid. You identify and confirm your most appropriate education challenge. Then you explore the options in the design space to build or adapt one or more high-probability interventions based on the *what works best* research and fit this with your local context. However, you acknowledge that you have no idea whether your program logic model will be successful, will need to be iterated, or will even need to be canned until you get going. So, you deliberately build in evaluative pause points to review the data and decide how to move forward. To us, this iterative approach is the default way of implementing the 5D methodology. You would only not iterate if there is some reason why you can't (e.g., once it's up, it becomes entrenched and almost impossible to take back down), when the stakes are low (e.g., you are trying a new approach in a single classroom, once or twice, just to informally gauge the reaction and to decide whether to add it to your repertoire), or if your selected approach is obviously the only correct solution (e.g., calling the fire department).

DELIVERY APPROACH DOUBLE-BACK

1. Have we explicitly identified which type of delivery approach we are adopting?
2. Do we have a clear rationale for that approach?
3. Have we fully considered the risks and opportunities of using other approaches?
4. Are we sure?

THE DELIVERY PLAN

With your delivery approach decided, the next step is to map out your delivery plan. Outside of education, there are already a range of project management methodologies and tools that you can choose from. We have cataloged many of the common ones in Appendix 1, including PRINCE2 (PRojects IN Controlled Environments), **Project Management Body of Knowledge (PMBOK)**, PMP (Project Management Professional), Waterfall, Scrum, and Agile. Some of the key differences in these approaches relate to whether they advocate a rigid or iterative approach to delivery and also whether the methodologies themselves are open to interpretation and cherry-picking or whether they have to be followed in a stepwise fashion.

If you are working at the system or district level, more likely than not you will have access to in-house professionally accredited project or program managers who work to whichever methodology you have selected as your organizational standard. It's perfectly fine for you to then use the 5D processes to Discover and Design your initiative and then to leverage your preferred project management methodology to Deliver.

However, if you have no in-house approach, the PMBOK is a good place to start. This formally documents the range of processes, terminology, and tools that have evolved in project management over time and that are generally recognized as good practices. PMBOK is also compatible with both rigid and iterative approaches. Some of the common tools or assets cataloged by PMBOK and other project management methodologies that you may find it useful to use both in delivery planning and actual delivery include those listed in Figure 3.2.

If you are implementing a 5D project at scale (i.e., across many, many schools) and if it will be difficult or costly to reverse or overrun, you are probably going to use most or all of these tools to support effective delivery. And you are also likely going to set up a dedicated project office staffed by professionally trained and certified project managers.

If you are working at the school level, you are less likely to have the luxury of access to this level of continuous expertise. You also need to strike the right balance between getting things done and filling in forms and documentation that merely give you the illusion of progress and impact. Therefore, at the school level, you are likely going to have to be more selective and focused in your use of the various PMBOK tools.

However, at the school level, the minimum tools that you should consider using are some form of a **project plan** and a **highlight report**. We describe these next.

PROJECT PLAN

A project plan gives you a concrete roadmap for how you are going to execute your program logic model—that is, your anticipated journey from getting from A to B to C to impact.

For more complex whole-school initiatives involving many strands of activity with participants, we recommend that you develop your project plan as a **Gantt chart**. There are many free online Gantt chart templates that you can download in spreadsheet format to

FIGURE 3.2 ● Common Project Management Assets and Tools

TOOL	DESCRIPTION
STRATEGIC TOOLS	
Business case	Outlines the value proposition for the proposed project. This often includes the rationale, intended benefits, risks, and resourcing requirements. In the context of the 5D framework, the business case would emerge from the Discover and Design activities and the sponsor(s) would review the business case to decide whether to proceed to the Deliver Stage.
Project charter	Once a business case is approved, the project charter formally authorizes the project, gives the backbone organization authority to implement, and sets out the timelines, budget, deliverables, acceptance criteria, and intended benefits.
Roadmap	A high-level timeline of key activities. This is used by the sponsor(s) to keep track of the project, without getting into the weeds.
LOGS	
Risk register	This details all the things that could go wrong in the delivery of your initiative, usually ranking both the probability and severity of impact. The risk register is used to plan mitigations and contingencies so that you are prepared before the risk turns into a live issue. Within the context of 5D, you will have already identified many of the risks during the stress test (Step 2.3) of your program logic model.
Issues log	This lists risks that have materialized and turned into live issues. It also details the actions being taken to remediate the issue.
Change log	During implementation, stakeholders often ask for changes and these can result in scope creep. The change log allows you to formally record all changes that have been asked for, the rationale and implications of change, and the decision made by the sponsor(s).
Lessons learned log	As you implement your initiative, you are bound to fall into many bear traps. The lessons learned log is used to record what you have learned from these experiences, so that you can share this with the wider organization and remember it yourself!
Stakeholder register	This lists all the project stakeholders, their roles, and their responsibilities. It can sometimes also be used to classify their level of engagement and the push/pull factors that might enhance their levels of participation.
PLANS	
Project plan	This is a detailed timeline of tasks, subtasks, start and end dates, and task owners. It is used by the backbone organization to monitor and manage delivery activity and is often presented as a Gantt chart. It is often accompanied by a process statement related to how frequently it will be reviewed and/or updated and by whom.
Change control plan	This explains what will happen if someone requests a change to the project scope or requirements (e.g., who will agree/decide).
Communications plan	This outlines how, when, by whom, and to whom information about the progress of the project will be disseminated.

TOOL	DESCRIPTION
PLANS	
Cost management plan	This explains how budgetary costs will be monitored, managed, and controlled.
Monitoring and evaluation plan	This details what will be monitored and evaluated and the methodology and timelines for doing so. You undertook this activity in Step 2.5.
Risk and issue management plan	How frequently you will review risks and issues, who does so, and what is the escalation process.
Resource management plan	This describes how you will acquire and manage project resources (e.g., people, budget, time. etc.).
REPORTS	
Highlight report	A high-level summary of project progress that is circulated to sponsor(s) at pre-agreed intervals. This usually contains details on activities completed; whether the project is behind/ahead of schedule; budget burn rate; top risks; live issues.

Source: Adapted from the Project Management Institute (2021).

enable you to do this. Or you can access more specialist project management software that also includes this functionality.

Figure 3.3 illustrates how a Gantt chart is laid out. You will see that this example project plan is only for a single "work package." The figure covers the tasks and activities for just one of the four rows in the program logic model we introduced in Chapter 2—in this case, for the procurement and rollout of an intelligent tutoring system to enhance children's literacy skills. As you look at this worked example, you will further see that it has been subdivided into a

FIGURE 3.3 ● Gantt Chart Illustration

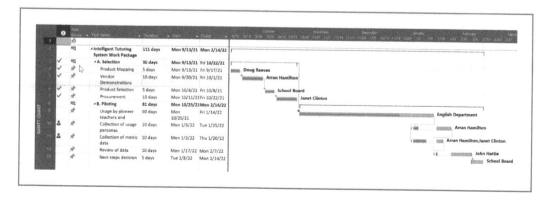

range of tasks, including selecting the system and piloting it. For each task, the Gantt chart also details a range of subtasks, each with their start and end dates and the action owner. The other benefit of a Gantt chart is that you can explicitly link the tasks together so that you can see which have to be done first; this is called the *task dependencies* or the *critical path*.

Obviously, this is just a worked example. The full Gantt chart for the implementation of the intelligent tutoring work package could have 100 or more tasks or subtasks within it. It will take you some time to map this out, check the dependencies and durations, and confirm whether the time allocations seem reasonable. You also need to repeat the process for each of the other work packages in your program logic model, including for each of the things you have decided to start and for those you have decided to stop.

If you are part of a professional learning community in which you are using more fluid/hunch-based protocols to try an idea and solicit quick feedback, then a Gantt chart is likely to be overkill for you. A good alternative is a **Kanban board**, which enables you and your small group of colleagues to agree and track key actions without "boiling the ocean." Figure 3.4 provides a Kanban board illustration, and it breaks down activities into three categories:

- Things to do
- Things you are currently doing
- Things you have done

You can draw this on a whiteboard, use sticky notes to record the key tasks, and then move them between the three columns as you undertake your project.

FIGURE 3.4 ● Kanban Board Illustration

To Do	Doing	Done
Confirm Leadership Approval JH	Localize Protocol to Trial with Students AH	Review Student Achievement Data JC
Trial Agreed New Protocol ALL	Developing Aligned Evaluation Questionnaire DR	Identify Suitable Improvement Protocols JH
Collect Evaluation Data JC		

You will see that within the Kanban board, the activities are cataloged at a much higher level—that is, without a long list of all the associated subtasks needed to make the activity happen. You might also notice the initials in smaller print in the corner of each sticky note. These identify the action owner (e.g., JC means Janet Clinton). However, a disadvantage of the Kanban approach is that it is more difficult (but not impossible) to track deadlines and task slippages.

HIGHLIGHT REPORT

For whole-school initiatives, a second very useful project management tool is the **highlight report**. This report summarizes information, such as activity progress, key risks, issues, budget burn rate, and decisions that need to be escalated, in a single template. Its beauty is that for smaller projects you can use this as a single integrated tracking and reporting tool and sidestep many of the other logs and tools. We illustrate this in Figure 3.5.

If you are collaborating informally with colleagues or via a professional learning community and have opted for a more fluid mode of engagement, then it might be perfectly sufficient for you to come together briefly every few days to review your Kanban board and give verbal progress updates to one another—rather than using a highlight report for formal reporting.

DELIVERY PLAN DOUBLE-BACK

1. Have we explicitly identified which project management tools and processes we are going to use?

2. Do we have a clear rationale for our selected project management approach, including its alignment with our proposed delivery approach (i.e., rigid vs. iterative vs. fluid)?

3. Have we fully considered the risks and opportunities of using other project management approaches?

4. Are we sure?

5. Have we developed our delivery plan to a suitable level of detail, based on the considerations above?

FIGURE 3.5 ● Highlight Report Illustration

Overall Project Status	Trend Since Last Report	Program Highlights
Amber Red / Green	Same Worse / Better	1. Focus Group Completed 2. A Range of Intelligent Tutoring Systems scoped 3. Budget savings have been identified

Work Package: Intelligent Tutoring System

Red Amber Green	A review of potentially suitable systems has been undertaken. Still awaiting costed proposals

Work Package: Response to Intervention Program

Red Amber Green	Program has been selected and staff training is already underway

Work Package: Stop Student Co-Curricular Project

Red Amber Green	Significant pushback from teachers, students and some parents

SLIPPAGE OF PLANNED TASKS		ISSUES/RISKS	
Item Description	Action Take/ Required (Including Revised Dates Where Applicable)	Item Description/ Strand	Comment on any counter measures or contingency plans (where applicable). Please indicate whether the risk effects one or more of the following areas: FINANCIAL, DELIVERY AND IMPACT
Costed Intelligent Tutoring System Proposals Disestablishment of co-curricular project	We have chased all vendors – revised date **6/1/22** **Escalating as an ISSUE**	**ISSUE:** pushback on disestablishing co-curricular project	**Delivery:** we are banking on leveraging the saved time
		RISK RTI Program might not be effective	**Impact:** student literacy rates will not increase. We are monitoring via evaluation plan and metrics

COMPLETED BY			
Name	Janet Clinton	**Date**	03/03/22
Position	Delivery Leader		

Source: Copyright © Cognition Education (2022). All rights reserved.

Source: Copyright © Cognition Education (2022). All rights reserved.

3.2 UNDERTAKE DELIVERY

Now you really have reached the point of delivery! After having confirmed your education challenge, undertaken your path analysis, built your program logic model, developed your monitoring and evaluation plan, and crafted your delivery plan, you are ready to go.

So, what happens here? We have absolutely no idea. Only you can know.

All your delivery activity will be shaped and determined by your prior investigating and decision-making during the Discover (D1) and Design (D2) Stages. And this could lead you in many different directions. In one school or system, your focus might be on teacher recruitment and retention. In another context, it might be about student absence and achievement rates or health and well-being. Your education challenge could literally be (almost) *anything*. The only thing we are adamant about is that you should have gotten to this point through systematic checking and cross-checking and not through a magical mystery tour that sees you committing resources to kneejerk agendas that you are not really sure about or to interventions that you have not carefully identified and confirmed.

Your delivery activity is a black box to us, and it will be a black box to you until you have worked through the previous stages and steps of the 5D process. Therefore, we have three generic things to proffer about considerations that *may* be relevant during your delivery activity.

Your delivery activity is a black box to us, and it will be a black box to you until you have worked through the previous stages and steps of the 5D process.

GENERIC THING 1: FIDELITY OF IMPACT

Often leaders of new educational programs hear that the key to success is *fidelity*—that is, implementing the program as it was designed. This conveniently shifts the blame from program designers and salespeople to those who bear the responsibility for implementing the program. There is always going to be variation in implementation, and an essential element of the stress test (Step 2.3) is to determine, in advance, where variation is acceptable and where it is not.

There are three levels of decisions in every school: teacher discretion, teacher collaboration, and administrator decisions. The common stereotype of decision-making in schools today is that there are very few areas of discretion remaining, as school officials are relentlessly micromanaging the activities of teachers. Nevertheless, our observations of classrooms at the same grade level, and where the same subject is taught by different teachers, reveal an astonishing amount of variation. This suggests that discretionary decision-making is alive and well. Some of this professional discretion is essential, such as making in-the-moment decisions to check for understanding, stopping and reteaching, creating small groups where necessary, and using constant checks to respond to the immediate needs of students.

Some of this discretion, however, undermines even the most promising educational practices. For example, there is very strong evidence that collaborative scoring of student work leads to consistent feedback for students, improved quality of student work, fewer disparities among students from historically disadvantaged groups, and even faster work by teachers, as they gain speed in scoring student work with more frequent collaborative scoring (Reeves, 2020b). Yet no matter how well designed collaborative team agendas may be, no matter how much time is allocated for them, and no matter how great the expenditures on teacher training, many teams fail to implement this essential practice (DuFour & Reeves, 2016).

The program logic model (Step 2.2) establishes the links between causes and effects; the stress test (Step 2.3) provides the details of implementation, including consideration of design features and setting levels. It is essential to note that the stress test does not eliminate teacher professional discretion; rather, it specifies clearly where discretion can be helpful and where it undermines student learning and educational equity.

GENERIC THING 2: BARRIERS TO IMPLEMENTATION

Any innovative implementation inevitably runs into resistance, including physical, technological, organizational, interpersonal, cultural, and parental barriers. The value of the innovation and the power of the evidence are often insufficient to remove barriers (Nordgren & Schnonthal, 2021). Once the barriers have been identified, backbone teams must choose one of two starkly different paths: either the doomed quest for buy-in based on emotional appeals (Theory 1) or the path of inside-out change in which the evidence of impact precedes the request for buy-in (Theory 2). Perhaps it is possible that the strategy of begging and pleading with the guards upholding the barriers to innovation could be effective, but the preponderance of the evidence on change leadership suggests that this is a fool's errand. The path to buy-in lies not in rhetorical appeals but in local evidence of impact. This suggests, contrary to the prevailing wisdom about leadership, that we must rethink the leadership–management dichotomy. We will challenge the notion that leaders think great thoughts while the hapless managers are just those who carry out low-level tasks ill-suited to the genius of leaders.

The path to buy-in lies not in rhetorical appeals but in local evidence of impact. This suggests, contrary to the prevailing wisdom about leadership, that we must rethink the leadership–management dichotomy.

PHYSICAL BARRIERS

The physical barriers to change include not only the architecture of the school itself but also how physical space is used in the classrooms, hallways, and offices. If school leaders desire visibility and personal connection, they can, as we have seen, turn their office into a parent welcome center and conference room, move their desk to the hallway where they will greet students by name, and conduct nonconfidential business in a place where everyone knows they are fully present. When the leaders need quiet time for focused work on projects, people, and tasks, they can find a quiet spot in the library or other uninterrupted space. When they want to ensure orderly transitions and student behavior, they can choose to be completely visible in the hallways, cafeterias, playgrounds, and other places students assemble.

Classrooms also have physical barriers to innovation. Classrooms of the 19th century had desks in rows facing the teacher, with the teacher invariably positioned at the front of the room. While the color of the teacher's writing surface may have changed from black to white, and the writing instrument may have changed from chalk to a keyboard, the physical configuration of classrooms has been astonishingly impervious to change. Half a century of research on cooperative learning (Slavin, 2011) does not overcome the command-and-control architecture of most classrooms. There are clearly exceptions, with the furniture arrangements and classroom architecture more conducive to collaboration, but our collective visits to thousands of classrooms, including in the current pandemic environment, show little evidence that the majority of classrooms are physically different from those of centuries earlier. In Boston Latin School, the oldest public school in the United States established in 1635, the desks are bolted to the floor in many classrooms, maintaining the same physical barriers to collaboration in the 21st century that prevailed in the 17th century.

We recognize that architecture alone does not guarantee innovation. In school buildings of a certain age, long-term teachers and administrators can remember when the cinder block walls were removed to provide for the "open classroom," only to be rebuilt years later when the only observable impacts of the removal of walls were more noise and less concentration by exasperated teachers. Our claim is not that the removal of physical barriers to innovation will alone lead to effective results, but rather that identifying and removing physical barriers helps to make the implementation process less onerous.

TECHNOLOGICAL BARRIERS

Technological barriers to effective implementation include not only access to computers but also access to connectivity and support. During the school closures associated with the global pandemic, purchases of educational technology increased almost five-fold, from $7.5 billion in 2019 to almost $36 billion in 2021 (Cauthen, n.d.). However, the mere delivery of machines provided little in the way of meaningful learning in homes without internet connectivity.

Despite the common stereotype that students of today are digital natives, many students lack essential skills such as keyboarding, taking notes, interacting with classmates, and taking assessments on a computer. Even as students return to the physical school building, technology barriers remain in place for instructional innovations that are premised on student and teacher skills in using technology. Even in cases where technology skills are high, the persistent interruptions associated with constant tech access create what Georgetown computer scientist Cal Newport (2021) refers to as the hyperactive hive mind, in which students and teachers flit from one task to the next without sufficient focus and concentration to accomplish real learning and work. In the halls of the Massachusetts Institute of Technology, where they have a special affinity for computers, Sherry Turkle (2016) warns that students must have what she refers to as *human time*—personal connections that are uninterrupted by technology distractions.

ORGANIZATIONAL BARRIERS

Organizational barriers to implementation reflect the hierarchical nature of school systems in which different silos compete for resources, time, and visibility. We continue to observe systems in which responsibility for and authority over technology resides not in the instructional leadership division but in the business office, precisely where it was in the 1950s when the school system owned one computer to do the payroll. While professional learning initiatives depend on coherence and consistency, we observe with dismay districts in which the authority to require teacher attendance at training programs is spread among the departments of human resources, teaching, leadership, and accountability, each providing separate and sometimes contradictory messages. This organizational confusion extends from the district to the school level when, despite clarion calls for curriculum coordination, there is little or no communication among elementary and secondary schools. As each principal reports to a different supervisor with different priorities, the need for coordination becomes quickly lost amid the demands of each principal's direct supervisor. Within the school building, there are districts where the principal is the titular instructional leader, but department heads, grade-level leaders, and other informal influences on curriculum, instruction, and assessment displace the principal's instructional leadership aspirations.

INTERPERSONAL BARRIERS

Interpersonal barriers are widely known but rarely labeled as leaders implementing change. One central problem is that leaders fail to distinguish between skeptics, who want to see evidence before embracing a change, and cynics, who oppose any change based on their primary value of personal convenience and comfort. While both of these groups may appear to constitute barriers to implementation, our experience is that the skeptics can support innovation when they perceive a combination of respect, experimentation, and local evidence of impact. We have seen multidecade veterans in secondary school math and science—the stereotypical opponents of change—become strong advocates when they were the full partners in innovation and implementation and not merely the recipients of commands. We have not, however, seen cynics change. These are the toxic few who oppose implementation, undermine leadership, and take pride not in advancing the cause of learning but in their ability to defeat it. If skeptics are the Galileos of change, guided by evidence rather than commands, the cynics are the Inquisition, willing to go to any lengths to suppress effective implementation of change.

CULTURAL BARRIERS

Cultural barriers to effective implementation are part of the personal and psychological identity of teachers as experts, parents as the first and most important teachers of children, and leaders as visionary change agents. The cultural contexts of teachers, parents, and leaders are often at odds, not only creating barriers to the implementation of one innovation but also maintaining an atmosphere of doubt that any change can be sustained. Most readers of this book became teachers for the same reasons as the authors—a deep love of learning and a desire to share our learning with others. Over time, teachers develop a personal and psychological identity that is deeply rooted in their hard-earned role as the expert from whom others learn. Having labored, often for decades, to acquire that expertise, teachers are therefore understandably reluctant to have that expertise challenged. Any suggestion that a new change should be implemented carries with it the implicit message that the experienced professionals are wrong, inadequate, unprofessional, and not quite as great an expert as they thought.

For example, Doug was weaned on learning styles theory, the apparently self-evident position that every child could be assessed and labeled as an auditory, kinesthetic, or visual learner. When Doug accepted John's assembled evidence that concluded that learning styles theory was bunkum and shared it with audiences of teachers around the world, it was as if he had exposed the Tooth Fairy as a fraud. "I was with you," audience members wrote in critiques, "until you criticized learning styles theory. I think it's true and I still believe it." When the culture of opinion becomes an excuse for imperviousness to change, then educators cannot claim to be professionals. In a profession, standards of practice change as new evidence emerges. That is why physicians, engineers, lawyers, and truck drivers have different standards of practice today than they did 20 or 30 years ago. Moreover, the adequacy of their performance is not determined by mere self-perception and personal satisfaction, but rather by their adherence to generally accepted standards of practice.

When the culture of opinion becomes an excuse for imperviousness to change, then educators cannot claim to be professionals.

PARENTAL BARRIERS

Just as teachers hold strong cultural values that can sometimes militate against effective implementation, the same is true of many parents. They rightfully claim that they are the first and most important teachers of their children and doubt the ability of any other individual or institution to know their children as well as the people who nurtured and raised them. The judgments that parents make about schools and the practice of teaching are colored by their own personal experiences. Thus if parents learned best in a classroom and home environment that included strict order and corporal punishment (Harris, 2010), then they are likely to replicate that environment. Parents raised in a lenient environment with few rules and behavioral expectations may reason that this approach will suit their own children well.

In late 2021, a parents movement began to emerge in the United States, with an agenda that includes the elimination of unpopular ideas, such as critical race theory, and the banning of books to which parents object. While these attitudes are not representative of all parents, they are reflective of a culture in which parents have an understandably strong interest in the physical safety and moral development of their children. We argue that parental interest in education is certainly not a barrier to be overcome, but rather a phenomenon to be understood and respected. It is possible to reason with skeptical parents who insist that their children must be prepared for the real world that awaits them after the completion of their education. That dialog requires a comparison of the real world that parents experienced upon graduation from secondary school and the real world that students face today. One example of the contrast between these two worlds is the widespread presumption that in the real world of college and work, students must get things right the first time. But research with employers and college professors reveals precisely the contrary to be true, in that they expect students to not only make mistakes but, most importantly, to take and receive critical feedback (Reeves, 2019).

PSYCHOLOGICAL BARRIERS

Schools are understandably impatient to see results when they implement a program or practice. But this impatience often leads to a cycle in which every few years, educational leaders and teachers will become weary of the wait for results and say, "That obviously didn't work. Let's buy another program." This prevents schools from the deep implementation that results in genuine gains in student achievement. Consider the examples of collaborative scoring and nonfiction writing, two very consistent high-impact strategies. But the results are not immediate and, in fact, can be frustratingly slow. The first time that teachers engage in collaborative scoring by looking at the same piece of anonymous student work and then struggling to gain consensus on what the correct evaluation is, they may experience disagreements that are unpleasant and exhausting. With persistence and deliberate practice in collaborative scoring, however, teachers can reach very high levels of consistency—inter-rater reliability. But if they will not endure the discomfort of disagreement, they will never make the necessary improvements to scoring protocols that lead to greater effectiveness. Where does this leave students? If the rules of the game—that is, what successful student work looks like—change from one hour to the next, it doesn't take the students long to determine that the officials scoring the game are inconsistent and unfair. Under these conditions, they stop playing the game.

Similarly, a robust program of nonfiction writing in every subject at every grade is strongly associated with improved achievement, but getting busy teachers to see the value in a practice that is outside of their expertise— "I'm a math teacher, not a writing teacher!"— requires time and the opportunity to observe the impact over time. The patience of busy teachers often expires before the impact is understood. The attitude for these challenges is to dramatically shorten the interval between the application of a practice and the observation of impact. In *Visible Learning for Teachers*, there are straightforward guidelines for assessing impact in as few as 6 weeks (Hattie, 2012). If leaders wait for the end of the year or longer-term formal evaluation, they are likely to hear the refrain, "We tried that, and it didn't work."

THE LEADERSHIP–MANAGEMENT DICHOTOMY

In order to identify and address the barriers to implementation, we must rethink the traditional dichotomy between leadership and management. Originally articulated in a famous *Harvard Business Review* article (Zaleznik, 1992), the conventional wisdom is that leaders are visionaries who do the right thing, while managers are responsible for executing that vision and doing things right. A more stark division of attributes between the leader and manager includes the following: "The manager relies on control; the leader inspires trust." "The manager is a copy; the leader is an original." "The manager accepts the status quo; the leader challenges it" (Boynton, 2016).

We find this dichotomy not only to be unhelpful but also to actively undermine the qualities necessary for the deep implementation of change. In fact, one cannot be a great leader without also being a great manager. Leaders must manage time, projects, and people, all of which are not mundane chores unworthy of the exalted leader but rather are essential elements in the delivery of effective implementation and the 5D framework generally. As this book makes clear, implementation is serious and complex work, requiring focused energy and deep work (Newport, 2016). That means uninterrupted time to design and deliver effective implementation while avoiding the incessant interruptions that afflict knowledge workers—that's everyone in education—every moment of the day.

The management skills that are essential for effective leadership include establishing priorities, monitoring what matters, and communicating clearly and consistently throughout the organization. In sum, gauzy visions are insufficient, and vacuous mission statements may be the stuff of leadership retreats in the woods but are not what is required to actually implement change. Real leadership requires a backbone (organization).

PREREQUISITES TO DELIVERY

The next barrier to implementation is the failure to identify the prerequisites to delivery, such as the program logic model or the Rube Goldberg machine (Step 2.2). Even when the need to implement a practice is clear, the inability or unwillingness of leaders to identify the prerequisites can undermine even the most well-planned implementation. Consider the example of the use of interim assessments by collaborative teams of teachers. These teams are at the heart of the common educational practice around the world known variously as professional learning communities or variants on the name, but the actual conduct of those teams varies wildly. When collaborative teams fail to use and learn from interim assessment data, they disconnect teaching from learning and thus have little to exchange in their meetings except for opinions unburdened by evidence. Examples of the conditions necessary for the effective use of interim assessments include the following (Marshall, 2008):

- Build understanding and trust.
- Clarify learning outcomes.
- Select quality interim assessments with a variety of item types, including constructed response items.
- Schedule time for immediate follow-up.
- Involve teachers in making sense of the assessment data.
- Display data effectively so that teachers understand performance on items and standards, not just a score on the entire test.
- Hold candid data meetings with clear action steps to follow up on the information gleaned in the meetings.
- Involve students in the process, including the establishment of learning goals and a clear understanding of the distance from where they are to where they want to be. Marshall says that student engagement in the data process is one of the greatest untapped resources in education.
- Follow up relentlessly.

The last prerequisite in this particular logic model is especially important, as many assessments, including those designated as "formative," are better described as "uninformative assessments." Unless an assessment informs teaching and learning, it holds no more value than the patient who endures time-consuming and painful tests in the physician's office and then departs without either the physician or the patient having a clue about how to use the information in those tests to improve the health of the patient.

GENERIC THING 3: INSIDE-OUT CHANGE

When it comes to the implementation of effective educational innovations, evidence can start the conversation but the delivery of implementation requires inside-out change. That is, teachers attempt an implementation even before there is buy-in or belief, skeptically observe the results, and then and only then are they ready to be convinced and to share their convictions with their equally skeptical colleagues. We have seen this scenario play out again and again, even in the most change-resistant environments. When emotional appeals and administrative mandates have failed, the most effective implementation delivery practice is inside-out change. We colloquially call this method the "science fair" approach, because the method of data gathering and the presentation of the data to school colleagues look in every respect like a student science fair. The room is full of simple three-panel displays and shows the challenge to be addressed, the practice to be implemented, and the results that were achieved. Each of these displays represents only small subsets of a larger implementation model. Taken as a whole, they demonstrate (1) the relationship between the theory of action and the stress test model in the Design Stage of the D5 model and (2) the impact at the classroom level. Here are some real-world examples:

- From a large urban high-poverty high school
  - **Education Challenge:** Excessive failures in Grades 9 and 10 math and science.
  - **Program Logic Model:** Move student practice problems (formerly homework) to in-class practice with immediate feedback and support from the teacher. Evaluate students based on their final performance and not the average of their performance throughout the marking period.
  - **Results:** Greater than 80% reduction in Ds and Fs, improvements in classroom climate and culture, and reduction in tardiness and absenteeism.

- From a rural high school
  - **Education Challenge:** Excessive failures due to missing student work.
  - **Program Logic Model:** Catchup Fridays, with mandatory morning work sessions to make up any missing work.
  - **Results:** Student course failures reduced from 385 to 15. Suspensions down 55%. Attendance increased.

- From an urban elementary and middle school
  - **Education Challenge:** Majority of students reading and writing below grade level.
  - **Program Logic Model:** Interdisciplinary writing in every subject—English, math, science, social studies, art, music, technology, and physical education. Monthly writing assessments, linked to the curriculum, were assessed with a simplified rubric that all teachers in all subjects could use.
  - **Results:** Doubled the number of students writing and reading on grade level. Same-student-to-same-student comparisons showed dramatic gains in the complexity, quality, and length of student writing.

Teachers who were unpersuaded by speeches and who could find ways to evade or delay administrative commands saw the benefits not merely for students but also for the teachers and the community. As high schools reduced the number of course failures, for example, the number of electives increased correspondingly. As misbehavior decreased, staff morale improved.

Inside-out change represents a repudiation of the traditional change models whose popularity has exceeded their utility. It replaces superficial enthusiasm, rallies, and emotional appeals with evidence of impact. It supplants the revolving door of short-term changes with the sustainable implementation of effective practices. It forgoes the mythology of buy-in and the cynical opposition with practical steps and professional practices that yield observable results that benefit all stakeholders. Nothing in these pages will make the change and the deep implementation it requires easy, but it is certainly possible to make implementation more effective and, as a result, more attractive and sustainable in the long run.

3.3 COLLECT MONITORING AND EVALUATION DATA

As you undertake delivery, it is also imperative that you collect monitoring and evaluation data against the plan that you developed in Step 2.5. In that plan, you will already have identified both indicators, timelines for data collection, and performance targets. **Note:** Right now, you do *not* need to think about interpreting the data. We just want to make sure that you are *indeed* collecting it, as you originally set out to.

We need you to make sure you do this because rigorous monitoring and evaluation are often resisted by program advocates and implementors. They claim, quite correctly, that perfection is the enemy of progress and that the urgency of the needs of students should take precedence over the elegance of evaluation design. This sets up, in our view, a false dichotomy between systematic and rigorous evaluation and the impulse to do *something*—*anything*—to help children in need. It pits implementors, the heroes of the story, against evaluators, the pedants who obstruct progress. The 5D framework embraces rigorous evaluation, but we contend that evaluation is too important to be encumbered by this sort of toxic animosity.

When monitoring and evaluation systems are designed well, the implementors and evaluators are *on* the same team (and ideally *are* the same team, just wearing different hats). Both have a vested interest not merely in the program as originally designed, but in the impact that the program has on students and communities. That is why we reject the traditional notion of end-project evaluation, which we liken to a funeral oration delivered after the program has died or an elegy to a program whose success is already acknowledged. Rather, we call for real-time feedback that makes monitoring and evaluation an inherent part of the implementation process. This allows, for example, evaluators to notice ambiguities in implementation design before the delivery even begins, through continuous double-back. It makes the evaluator an ally (and hopefully a co-deliverer) rather than an opponent of the implementation leaders. Moreover, it changes the culture of evaluation from one in which the authors of a document free of criticism can be suspected of being in the pocket of program designers to one in which the mutual goals of designers and evaluators is to do more of what has an effective impact on students and less of what does not.

Rigorous monitoring and evaluation also helps to counteract the *sunk cost fallacy* (Kahneman, 2013). This fallacy is a well-documented cognitive bias that occurs when implementors continue to invest resources of money and time into initiatives after it is clear that these investments are unsound. "I've already put a million dollars into this plan," the leader reasons, "so if I don't follow through now, that money will have been wasted." This is the same logic by the investor who unwisely chose a stock that plummeted from $100 per share to $5, yet continues to hold this turkey of an investment because to sell it would be to admit loss.

The same happens in education when schools invest in technology, curriculum, assessment regimens, and workshops that fail to produce the desired results. We have encountered, for example, curriculum programs that seemed impressive when the acquisition decision was made, leading to a very expensive purchase of licenses for every teacher in the system. But a persistent inquiry a few years later revealed that fewer than 1% of teachers were using it. The district nevertheless continued to maintain and pay for the unused technology, because the person making the decision remained convinced that the schools *needed* the program.

The first step to monitoring and evaluation is to *collect the data in the first place*. The critical next step is to then *look at* and *interpret* these data to decide what to do next. This is the heart of Chapter 4 (D4: Double-Back), in which we explore how successful implementation requires doubling-back to align implementation action with design.

D3: Deliver Summary

You have now reached the end of the D3 Deliver Processes. During this stage of your inquiry:

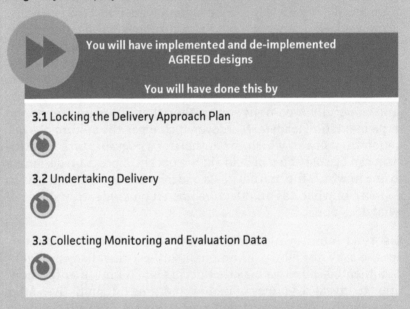

You will have implemented and de-implemented AGREED designs

You will have done this by

3.1 Locking the Delivery Approach Plan

3.2 Undertaking Delivery

3.3 Collecting Monitoring and Evaluation Data

Your next step is to double-back (i.e., evaluate) in order to confirm and grow your impact!

CHAPTER 4

D4: Double-Back

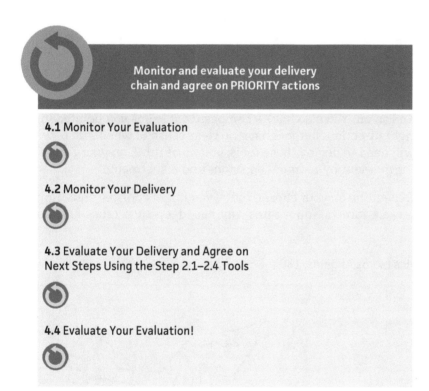

Monitor and evaluate your delivery chain and agree on PRIORITY actions

4.1 Monitor Your Evaluation

4.2 Monitor Your Delivery

4.3 Evaluate Your Delivery and Agree on Next Steps Using the Step 2.1–2.4 Tools

4.4 Evaluate Your Evaluation!

INTRODUCTION

In their brilliant book *Building State Capability*, Matt Andrews, Michael Woolcock, and Lant Pritchett (2017) distinguish between goals that are fiendishly hard to progress and those that are relatively easy. The hard ones they call "1804 problems" and the easier ones "2017 problems" (because they wrote the book in 2017). They illustrate the difference between the two types of problems in the context of attempting to travel from St. Louis in Missouri to Los Angeles, California.

In the 2017 version of the travel task, the actions are straightforward. If you have a car, a GPS system, a credit card or means of payment, some refreshments, and (ideally) a cell phone, you are (pretty much) good to go. Yes, the journey is long. According to Google Maps, the distance is 1,826 miles along I-44 and I-40 and driving nonstop would take 26 hours. So, you might also want to book a motel room along the way to break up the journey. In the unlikely event that your car breaks down (modern cars don't), you can use that cell phone to call for roadside assistance.

As you might have guessed, in the 1804 version, all you have to go on is a map like the one in Figure 4.1.

This map gives you reasonable insight into the (lack of) main highways of the East Coast of North America. It also shows the Californian coastline, which had already been mapped by cartographers. But in between, there could be dragons. For the 1804 version of this task, you have a good sense of the main inputs you will need: horses, wagons, feed, shovels, muskets, medical supplies, and so on. You also have a compass that keeps you pointed in the right direction. But you have no clear sense of when and how you will need to deploy these tools; you must think on your feet, making moment-by-moment decisions and adjustments.

Depending on your chosen route, you might confront thick impenetrable forests, mountains, ravines, deep river crossings, and a

FIGURE 4.1 ● St. Louis to Los Angeles, 1804

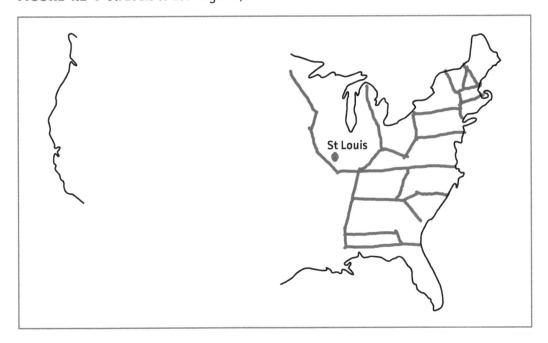

Source: Adapted from Andrews et al. (2017).

seemingly endless number of grizzly bears. As you inch forward across the uncharted map, you continuously have decisions to make. For example, if you can't get the wagons across the river, do you abandon them and swim across with just the horses or do you follow the river possibly for days to try and find a shallow part that the wagons can traverse? There will be many times during the 1804 version of the journey where you feel like you are going 10 steps forward and 25 steps back—where you travel in a straight line to then hit a mountain range that requires you to either double-back or to double-down. During implementation, you are constantly confronted with new information that you have to consider in the context of your original strategy. Occasionally that information may make you abandon the goal altogether; other times, it may make you reconsider your strategy—and yet other times, just your tactics.

There is an analogous idea in computer science called the *halting problem*. From the work of Alan Turing (1937), we know that it is mathematically impossible to predict in advance whether a new computer program will finish running or continue running forever, let alone *when* it might finish running. We only know the outcome when it actually happens. We know by running the program and *seeing* what happens.

These exact same ideas apply to many forms of education improvement. Many of the goals that we might seek to progress are at the 1804 end of the spectrum. Yes, we might have data showing that certain types of interventions are likely to be more effective than others (our equivalent of selecting horses and wagons rather than traveling on foot with a backpack). However, we might not (fully) know the optimal sequencing technique during implementation (i.e., the 1804 problem) or how long before we will see an impact in our context (i.e., the halting problem). And this is precisely why we need rigorous and ongoing evaluation. Otherwise, we might just keep on going—driving our (educational) wagons deeper and deeper in the water, getting stuck on the bottom, whipping the horses yet harder, and being astonished when nothing good comes of it.

The kinds of education challenges that are worth you establishing a backbone organization to progress are almost always going to be at the hard and super-hard end of the continuum.

Indeed, the kinds of education challenges that are *worth* you establishing a backbone organization to progress are almost always going to be at the *hard* and *super-hard* end of the continuum presented in Figure 4.2.

And this is exactly why we spent so much time during Stage D2 establishing evaluative systems (Step 2.5), so that we have preselected appropriate measuring tools (i.e., indicators) and realistic (but stretching) targets. Those targets put the pressure on, but they also give us evaluative data. If we undershoot these targets, we need to know why. If we overshoot them, we also need to know why. In both cases, the purpose is to decide what we should do next.

FIGURE 4.2 ● Easier, Hard, and Super-Hard Education Challenges

	EASIER	HARD	SUPER-HARD
	Addressed by educators as part of what they do in their classrooms	*More complex; addressed by local groups of educators (e.g., professional learning community or school-level backbone organization)*	*Highly complex and high risk; requires highly structured activities (e.g., Building to Impact 5D approach and additional resources)*
Potential impact on children's life outcomes	Possible risks to quality of life (e.g., life chances, health, well-being, etc.)	Moderate risk to quality of life	Significant risk to life or quality of life (e.g., die younger, live in poverty, spend time in prison, etc.)
Confidence in the data	Data often white noise or statistical anomalies	Often long-term underlying pattern in the data	Usually, incontrovertible evidence
Stakeholder consensus	No agreement that a widespread need/goal/problem exists	Agreement that the need/goal/problem exists but differences of opinion about how to solve it	Strong agreement that the need/goal/problem exists, strong differences of opinion about how to solve it, and often limited time
External/ additional resourcing required?	Does not require additional resources/ support	May benefit from additional resources/ support	Unlikely to be progressed without additional resources and support
Will it self-improve?	Sometimes self-improving (i.e., automatic reversion to the mean)	Rarely self-improving	Almost never self-improving
Complexity	Relatively easy to make progress	Difficult to make progress; lots of interconnected moving parts to consider	Fiendishly difficult to make progress; actions often generate devilish unanticipated consequences
Scale	Classroom	School	Multiple schools/ systemwide
Urgency	A priority for individual teachers but less so for schools and systems	A priority for individual schools but not systemic	Systemic (it cannot wait)
Will we get it right first time?	Maybe	Unlikely	Hell, no!
Do we need to systematically evaluate our actions?	Probably	Definitely	Hell, yes!

Source: Adapted from Hamilton and Hattie (2021).

In fact, as we highlighted in the Introduction and reiterate in Figure 4.3, evaluative processes have been deliberately embedded in various places throughout the *Building to Impact* 5D framework.

The good news is that if you have implemented all these steps properly and have not cut corners, much of the heavy lifting has already been done. And your core remaining task is to evaluate all these rich data to decide where to drive the wagons to next!

In the following sections, we outline what you should now do with all these data and insights to grow your impact in **Stage D4: Double-Back**.

FIGURE 4.3 ● Embedded Evaluation Processes (i.e., Double-Back)

Embedded Evaluation Processes (a.k.a. Double-Back)		
D1: DISCOVER	**D2: DESIGN**	**D3: DELIVER**
1.2: By searching for and ranking potential education challenges, you are pre-evaluating which are most worthy of resolution	**2.1:** By sifting global research data, local positive outliers, and existing local practice, you are pre-evaluating which overarching activities have the highest probability of generating impact	Through the use of project management and evaluation tools, you will be able to measure these:
1.3: By developing a path analysis, you are building and then evaluating a theory of the present	**2.2–2.3:** By systematically reviewing all the different design features, setting levels, and undertaking stress testing, you are pre-evaluating the design features most likely to generate impact	— **Milestones/outputs/ deliverables** (i.e., Are we doing the things we said we would do? Are these being delivered on time/ budget to the agreed quality standard?)
1.4: By setting provisional improvement goals, you are collecting baseline data and setting improvement targets to evaluate against	**2.4:** By developing **Step 1.4** into a full success map that identifies the key indicators, targets, and data collection protocols, you have ready measuring sticks for evaluation	— **Evidence of impact** (i.e., Are the things we are doing resulting in tangible improvement on our **Step 2.4** leading and lagging indicators?)

4.1 MONITOR YOUR EVALUATION

The first key task is to reconfirm that the evaluative systems that you decided during Step 2.4 are *actually* being used and implemented. We explicitly need you to do this because (unfortunately) we often see these evaluative plans languishing in desk drawers, forgotten and discarded.

So, on at least a monthly basis, we want you to monitor (i.e., check) that you are putting all those (Step 2.4) evaluative plans into action. Ask yourself whether you are engaged in *zombie evaluation* or *real evaluation*, as illustrated in Figure 4.4.

FIGURE 4.4 ● Zombie vs. Real Evaluation

ZOMBIE EVALUATION	REAL EVALUATION
<ul><li>Happens sporadically (perhaps not at all)</li><li>Stakeholders are confused about the purpose</li><li>No clear responsibilities and accountabilities for the evaluative tasks</li><li>Key stakeholders are rarely involved</li><li>Data are not regularly reviewed for improvement</li><li>Data are ignored if they show no improvement</li><li>Stakeholders cherry-pick positives to justify plan continuation</li></ul>	<ul><li>Happens continuously</li><li>Everyone knows that without evaluation there is no point in implementing</li><li>Clear responsibilities for each evaluative task and equally clear accountabilities at the program level</li><li>Key stakeholders deeply involved</li><li>Data informally interrogated (e.g., daily/weekly) and systematically reviewed (e.g., monthly)</li><li>Seeing no improvement is seen as a positive; it tells you that the current approach (probably) isn't working and that you (may) need to go back to the drawing board</li><li>Stakeholders take a *warts-and-all* approach, digging deep into any negative data</li></ul>

If, after undertaking this monitoring activity, you conclude that you are engaged in real evaluation, all good. You can then progress to the Step 4.2 activities. However, if you conclude that you are engaged in zombie evaluation, then you need to ask yourself some hard questions:

1. **Why are we NOT evaluating?** Is your answer similar to one of these?

   a. We would like to evaluate but the systems that we have established are too hard/complex/time-consuming for us to collect the data.

   b. We don't see the need to evaluate. It's obvious to everyone that the initiative is generating impact. We can *feel* it.

   c. We know the project isn't working but no one has the heart to kill it. Everyone has spent so much time working on it and we don't want to hurt anyone's feelings.

2. **What are we going to do about it?** Here, your answer is contingent on your reason (in question 1) for not properly implementing your evaluative process.

   a. **If you chose answer a** ("We would like to evaluate but the systems that we have established are too hard/complex/time-consuming for us to collect the data"), **then**

      • Move to **Stage 4.4** and evaluate your evaluative systems to identify whether there are efficiencies you can make that will give you good (enough) data.

   b. **If you chose answer b** ("We don't see the need to evaluate. It's obvious to everyone that the initiative is generating impact. We can *feel* it"), **then**

- You really need your heads examined. History is littered with follies that were pursued because of the echo chamber of (delusional) beliefs that had no empirical basis. Feelings/perceptions/anecdotes are NOT good enough yardsticks to know the impact.

- If you still cannot commit to systematically evaluating your impact, you need to **STOP** your improvement initiative immediately. Just stop. Do not waste any further time on something that you are not prepared to evaluate and are not evaluating.

c. **If you chose answer c** ("We know the project isn't working but no one has the heart to kill it. Everyone has spent so much time working on it and we don't want to hurt anyone's feelings"), **then**

- You need to hold the mirror up and ask those difficult questions immediately. It's a disservice to your students and to your community to carry on with something that in your heart-of-hearts you know isn't working. Even if you conclude that your initiative isn't "causing any harm," this also isn't good enough. While it might not be doing damage, it is sucking up your valuable time—time that could be repurposed for other more impactful activities.

4.2 MONITOR YOUR DELIVERY

Now that you have monitored your evaluation, the next key task is to monitor your delivery. This is about you checking that you are doing the delivery-focused things that you said you were going to do in your program logic model and your implementation plan. It's also about checking that you are doing them in the *way* that you originally set out to. It builds on the activities you will already have been undertaking in Step 3.3 (i.e., collecting monitoring and evaluation data). Now you are going to review these data to monitor your progress.

Your program logic model contains a range of resources, activities, assumptions, and outputs, as recapped in Figure 4.5.

FIGURE 4.5 ● Recapping the Program Logic Model

RESOURCES	ACTIVITIES	ASSUMPTIONS	OUTPUTS
e.g.:	e.g.:	e.g.:	e.g.:
• People	• Development of programs	• We will be able to develop the programs	• Products developed
• Time			
• Money	• Implementation of programs	• Wider stakeholders will participate	• Training delivered
• Equipment	• Quality assurance of delivery	• *Their participation will improve outcomes*	• Number of people engaged/reached
• Goodwill			

There are many standard project management tools that you can leverage to monitor the implementation of your program logic model. Here are some examples:

- **Project plan.** You will have developed some version of this in Stage D3, whether this is a Kanban board or a Gantt chart. The most comprehensive version lists all your workstreams/subprojects and then all the activities for each (task by task), the intended start and end dates, the allocated resources, and the critical path (i.e., which tasks need to be completed first, second, third, etc., or the task dependencies). As you implement your project, the idea is that you then update this in real time, so that you can see what percentage of each task has been completed and what is still left to do.

PROJECT PLAN MONITORING ACTIVITY

Are we on track, ahead, or behind? Are we hitting our key milestones?

- **Time tracking.** In the private sector, many professional services organizations use time-logging software to monitor how much time staff spend on different projects and activities. They often use these tools or apps to support client billing. Depending on the complexity of your project, it may be important and useful for you to know and monitor how much time each of the project team members is spending on a task. This will help you to understand whether your assumptions about time were correct, and it may also give you wider insights into what proportion of their time they are spending on different initiatives. We provide an illustration in Figure 4.6.

TIME-TRACKING MONITORING ACTIVITY

Are we spending more, less, or the same amount of time on this project as we anticipated?

- **Product acceptance criteria.** In project management it is common to explicitly describe the acceptance criteria for each output. For example, if the "product" is a set of

FIGURE 4.6 ● Time Tracking

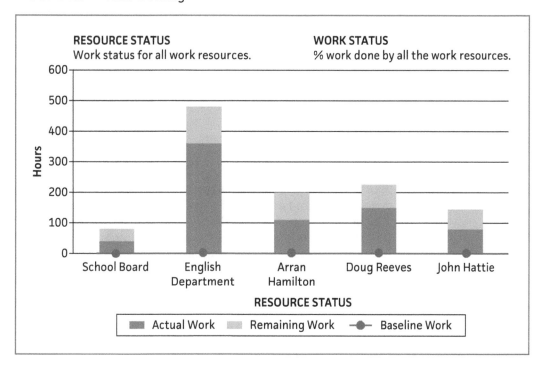

RESOURCE STATUS
Work status for all work resources.

WORK STATUS
% work done by all the work resources.

Legend: Actual Work | Remaining Work | Baseline Work

curriculum materials, you might define the topic areas, the age appropriateness of the content, the number of pages or images, or even just include a worked example and state that "the finished product must be like this."

ACCEPTANCE MONITORING ACTIVITY

Do the artifacts, products, and/or outputs that we have created meet or exceed the acceptance criteria that we described?

- **Budget tracking.** This is about monitoring what you have spent versus what you intended to spend. During the Design (D2) and Deliver (D3) Stages, you will have already set out your financial requirements for the procurement of any goods and services to support your implementation. However, you now need to keep track of that spending. Is it more, less, or the same as you anticipated? And is the spending happening at the times that you anticipated it would? Do you forecast that the budget allocation will be sufficient or are you likely to need more?

BUDGET MONITORING ACTIVITY

Are we spending more, less, or the same as we expected? Are we spending when we expected to spend?

- **Implementation metrics.** These will vary depending on what it is you are implementing but they enable you to track your outputs. For example, if your logic model envisages the development and delivery of teacher professional development programs, your metrics might relate to the percentage of programs that have been developed, the number of training sessions delivered, and the number of educators that have participated in the training.

IMPLEMENTATION ACTIVITY

Are we meeting our implementation metric targets?

The complexity of the monitoring systems that you put in place and your frequency of monitoring will be directly proportional to the scale and importance of your initiative. If you are working at the district level or beyond, you will very likely want to set up robust and professional monitoring processes. You will probably also seek to leverage specialized software to support this. If you are working at the whole-school level, these tools and systems are also likely to be useful to you but are less essential. However, at the level of a professional learning community, it's probably sufficient to just record your progress in a notebook or to maintain a tracking spreadsheet.

In this monitoring stage, you are checking whether you have done the things you said you would do. In addition, you are checking that you leveraged the resources, undertook the activities, and achieved the outputs. Most importantly, you are checking that you did this on time, on budget, and to the required quality standards. This is important.

To know your impact, you now need to move beyond mere monitoring and toward systematic evaluation.

However, getting things done is not the same as those things generating impact. You might successfully do all the things you set out to do but find that it contributes little or nothing to your longer-term improvement trajectory. To know your impact, you now need to move beyond mere monitoring and toward systematic evaluation.

4.3 EVALUATE YOUR DELIVERY AND AGREE ON NEXT STEPS USING THE STEP 2.1–2.4 TOOLS

Way back in Stage D2 we introduced our six levels of evaluation, which builds on the work of Kirkpatrick (1993) and Guskey (2000). We also suggested that you need to establish select appropriate tools (i.e., indicators) to help you glean answers to each of these focus areas and to set targets for your trajectory of improvement.

This is so important that we are, again, illustrating these six levels here in Figure 4.7. Level 1 is shaded gray because it relates to the monitoring activity that you progressed under Step 4.2. However, the remaining five levels are all about giving you insight into whether your program logic model *works* and what you should do next.

FIGURE 4.7 ● Recapping the Six Levels of Evaluation

LEVEL	FOCUS	TIME HORIZON	EVALUATIVE TOOLS
1	**Monitoring** Did we do the things we said we were going to do? Did we do them according to the anticipated timelines and with the anticipated level of resources?	Short term	● Project plan monitoring ● Budget monitoring ● Time tracking ● Product acceptance criteria
2	**Engagement** Did stakeholders engage positively with the improvement initiative? Did they *like it*, and did they participate at the expected level/frequency?	Short term	● Satisfaction surveys ● Interviews ● Focus groups
3	**Learning** Did stakeholders (usually teachers) successfully learn new skills/techniques/approaches that have the *potential* to enhance their collective performance?	Short term	● Portfolio evidence aligned (e.g., to teaching standards) ● Lesson observation ● Interviews and focus groups ● Questionnaires
4	**Change** Was there a noticeable change in stakeholders' performance behaviors? Did they (usually teachers) put the learnings into practice in their classrooms/work practices?	Medium term	● Lesson observation (e.g., with video tools) ● Questionnaires ● Structured interviews ● Self-/collective efficacy psychometrics

(Continued)

FIGURE 4.7 ● (Continued)

LEVEL	FOCUS	TIME HORIZON	EVALUATIVE TOOLS
5	**Impact** Did the (L2) engagement, (L3) learning, and (L4) change actually result in improvement in the targeted area? Did outcomes from the students improve?	Longer term	• Student achievement data • Student attendance data • Student voice • Structured interviews with teachers, parents, students, and leaders
6	**Improvement and Sustainability** How can we further enhance the impact, and what do we need to do to stop backsliding?	Continuously	• All of the above—for the purpose of reviewing and enhancing your program logic model

Some of these data come quickly. They are what economists call *leading indicators*. You can quickly and regularly take pulse surveys, run focus groups, or have even more informal design huddles to measure engagement and enjoyment. You can talk to people to see if they understood the theory behind what they are supposed to be doing and whether they agree with it. You can also get into classrooms within a couple of months of implementation to look for signs of changes to educator practice. However, whether your program logic model leads to improvements for students is more of a *lagging indicator*. It often takes time for changes in teacher behaviors to percolate through to improvements in student learning, engagement, or attendance. Usually, it takes a minimum of 6 months to see the needle start to inch upward. In fact, you may face an immediate implementation dip in which the initial rollout causes stress, confusion, and even resistance, resulting in a decline in performance on some of your outcome measures (Herold & Fedor, 2008). And this is the time when you need to hold your breath and see whether the niggles will subside or whether you need to iterate (or even abandon) your logic model.

LEVERAGING LEVEL 2 ENGAGEMENT DATA

One of the easiest forms of **leading indicator** data that you can capture, while holding your breath for impact, is level 2 engagement data. By leveraging the Stages of Concern framework (Hall, 1979; Straub, 2009), you can begin to categorize the *type* of engagement, based on stakeholder feedback. You may also find that you begin to get qualitative perceptual data on impact and outcomes too, that give you Gray-Box and Clear-Box insights. We illustrate this in Figure 4.8.

FIGURE 4.8 ● Level of Engagement

ENGAGEMENT LEVEL	ENGAGEMENT DESCRIPTION	MAPPING TO EVALUATION FRAMEWORK
Unaware	I'm not sure what the initiative is or what it has to do with me	L2
Aware	I've got a basic understanding of the initiative and its purpose but haven't thought through how I will engage with it	L2, L3
Personal	I'm concerned about personal costs and sacrifices required to implement	L2, L3, L4
Procedural	I'm focused on the technical and logistical processes of implementation	L2, L3, L4
Personal Outcomes	I'm focused on collecting informal data on whether the initiative works	L5
Collective Outcomes	We are focused on comparative outcomes (i.e., my impact vs. yours vs. our collective impact)	L5
Enhancing Outcomes	We are focused on exploring the adjustments we make to the design features and setting levels that will further enhance impact	L6

Source: Adapted from Straub (2009).

We suggest that on at least a monthly basis you review and interpret the evaluative data that are being collected. Here are the questions you need to ask:

1. **Is the evidence of impact sufficiently positive for us to continue without making adjustments to the program logic model?** Your answers are likely to be one of the following:

   a. It's too soon to know. We need to hold our breath a bit longer.

   b. Evidence of impact is promising, but there are minor adjustments we could make to enhance delivery.

   c. Evidence of impact is strong. We should avoid the distraction of fiddling and iterating for now.

   d. Things are not looking promising. We need to consider radical adjustment and possibly even stop completely.

2. **What are we going to do?** Your options are likely to be one of these: ↻

   a. Carry on for now, and Double-Back again in another month.

   b. ITERATE the program logic model (i.e., crawl the design space).

   c. STOP.

We illustrate this as a process flow in Figure 4.9.

FIGURE 4.9 ● Iterative Implementation

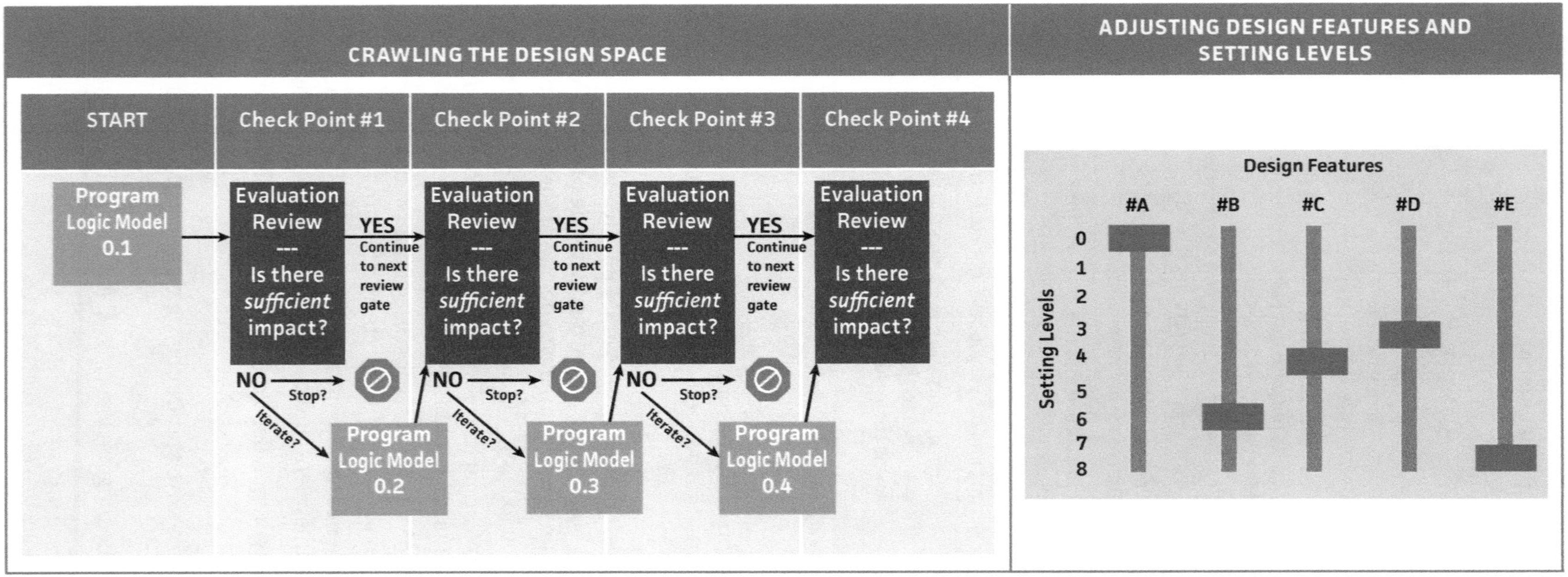

ADJUSTING DESIGN FEATURES AND SETTING LEVELS

CRAWLING THE DESIGN SPACE

Source: Copyright © Cognition Education. (2022). All rights reserved.

CONSIDERATIONS ABOUT ITERATING

If, after conducting your evaluative review, you conclude that your initiative is "working" but that the *sufficiency* of impact could be improved, then you need to consider iterating (or wiggling) your program logic model to enhance that impact. You can do this by going back to and reviewing the tools we introduced in Stage D2 (Design).

For each relevant row in your program logic model, you can start by revisiting your accompanying analysis of design features and setting levels. Here, you mapped all the relevant design features and all the positions that you could move the various "music sliders" to. Some of those core considerations were about the following:

- **Dosage** (How much "medicine" do we give?)
- **Duration** (How long do we give it for and at what spacing between "doses"?)
- **Target group** (Who is selected for "treatment"?)
- **Delivery group** (Who implements the initiative?)
- **Fidelity** (Is it essential that the implementation protocols are followed exactly? Should we tighten or loosen them?)
- **Regimen** (Do we need to alter some of the contents, features, and/or design properties of the "medicine" or of the administration procedures?)

The good news is that you have already done the analysis. Yes, from the experience of implementation, you might identify additional design features and setting levels that you had not previously considered. And you can add these to your matrix. Then, with your matrix updated, the next step is to identify the iterations that are most likely to improve your impact.

We suggest that you start incrementally and that you focus initially on ONE (or two) high-probability variations that are easier to implement. We illustrate this in the four-quadrant matrix in Figure 4.10,

FIGURE 4.10 ● Four-Quadrant Matrix

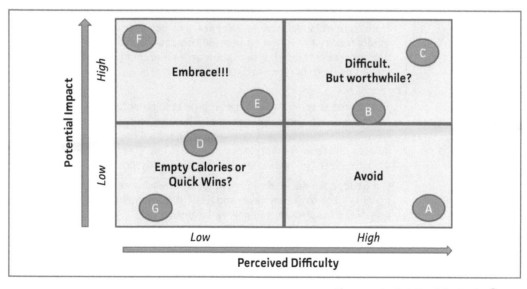

where you can see that options F and E look to offer the best return on investment.

The idea is that after you select the highest-probability (for lowest-effort) modifications, you then update your logic model and your delivery protocols to reflect those changes. Then you press "play" again, implement, and then (again) review the evaluation data to look for the next high-priority wiggle. This means that in another review cycle you will be back to this point again. When you return, you will be considering (1) whether those changes did deepen the impact, as intended, and (2) whether to attempt additional iterative changes to other aspects of your program logic model, as you crawl and learn. We illustrate this in Figure 4.11.

FIGURE 4.11 ● Adjusting the Design Features and Setting Levels

After 6 months of implementing the intelligent tutoring system and seeing some impact, the backbone team is focused on how they can grow it yet further. So, they go back to their map of design features and setting levels to identify appropriate areas for iterative enhancement.

After reviewing the map, the backbone team concludes that shifting from Tutoring Platform E to another system will be too complex and costly. In fact, the reason the platform was selected was that it had so much evidence of impact in other contexts. So, no change here.

The backbone team therefore wonders whether adjustments to how the existing platform is used and how that use is supported will enhance impact. Recognizing that the platform's task difficulty is too low for the highest-performing students and that it is generating boredom and disengagement for them, the team considers varying this setting level and making use optional, except for students who have fallen behind.

The team has also noticed that when students access the system from their personal devices, they seem to get distracted by social media feeds. One way of addressing this could be to only allow system access through school computer equipment, which has been locked down to prevent social media access. They decide to carry this forward.

The backbone team also wonders if increased parental engagement might help with student engagement. But having decided that the tutoring platform will only be used during school hours and on school devices, the team ultimately decides not to implement this potential adjustment to the setting level of this design feature.

Once they have decided which design features and setting levels will be varied, the backbone team updates the program logic model and prepares to implement the new variations.

(Continued)

FIGURE 4.11 ● (Continued)

	Design Feature 1: Which system do we select?	Design Feature 2: Is it Mandatory?	Design Feature 3: Hardware	Design Feature 4: Parental Engagement	Design Feature 5: Dosage Level
			ACTIVITY: INTELLIGENT TUTORING SYSTEM		
Setting Level 1	Tutoring Platform A	Mandatory for All students	Students' own devices—any	None –all done in school	Left to personal choice
Setting Level 2	Tutoring Platform B	Optional for All students	Students' own devices–non-smartphone only	None –but used home and school	Minimum 60 minutes per week
Setting Level 3	Tutoring Platform C	Mandatory for students that have fallen behind. Optional for all others	School tablets	Parent newsletter	Maximum of 90 minutes per week and minimum of 60
Setting Level 4	Tutoring Platform D		Hybrid	Parent briefing session	
Setting Level 5	Tutoring Platform E			Telephone call to parents	
			ANALYSIS		
	Platform E has been used in other schools locally. Staff very positive. Also, strong independent evaluation data.	If it's optional no one will take seriously. If it's mandatory only for students that have fallen behind –creates stigma	We are not sure it will make much difference. Let's start with Hybrid and see what happens	It would probably be helpful to inform parents!! Let's start by putting it in the newsletter and see if any request more information	The global research suggests that 90 minutes a week spread over 3x30 minute sessions is about optimal
			CONCLUSION		
	Platform E	Mandatory for All	Hybrid	Parent Newsletter	90 minutes –split between three sessions

Source: Adapted from Hamilton and Hattie (2022).

CONSIDERATIONS ABOUT STOPPING ⟳

If, however, you conclude that your program logic model is beyond redemption, then you really need to stop. You might not come to that conclusion quickly or easily, and there might be a few rounds of iterative wiggling of your design features and setting levels before you get to this stage. But, if after doing all this, you see no improvement on your outcome indicators, you need to call it a day.

Of course, it will be hard and gut-wrenching. There are well-documented cognitive biases that suggest we are potentially hardwired to double-down rather than stop and rethink.

- **The sunk cost fallacy.:** "We've spent so much time/money/effort on this. We simply *caaaan't* give up, with all we invested."

- **The plan continuation bias:** "Okay, we haven't seen any progress on our outcome measures during these past 18 months. But I'm sure if we keep going another 5 years, we'll get there in the end" or "Everyone has gotten used to this new (but totally ineffective) way of doing things. It took a lot of kicking and screaming to get us here. Getting to this point is an achievement in itself!"

It may also involve difficult conversations, particularly with the early adopters or idea pioneers. It can be crushing for them to see the project they have been championing suddenly tossed into the deep freeze. However, one way you circumvent the loss of face dimension is to frame all your initiatives as 1804-type science experiments from the get-go. Then you depersonalize from the beginning if you start by saying something like this:

> We selected these activities because they worked extremely well in other contexts. So there is a high probability that if we implement them appropriately, we will see similar success in our organization. However, we can never be 100% sure that they will work. And even if they do, we are unlikely to implement them optimally the first time. So, we evaluate as we go to make sure we are spending our time on worthwhile initiatives and that we are implementing them in the best possible way for our context.

The initiative is seen as an algorithmic crawl through the design space. You searched for viable interventions. You selected the most likely. You implemented. Then you evaluated. And if it didn't work out, you can stop digging the hole deeper. Instead, you can fill it in and move on to Idea 2 and start again. It's not personal. It's how we do implementation science around here.

This is also how the metaphorical wagon riders would have approached their trek from St. Louis to California. Using their telescope, they might have initially concluded that the best path was straight West. That decision would have made sense at that moment in time—with the information they had at hand. But after they have traveled it for a bit, they might be presented with new information (e.g., the Grand Canyon) that makes them decide to turn around and try something different.

In our implementation, we need to be equally rational as we evaluate our implementation pathways and find that they are not working. And in making our decision to stop, we also need to get to the bottom of which element of our logic was faulty. Was it one of these?

1. **The education challenge.** Perhaps it didn't really exist, was self-correcting, or was a lower priority than we originally thought.
2. **The theory of the present.** Maybe we misunderstood the causal drivers. We had the wrong influence bubbles on our path analysis or the arrows were pointing to the wrong places, so we selected inappropriate initiatives to deliver.
3. **The program logic model.** Perhaps the initiatives we selected were not the right fit for our context, our starting point, our latent capabilities, or our beliefs.
4. **The implementation.** Maybe we struggled to maintain momentum with all the other things we had going on. It "fell down the back of the sofa," so to speak.

With these insights in mind, you go all the way back to Stage D1 and start anew. But make sure that you gather up all the lessons learned so that you don't walk right back into the same bear traps again. As Einstein apparently once said, "Stupidity is doing the same thing over and over and expecting a different outcome."

FIGURE 4.12 ● An Example of Program Logic Model Implementation, Iteration, and STOPPING

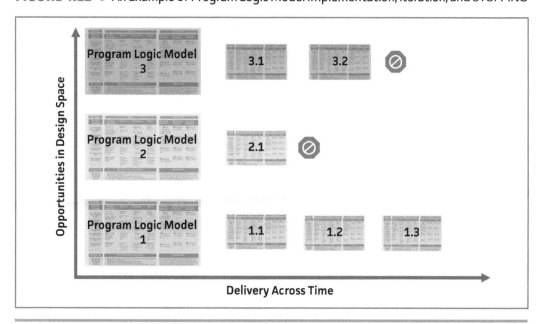

Source: Copyright © Cognition Education. (2022). All rights reserved.

In the example in Figure 4.12, a school district has developed three program logic models that the backbone team concludes are all technically feasible and that have potential for similar levels of impact. Rather than picking one and pressing play, the sponsors agreed to pilot all three across different schools in order to crawl and learn. At the first review gate, all three still look promising but variations are made to the design features to enhance their impact. At the second review gate, program logic model 2 is dropped because it is proving too complex to administer. At the next review gate, program logic model 3 is discontinued—this time because the outcome data are not as promising as model 1 and the costs of implementation are higher. Only logic model 1 makes it to the end of the "race" and several design features have been adjusted, so it's not quite the same "horse" that left the stalls at the start!

4.4 EVALUATE YOUR EVALUATION! ↻

If you opted for either the continuation of the existing program logic model without change *or* for iteration, we now come to our final highly recommended evaluative step. Evaluate your evaluation!

Now, you might think, "But we did this already in Step 4.1." Almost but not quite. What you did back then was monitor (or check) whether you were actually implementing the evaluative processes that you said you were going to. Now we want you to consider whether those systems and tools are giving you useful answers that enable you to confirm and to grow your impact.

You might do this on a term and/or semester basis, using the three lenses illustrated in Figure 4.13.

FIGURE 4.13 ● Three Lenses for Evaluating Your Evaluation

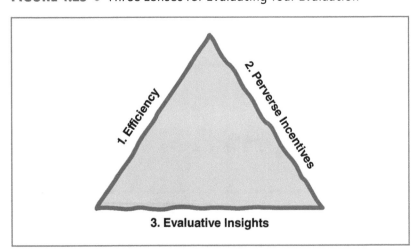

EFFICIENCY

This addresses the "we don't have time to evaluate" response. And even if you are making the time, there might still be some areas where you can make your evaluative activities leaner, easier, and quicker. Here are some areas you could consider.

EVALUATIVE INSTRUMENTS

- Do you have too many tools that all give you similar types of data? Can some of these be decommissioned without (significantly) reducing the evaluative insights that you generate?

- Are you deploying these tools too frequently (e.g., collecting student achievement data for evaluative purposes on a weekly basis) when it might be more appropriate to do so on a longer cycle?

EVALUATIVE INTERPRETATIONS

- Consider the frequency with which you are coming together to review the data. Too frequently and you won't be able to see the signal in the noise. Too infrequently and you won't be able to respond to what you see and iterate your initiative design. Are you getting this "just right"?

- Assess the depth of your evaluative reporting. Are you producing a dashboard-style highlight report or writing a 60-page report with complex appendices that no one is going to read or understand?

PERVERSE INCENTIVES

This is about whether the evaluative systems you have established are altering stakeholders' behaviors in unanticipated but problematic ways. For example, some of our work has been in developing countries where it is not uncommon for teachers to not show up at school and where, if they do attend, not to be in class and teaching. Sometimes we see ministries of education implementing new programs that use the evaluative tools for accountability purposes too, and this can create perverse incentives, including the examples detailed in Figure 4.14.

FIGURE 4.14 ● Generating Perverse Incentives

TOOL	IMPACT
Standardized lesson observation instrument	Teach best lesson when being observed, even if students have already had it 17 times already. Reinforcement is always good!
Standardized student achievement tests	Lots of test prep. Encourage weaker students to stay home on testing day. Accidentally lock any who forget not to attend in the stationary closet
Teacher daily attendance register	Make sure you clock in at the start of the day before going off to your second job

These examples are harrowing but all too real in places like South Asia and Sub-Saharan Africa. We are sure that the evaluative tools that you deploy will not result in these kinds of perverse incentives. But you still need to think about the potential that stakeholders are dancing to the tune of the tools you have implemented and this does not result in an impact on your ultimate outcome measure. Of course, dancing is fine—if the steps are aligned with what pushes the needle on your education challenge. This is the evaluative equivalent to the adage that *teaching to the test is fine if it's a test worth teaching to.*

EVALUATIVE INSIGHTS

The final perspective you want to think from is whether the tools you are using and the data you are collecting are helping you to answer useful questions that help you determine and improve your impact. You can consider this against our six levels of evaluation and use the tool in Figure 4.15 to record your answer, your explanation (i.e., the justification for your response), and your next steps. For example, your next step might be to do nothing if you already have it covered or if you have decided for efficiency purposes not to collect data against all six of the levels.

You especially need to do this if you have iterated your program logic model. Otherwise, it may be that you are collecting data about

FIGURE 4.15 ● **Meta-Evaluative Questions** ↻

LEVEL	EVALUATIVE QUESTION	CAN WE ANSWER IT?
1	**Monitoring** Did we do the things we said we were going to do? Did we do them according to the anticipated timelines and with the anticipated level of resources?	**Yes/No** **Explanation:** [i.e., why/why not] **Next Steps:** [i.e., what are we going to do about it]
2	**Engagement** Did stakeholders engage positively with the improvement initiative? Did they *like it*, and did they participate at the expected level/frequency?	**Yes/No** **Explanation:** **Next Steps:**
3	**Learning** Did stakeholders (usually teachers) successfully learn new skills/techniques/approaches that have the *potential* to enhance their collective performance?	**Yes/No** **Explanation:** **Next Steps:**

LEVEL	EVALUATIVE QUESTION	CAN WE ANSWER IT?
4	**Change** Was there noticeable change in stakeholders' performance behaviors? Did they (usually teachers) put the learnings into practice in their classrooms?	**Yes/No** **Explanation:** **Next Steps:**
5	**Impact** Did the (L2) engagement, (L3) learning, and (L4) change actually result in improvement in the targeted area? Did outcomes for the students improve?	**Yes/No** **Explanation:** **Next Steps:**
6	**Improvement and Sustainability** How can we further enhance the impact, and what do we need to do to stop backsliding?	**Yes/No** **Explanation:** **Next Steps:**

things you have stopped doing or that you have started doing something that you are not measuring and have no means of evaluating.

Most of all, remember that you are evaluating to learn, iterate, and grow your impact. We illustrate this in Figure 4.16.

FIGURE 4.16 ● Iterative Adaptation Across Time

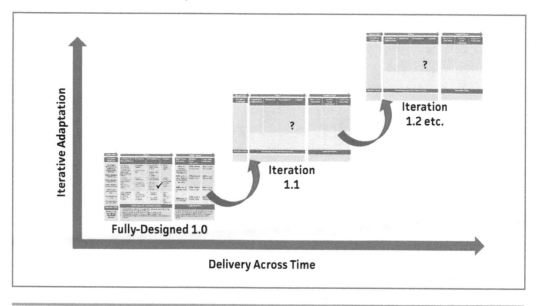

Source: Hamilton and Hattie (2022).

D4: Double-Back Summary

You have now reached the end of the D4 Double-Back. During this stage of your inquiry:

You will have monitored and evaluated your delivery chain and agreed on PRIORITY actions

You will have done this by

4.1 Monitoring Your Evaluation

4.2 Monitoring Your Delivery

4.3 Evaluating Your Delivery and Agreeing on Next Steps Using the Step 2.1–2.4 Tools

4.4 Evaluating Your Evaluation!

CHAPTER 5

D5: Double-Up

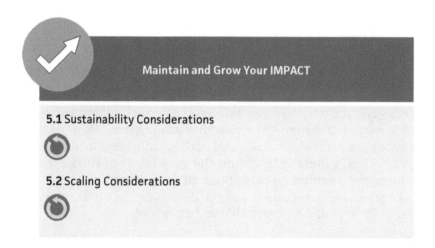

If your head is swimming from the range of processes and activities that we introduced during D1–D4 and you are worried about what more we have in store for you in **D5: Double-Up**, fear not. The reality is that if you follow the processes we have already unpacked and if you circle back to these continuously to evaluate, iterate, and enhance your impact, you have got it covered.

You can think of this chapter as a sort of after-show party or like the bonus material on a movie DVD, back when DVDs were a thing. Our focus in this bonus chapter is on two critical factors:

1. **Sustainability** (i.e., once you have got something going, how you maintain it)
2. **Scale** (i.e., how you move from 1, 2, 4, 8, 16, 32, 64, to 32,768 without your impact becoming a photocopy of a photocopy of a photocopy)

5.1 SUSTAINABILITY CONSIDERATIONS

Often in our work with school and system leaders we are asked, "How can we make this sustainable?" When we dig into what they mean by *sustainable*, it's usually some combination of these:

- Automatic
- Effortless
- Requires no further thought or sleepless nights
- It just happens
- I can now move on to put out the next fire or embark on the next moonshot priority and never look back.

You might not want to hear this . . . but there is no such thing as this form of sustainability.

Let us tell you why. The Second Law of Thermodynamics gives us the concept of *entropy*—the rule that any system left to its own devices gradually slows down and declines into disorder (Baierlein, 1999). This is literally built into the very fabric of the universe, which will (eventually) turn into cold soup. Thankfully this will take several billion years to happen. However, the same applies to our daily lives and on much shorter timescales.

When you buy a car, it does not run forever without servicing. There is an expectation that you will need to regularly check the tires and change the oil. And you will need to take the car to a mechanic at regular intervals to inspect and maintain the more complex inner workings. The same is true with your house. You need to mow the lawn, polish the interior, and occasionally call on contractors to fix the pipes or replace the roof. This is about keeping entropy at bay.

The same principles apply to people. Sometimes we just forget things we have learned (i.e., mental entropy). You will no doubt have seen this with your own students. Week 1 you teach the concept. Week 2 they get it. Week 3 they ace the formative assessment test. Week 6 they stare blankly. They've completely forgotten. What applies to students (obviously) also applies to adults undertaking professional development! You may (or may not) remember from your teacher training days that this is called the *forgetting curve* (see Murre & Dros, 2015).

We are more likely to form enduring memories that are less prone to entropy if our learning is spaced, if it connects with our prior learning, and if it conforms with our beliefs. And there is a whole literature on the essential features of teacher professional development that tells us that one-off workshops are exceedingly entropy prone and that instead, we need to (1) introduce a new protocol,

(2) model it in the context in which it will be deployed, (3) get people to deliberately practice implementation, and (4) provide feedback/coaching—all spaced over time (e.g., see Joyce & Showers, 2002; Timperley et al., 2007). Note that there is even a branch of computer science called information theory, which is focused on the fact that even digital data degrade and mutate as they are transmitted and restored, pioneered by the late great Claude Shannon (1948).

Sometimes we remember well enough but lose the motivation to maintain a strategy. Earlier in this book, we spoke about New Year's resolutions—that tradition of making life-altering promises to oneself on December 31. There are significant commonalities in those "binding" commitments: exercise more, lose weight, save more money, quit smoking, take up a new hobby, drink less, and so on. However, when we look at the longitudinal tracking data on people's ability to stick with and maintain their new habits, we also see entropy and degradation at play. For example, relapse rates are extremely high for people who join weight loss programs (Tsai & Wadden, 2005), attempt smoking cessation programs (Carpenter et al., 2013; Hughes et al., 2004), or try and reduce their alcohol intake (Moos & Moos, 2006). And that failure seems to be due to a mixture of having unrealistic goals or timeframes, not monitoring and evaluating progress, having too many goals, or just forgetting and losing interest.

There is remarkably little research on *long-term* habit maintenance that tracks people's adherence over several years. However, the findings from what is available are remarkably common sense (e.g., see Kwasnicka et al., 2016):

1. **Maintenance motives.** If we enjoy the outcomes of the new behavior and they align with our sense of self-identity, we are more likely to continue (Weinstein & Sandman, 1992).

2. **Maintenance monitoring.** If we gather data to track our progress and develop self-regulation protocols, we are also more likely to continue (Hofmann et al., 2008).

3. **Habit formation.** Over time and hundreds of repetition cycles, behaviors gradually become ingrained and automatic (Rothman et al., 2009). The higher the number of repetitions, the more likely we are to continue. Over the long run, there will be mutations, adaptations, and drift in how we implement the strategies and protocols. Some of these will be improvements; others will cause the educational equivalent of IV-line infections.

4. **Cognitive resources.** The initial maintenance of a habit (i.e., prior to habit formation) is cognitively taxing. If our cognitive resources are limited (e.g., we are attempting to make multiple changes at once or we simultaneously face significant outside stressors), we are less likely to continue (Hagger et al., 2010).

5. **Environmental context.** If others in our organizational environment are also attempting to acquire and maintain similar habits, we are more likely to continue (Mackenbach et al., 2014). And if we publicly declare our goals, we are also more likely to stick with them. For example, it's easier to stick to a diet if you publicly declare your intention and if your whole family goes on the same regimen. And it's considerably harder if you do it secretly and have to watch your family eating chocolate cake while you abstain!

Versions of these common-sense tricks can and should be built into your program logic model to increase the fidelity of transmission, uptake, and maintenance. But you cannot assume that once you have reached takeoff velocity, you will maintain momentum without adding further fuel and undertaking regular re-steering. It's a bit like driving a car at full speed up a hill and then jumping out at the downward leg. Yes, the car will continue down the hill at speed for some time, but it will gradually slow, will no longer follow the contours of the road, and will probably grind to a halt in the bushes.

Ergo, there is no such thing as *I can now move on to put out the next fire or embark on the next moonshot priority and <u>never look back</u>*. If the education challenge you have been working on is still an important priority for you, you have three options:

1. **Keep your backbone team on it.** In other words, you continue to strategically oversee the education challenge. And you continue to cycle through successive waves of Deliver, Double-Back, and iterative (re-)Design *for as long as it remains important to you*. This could be months, years, or forever.
   a. *Advantage:* This is the best way to slow entropy.
   b. *Disadvantage:* You do not have the bandwidth to put out other fires or take on new moonshot goals.

2. **Move on but monitor.** This is the equivalent of jumping out of the moving car to focus on other pressing priorities, while attempting to keep the car in view. Then, as required, run and jump back in to restart the engine, re-steer, and drive it up the next hill before jumping out again.
   a. *Advantage:* This enables your backbone team to focus on the next pressing need.
   b. *Disadvantage:* Entropy is swift, as you lose track of the car's location and (inevitably) cannot jump back in quickly enough.

3. **Delegate and empower.** Get the passengers to drive the car in shifts. Over time, however, their gear-changing technique can become sloppy, and new passengers enter the car without a

driver's license or with a different understanding of the rules of the road.

    a. *Advantage:* This builds and distributes capacity, especially if it has been designed into your program logic model from the get-go.

    b. *Disadvantage:* Entropy still occurs at a faster rate than option 1 but slower than option 2.

Our message is that there is no such thing as sustainability without maintenance. If you can accept a voltage drop and have other more pressing education challenges, then you need to jump out of the car or enlist other drivers. But at the same time, you cannot engage in the magical thinking that the car will indefinitely maintain its cruising speed and/or stay on the road by itself. The hidden hand of entropy always creates drag and resistance in the end.

> *There is no such thing as sustainability without maintenance.*

5.2 SCALING CONSIDERATIONS

On the important topic of moving from the one, to the few, to the many, we have Six Things to proffer.

THING 1: SCALING IS RELEVANT TO ALL SYSTEM LEVELS

Scale is usually thought of in terms of widespread use of a program or intervention (Adelman & Taylor, 1997; Fullan, 2000; Sloane, 2005; Stringfield & Datnow, 1998). The implication is that this is about system-level change—the implementation of a new activity across hundreds or thousands of schools. For example, Michael Fullan (2000), in some of his earlier work, defines scale as a *minimum* of 20,000 students across 50 schools.

However, the challenges of scaling can be just as common in the world of the small as the large. Imagine a small rural primary school with 10 teachers, one of whom has developed skills in an evidence-based practice that has high potential to improve student learning outcomes for the other nine. The act of getting these ideas to jump out of the brain of that one skilled practitioner to those nine and for them to agree with it, want to replicate it, implement it properly, and then see impact is arguably *more* challenging than scaling from one school to multiple schools. Yes, there will be a voltage drop as you engage more sites and stakeholders with your initiative. But for larger initiatives, you are also more likely to have a dedicated backbone organization in place—a machine that is solely focused on the transmission and replication of those ideas and that develops systematic codes, monitoring protocols, and systematically iterates as it goes.

Until we reach the era of brain-to-brain Bluetooth (and yes, this day will eventually come), there will always be significant degradation or reinterpretation as we transfer ideas from one brain to another. This is the messy and inefficient nature of learning, and it applies equally from the one to the few as it does from the few to the many. Ergo, scaling is relevant to ALL system levels.

THING 2: SCALING REQUIRES A COMMON NEED AND A SIMILAR CONTEXTUAL CAUSE

Here we present five levels of scaling to get your mental juices flowing.

LEVEL 1: WELL-RESOURCED NATIONAL OR INTERNATIONAL BACKBONE ORGANIZATION (e.g., a national ministry, a national department of education, or an international nongovernmental organization like teach for all)

Hypothetical Examples

- The Education Minister of a South Asian country is concerned that an average of 22% of teachers across the whole country do not turn up for work on any given day.

- The Secretary of State in the United Kingdom has been informed that, on average, children had 66% less teaching time during 2020, as a result of COVID-19 school closures.

A potential problem/focus area has been identified that seems to exist across ALL or MOST schools in the country or state.

LEVEL 2: SUBNATIONAL (e.g., education service areas, school districts)

Hypothetical Examples

- The local special school in a London borough has closed and 200 children with significant special educational needs are being mainstreamed into 10 secondary schools across the borough, with one or more joining almost every class in each school.

- In Kuala Lumpur, 40% of parents are sending their children to school-readiness classes when they subsequently arrive in the first year of primary education. These children are already near to the Primary 2 entry standard.

A potential problem/focus area has been identified that seems to exist across ALL or MOST schools in a smaller geographic area.

LEVEL 3: WHOLE SCHOOL

Hypothetical Examples

- A school in Auckland has just been inspected by the Education Review Office. The inspectors were highly critical of the rate of learning progressions across the whole school vs. comparator schools in the same decile.

LEVEL 3: WHOLE SCHOOL

- A school in the North of England has had a recent influx of Syrian refugee children who cannot speak English. At least one refugee child is now in every single class.

A potential problem/focus area has been identified that seems to affect most areas or departments within a single school.

LEVEL 4: WITHIN SCHOOL

Hypothetical Examples

- The Maths team at a school in Sydney has identified that the average student performance for the school in year 9 National Assessment Program—Literacy and Numeracy assessments has steadily declined over 3 years.
- Nine Grade 11 girls at a school in Boston have recently become pregnant.

A potential problem/focus area has been identified that seems to affect one department or area or age group of learners.

LEVEL 5: INDIVIDUAL TEACHERS

Hypothetical Examples

- A newly qualified teacher in Toronto has listened to a podcast about cognitive task analysis and cognitive load theory and wants to apply this to her teaching.
- A teacher at a school in a low-income New York City neighborhood is struggling with behavior management in his classes.

A potential area of inquiry or improvement has been identified that is specific to an individual teacher.

The question of scale (probably) applies much less at Level 5. Here, the need or goal remains at the individual educator level and the individual is seeking out sources of information and actions that relate principally to their specific circumstances. It may be that none of the other teachers in the school have the same behavior management challenges, that they are already applying the principles of cognitive load theory, or that they are doing something else.

The question of scale is highly relevant at Levels 1–4, as there is a common need or goal across multiple people, schools, or even systems. However, without further investigation, it is not (yet) clear whether the same treatments or actions will improve outcomes across all these different contexts. They may have similar symptoms (remember our previous example of backache?), but these might still emanate from different root causes and therefore respond to different treatment options. Therefore, scaling a response to similar symptoms often requires differential diagnosis and the development of more than one templated treatment plan.

Take, for example, the 22% of teachers who are missing from school in a South Asian country on a daily basis. This is a real statistic from an actual country (in fact, many developing countries suffer from high teacher absence rates). But it may be that when the backbone team undertakes their *Five Whys* and builds their path analysis, they discover that nonattendance varies across regions. Perhaps it's 55% in region A, 10% in region B, and 3% in region D, which averages around 22%. It's also possible that the reasons for nonattendance vary across regions. Perhaps, in some cases, the teachers are not getting paid, so they are not attending because they need to do other work to cover their expenses. In other cases, they might be getting paid regularly but might be significantly underestimating the contribution that their teaching makes to students' life outcomes. They are not attending because they don't believe they make a difference. Perhaps the reasons also vary within the regions and within individual schools. These different causal chains generate different path analyses and require different program logic models, or at the very least a single logic model that addresses ALL sets of whys.

THING 3: WE ALREADY KNOW A LOT ABOUT WHAT IS LESS LIKELY TO WORK FOR SCALING

Over the decades, many different approaches to scaling have already been trialed. Some are efficient in their management of inputs but suffer fast entropy on the outcomes. Others have slower entropy but much greater variation or local adaptation, as illustrated in Figure 5.1.

THING 4: PACKET SIZE

We also know that some types of practices are easier to scale than others. For example, it is easier to learn to sing the first verse of *Bohemian Rhapsody* than to sing the full eight verses. And, again, it is easier to learn to sing the eight verses than to also learn the guitar solo, bass guitar, and drum accompaniments. Each is a successively bigger "packet" and each of these additional packet elements requires mastery of different protocols—from memorizing lyrics, to vocal control, to the implementation of guitar and drumming techniques that even we don't know the technical words for.

This concept of packet size (and number of packets) applies equally to the scaling of education improvement. We can distinguish between the following:

1. **Small packet.** This is the equivalent of getting everyone who has already mastered the first verse of *Bohemian Rhapsody* to learn the second. It's a relatively self-contained change that is heavily codified and that therefore should be easier to implement. An education example of this would be moving

FIGURE 5.1 ● Different Models for Scaling

MODEL	DESCRIPTION	OUTCOME
Incremental growth model	Assumes that the act of providing teachers with training in a specific area will always and automatically result in them understanding what they are being trained in, agreeing with it, and putting it into practice in the manner intended	On average, teachers will remember 25% and put less than 10% into practice (e.g., see Joyce & Showers, 2002)
Cascade model	A variant of the incremental growth model. It makes the same assumptions but goes a step further, suggesting that each of those that have been trained in turn go on to train many others—creating a power law effect	Even worse than incremental growth model: a photocopy of a photocopy of a photocopy
Unbalanced growth model	Identifying high-performing teachers and sprinkling them like seeds across a range of schools to evangelize and to increase the transmission of ideas and changes in behavior	**Mixed.** Runs counter to the normal career progression trajectory where teachers move to better schools as their careers progress. Also requires the appropriate local critical mass to avoid crowding out
Cell division model	Asking teachers to innovate a new approach and then, like a break-away cell, move on to establish a new school from scratch that embodies the innovation	**Mixed.** There are limits to how often we can do this before we have too many schools. Diversity can also limit our ability to evaluate impact

Source: Hamilton and Hattie (2021), adapted from Elmore (1996).

from taking a student attendance register at the start of the day to also doing so at the start of every period. This is an extension of an activity that everyone already knows how to do and already does once per day. It also takes very little time to implement and very little time to explain to new teachers how to do it, why to do it, and how to record the data. It can also be supplemented with simple monitoring/auditing processes to check that implementation is occurring. Therefore, it (should) be much easier to scale.

2. **Big packet.** Here we move from singing *Bohemian Rhapsody* to learning multiple songs and to singing them in appropriate contexts: *Happy Birthday* on people's birthdays and *We Wish You a Merry Christmas* during the month of December. An educational example of this would be the introduction of success criteria at the start of each lesson. This involves

explaining to learners at the start of each lesson what they will be able to do and what is expected of them in order to get there. Establishing success criteria is a high-impact instruction approach ($d = 0.88$). Depending on how it is introduced, it might not take much more time than the act of taking attendance or singing a song. However, it needs to be repeated (or "sung") with greater frequency throughout the day and also contextualized to the specific learning objectives of each lesson; so, it's more like singing a different song several times a day that is written or at least localized by the singer. We should therefore expect more implementation friction during scaling, and our program logic model would need to explicitly build this in.

3. **Multiple packets.** This is a significant level of change that involves both more routines but also more localization of those routines—like the juggling of vocals, guitar solo, and drumming and across different songs for all occasions. An education example could be the implementation of five high-impact instructional approaches across all schools: Cognitive Task Analysis ($d = 1.29$) + Success Criteria ($d = 0.88$) + Differentiation ($d = 0.68$) + Jigsaw Method ($d = 1.20$) + Feedback ($d = 0.57$). Even if the scaling is accompanied by significant levels of training, coaching, peer learning, and scaffolded support, the level of scaling is highly ambitious. This is because the level of expected change is profound. It therefore also comes with a significant risk for voltage drop, mutation, and lack of maintenance. Some will be better at the vocals, others the guitar; and sometimes the wrong song will get selected and sung badly.

The key takeaway is that small packets scale big and that big or multiple packets have the greatest potential for entropy. You need to account for this and build for it in your program logic model and then through successive waves of Double-Back to further iterate it out by varying the design features and setting levels.

THING 5: TRANSMISSION MECHANISM

The next key dimension is about how the new ideas, protocols, or "packages" are disseminated. Here, we distinguish between viral transmission, replication, and adaptation (Morel et al., 2019).

VIRAL TRANSMISSION

Viral transmission is when a new idea, process, or tool is gradually and organically transmitted through the system and where it gradually infects more and more brains with its stickiness. In other words, it becomes a meme in the Richard Dawkins (1976) sense of the term.

The idea is spread through word of mouth, testimonials, Twitter, and by authority figures and influencers. More people understand it, talk about it, and accept it. An example of viral transmission at work is Bloom's taxonomy. When Benjamin Bloom devised it in the 1950s, it was only discussed in fringe circles. Yet knowledge and use of the taxonomy have since grown incrementally, and today its use is widespread in curriculum development, assessment, and classroom instruction (Schneider, 2014). However, it is worth noting that there is very little high-quality research on the efficacy of Bloom's taxonomy (Hattie & Larsen, 2020). Sometimes ideas persist even without confirmatory evidence!

If you are working at a system level, it is possible that one of your program logic models could be about change through the viral dissemination of ideas. The last two decades have witnessed the rise of education evidence "clearing houses" that are seeking to "market" and viralize the *what works best* research. If you are in the United States, you may have peaked at the What Works Clearing House, for example. The United Kingdom, Canada, Australia, and New Zealand have their own equivalents that we described earlier in this book.

Many of these platforms are brilliant at turning the research into plain-language digests and even at signposting codified programs that have strong evidence of impact. However, once an idea is transmitted, what happens next is fundamentally down to the discretion of the receiver. Is it relevant to their context? Do they like it? Will it be easy to implement? So, while viral transmission is highly efficient, it is prone to mutation and there is no guarantee the ideas will be implanted. Talk is cheap. Action is hard.

If you are working at the school or district level, these idea viralizers are among the best places that you can look for evidence-based initiatives that *might* be relevant to your context. However, you then need to use systematic search and evaluation protocols, such as those we outline in Step 2.2, to identify the highest-probability activities for your context.

REPLICATION

Replication is about explicitly codifying all the implementation steps—to the level of a Heston Blumenthal cooking recipe. First, preheat the oven to 180 degrees. Second, prepare the baking tray. Third, slice the Caracas carrots at 2-cm thickness. And so on. Of course, Blumenthal does not write these instructions on a whim. He's thoroughly tested all the oven settings from lukewarm to 240 degrees and all the different thicknesses of carrots in order to decide the optimal temperature, carrot thickness, type of carrot, and duration of cooking. And if you carefully follow the instructions for the quantity and type of ingredients and the cooking process, you should be able to replicate the *exact* same results. Yes, of course, there will be a little trial and error as you master some of the specialist techniques. But if you follow the instructions to the letter, the outcome will be identical to Blumenthal's.

If we applied the same principles to education, then like Blumenthal, we would pilot test all the design features and setting levels of our program logic model in a single "restaurant" (school) to refine and enhance them. We would then scale up to one or more additional schools to understand the practical realities of engaging with new stakeholders who had no stake in the original ideas. We would learn from that mini-scaleup by evaluating and adjusting our design features and setting levels once again. And we would repeat this process until we had a recipe that could be scaled with fidelity across hundreds of contexts.

Here are some of the productization levers that we might consider during that scaling process:

- **Process standardization** by providing explicit steps (or "clicks") to be undertaken during implementation. This might be scaffolded (e.g., recommended processes/checklists with discretion about how and when to use them) or scripted (e.g., mandated processes that are delivered with fidelity).

- **Process simplification** by reducing the number of clicks or points of friction in the implementation of the new standard work protocols.

- **Stakeholder capacity-building** by gradual release support, including training, spaced learning, modeling, coaching, feedback, and so on.

- **Staged implementation** or successfully juggling one ball and then graduating to two.

- **Stakeholder motivation** such as beliefs (hearts and minds) vs. incentives (carrot) vs. sanctions (stick).

- **Automation** using technology systems to automate process implementation.

Source: Hamilton and Hattie (2022).

Here, the idea is to develop a turnkey "playbook" much like the standard operating processes used by airline pilots or the franchisee management processes used by McDonald's or Burger King, which are designed to ensure uniform customer experience from outlet to outlet. However, novice teachers are likely to be more open to franchise/replication approaches than their veteran counterparts (Morel et al., 2019). The latter are more likely to feel deprofessionalized when asked to implement turnkey processes to the letter. This is perhaps why many education systems are opting to explore systematic inquiry cycles that mandate a local process for investigation, but which allow educators to select their own priorities for improvement and implement their own customized adventures.

ADAPTATION

Adaptation is about recognizing that not all supermarkets carry Caracas carrots and that household kitchens in Asia often don't have an oven. So, the idea behind adaptation is to distinguish between the essential components for effective implementation (i.e., must have carrots) to the areas that can be adapted to the local context. For example, you can use other varieties of carrot, but we recommend you substitute in this order: Danvers, Imperator, and then Nantes. If you have no oven, it's completely fine to boil and then pan-finish them but they will taste different.

Or to put it in our education context, this is about scaled implementation while allowing local stakeholders to make *appropriate* variations, so the activity or program can be adjusted to match what is possible in the local context (Clarke & Dede, 2009; Cohen-Vogel et al., 2015; Fishman et al., 2013; Means & Penuel, 2005; Sisken, 2016; Wiske & Perkins, 2005).

However, if you are explicitly building your program for scale, our advice is that you do not leave the areas that can be locally adapted entirely to chance and local discretion. Otherwise, your carrot cake may contain no actual carrots. Instead, as you iterate your program logic model, we suggest that you can map and tag the following:

- **Mandatory processes/design features** or those that cannot be deviated from in any shape or form and that therefore need to be locked in.

- **Flexible processes/design features** or those that need to be implemented but where the tolerance for local discretion/variation is high. One example is whether school attendance is taken in assembly for the whole grade level or whether teachers do it in their individual classrooms. What children shout out to signal their presence during rollcall may not really matter; it only matters that the attendance data are accurately captured.

- **Built-in areas for localization** or explicit design features for local stakeholders to "decorate" and make personal to increase buy-in/ownership and unlock the IKEA effect. This might be as simple as adding the school logo and vision to the front of a nationally standardized document. Or it might be as complex as a scripted direct instruction program that highlights areas of delivery that can be localized to be more relatable to students' lives, with suggested examples of how this could be done.

Source: Hamilton and Hattie (2022).

THING 6: THE SCALING CHECKLIST

What we hope should be clear from Things 1–5 is that there are many moving parts that affect the scaling potential of any activity, program, or initiative. These include those listed in Figure 5.2.

If your intention is to scale your initiative, then we recommend you use this framework to score your readiness. You can then use the outcomes of this assessment to enhance your program logic model and your own organizational readiness.

FIGURE 5.2 ● The Scaling Checklist

DOMAIN	ITEM	1	EASIER TO SCALE	2	HARDER TO SCALE	3
1. Education challenge (i.e., the need)	**1.1**		Relevant to most schools		Relevant to few schools	
	1.2		Status quo is not an option		One of many agendas we could consider	
	1.3		Strong sense of urgency		Weak urgency	
	1.4		Weak opposition to change		Strong opposition to change	
2. Environmental context	**2.1**		The causes of the education challenge are similar across all contexts		The causes of the education challenge are fundamentally different across many contexts	
	2.2		The local *resources* to implement are similar		The local *resources* to implement are highly variable	
	2.3		The local *capacities* to implement are similar		The local *capacities* to implement are highly variable	
3. Program logic model	**3.1**		Robust evidence it *works*, even across diverse settings and contexts		Limited evidence it *works*, even across similar settings and contexts	
	3.1		Strong independent evaluation data confirming impact		No independent evaluation data in the setting context	
	3.3		Implementation models strongly codified		Implementation models uncodified	
	3.4		Parameters for permitted adaptation strongly codified		Parameters for permitted adaptation uncodified	

DOMAIN	ITEM	1	EASIER TO SCALE	2	HARDER TO SCALE	3
	3.5		Modest departure from the status quo (i.e., evolution)		Radical departure from the status quo (i.e., revolution)	
	3.6		Low complexity, small number of moving parts and interactions		High complexity, large number of moving parts and interactions	
	3.7		Easy to monitor and evaluate		Hard to monitor and evaluate	
	3.8		Lower cost than status quo		Higher cost than status quo	
	3.9		Aligns with the beliefs about *what works* in most contexts		Contrary to the beliefs about *what works* in most contexts	
4. Backbone organization	**4.1**		Has sustainable funding for multiple years		Temporary structure that will be quickly dismantled	
	4.2		Strong organizational capacity to support scaling		Weak organizational capacity to support scaling	
	4.3		Strong and deep collaborative relationships between backbone organization and target adopters		Nascent relationships between backbone organization and target adopters	
	4.4		Has significant experience in scaling this or other initiatives		Has limited experience in scaling initiatives	
	4.5		Has strongly codified processes for scaling		Has weakly codified processes for scaling	

Source: Copyright © Cognition Education. (2022). All rights reserved.

KEY TAKEAWAYS FROM THE SIX THINGS

To scale, you need to do the following:

1. **Identify an education challenge that is pervasive.** You can only scale if the goal you are seeking to progress is widespread.

2. **Comprehensively map your ecosystem** (i.e., via path analysis) to determine whether the systemwide environmental context

is uniform or whether it is rugged and messy. If it is the latter, developing a single intervention that supports the different needs across the system is likely to be significantly more challenging.

3. **Build program logic models that respond to the key categories of similarity and difference** across the system.

4. **Stress test those logic models**, including performing careful analysis of the most appropriate design features and setting levels as well as the permitted *areas* of adaptation and a permitted *degree* of adaptation.

5. During delivery, **Double-Back regularly** to identify iterative enhancements that support effective scaling.

6. **Explicitly build scaling considerations into your initial program logic model.** Different strategies for scaling could include the following:

   ○ **"Go big"** and seek to uniformly roll out an activity/program across all schools/settings (works best when the packet size is small),

   ○ **"Snowball"** by testing and refining your program logic model and gradually sucking more schools/settings into the orbit of your program (this works best if your packet size is larger),

   ○ **"Go flexible"** by having a handful of prevalidated implementation models for different types of contexts (this works best if your path analysis suggests multiple complex causes to similar symptoms), and/or

   ○ **"Go meta-flexible"** by giving schools tools to design and evaluate their own local initiatives that respond to their self-identified education challenges. The *Building to Impact 5D* framework offers schools such a support framework.

Source: Adapted from Hamilton and Hattie (2022).

Conclusion

The *Building to Impact 5D* playbook is focused on an extremely perplexing dichotomy:

1. **We have more evidence about *what works best* for student outcomes than at any time in human history.** The collective stockpile exceeds 1.5 million studies on teaching, learning, leadership, and all the rest. It involves many hundreds of millions of children and most of it is conducted in developed English-speaking countries. And while, yes, there are still research gaps, we know *a lot* about the good leads for impact. We *might* even say that the era of evidence is over.

2. **The predominantly English-speaking countries have been busily enacting policies and processes to bring this evidence to life, but with underwhelming impact.** Since 1970, we have seen increasing effort expended on teacher licensing, professional development, curriculum materials, and professional standards and in educators working harder and longer than ever (Organization for Economic Cooperation and Development, 2020). However, when we track the subsequent improvements in student outcomes across English-speaking countries since 1970, we struggle to find it (Altinok et al., 2018). So much effort for so little.

The troubling dichotomy is that **Evidence + Effort = Inconsistent Impact**.

To rebalance the equation, we need to add a third driver:

Evidence + Effort + Systematic Implementation = Impact.

Of course, as should be clear by now, "implementation" is not just the doing part; it's everything from A to Z. It's structured processes that support educators to (1) *Discover* a pressing local need, (2) *Design* or localize appropriate evidence-informed interventions, (3) *Deliver* those designs with fidelity, (4) *Double-Back* to evaluate and enhance impact, and (5) *Double-Up* to sustain and scale.

Although the era of evidence is arguably over, the era of implementation is only just beginning. The major reason for this is that we still lack high-quality data on what works best *for* implementation. To put this in context, through the Visible Learning project, we have more than 1,800 meta-analyses on over 300 things that can be implemented. By contrast, we have only been able to identify a handful of meta-analyses on *how* to implement (including Dunst & Trivette, 2012; Durlak & DuPre, 2008; Meyers et al., 2012; O'Donnell, 2008).

This book contributes to this work in progress by sketching a practical approach for implementation that can be leveraged by schools and systems (i.e., *Building to Impact 5D*). To recap, we carefully designed this framework by doing the following:

- **Reviewing 50 existing implementation methodologies** (some of which provide protocols that cover the A to Z; others focus on one single aspect such as goal identification, design, project management, governance processes, monitoring systems, evaluation processes, etc.)
- **Identifying 23 (fairly) common implementation processes** across the 50 methodologies, covering the Discover, Design, Deliver, Double-Back, and Double-Up Stages.
- **Leveraging factor analysis studies** that include the handful of implementations meta-analyses and our own practice-based insights from our combined work across more than 50 countries, with over 100,000 educators.

But most of all, we sought to get into the detail of practical implementation processes and how to use them because, sadly, so many of the existing books for educators provide high-level models and pretty graphics but nothing concrete that can be put into practice. Yet others provide big-picture leadership considerations about how to drive change and keep people motivated. But neither type really tells you how to implement implementation! Our vision, by contrast, was for structured protocols that were easy to understand and with clear steps that could be followed.

This means that, yes, you need to follow the five stages—ALL of them.

And, yes, you also need to attend to ALL of the processes under each stage. None are optional.

We should add that if you relentlessly focus on Stages D1–D4, D5 will take care of itself as long as you plan for it from the start.

Of course, one of the common reactions to *Building to Impact 5D* is that the 5 stages and 18 key processes are extremely difficult and time-consuming to follow. That life is too short, and we need to get on with something/anything before the children are grandparents and the teachers are long in their graves. Our counter is that the current impact is falling short, depressingly so. And that more of the same will just lead to . . . more of the same.

FIGURE 0.3 ● *Building to Impact 5D*

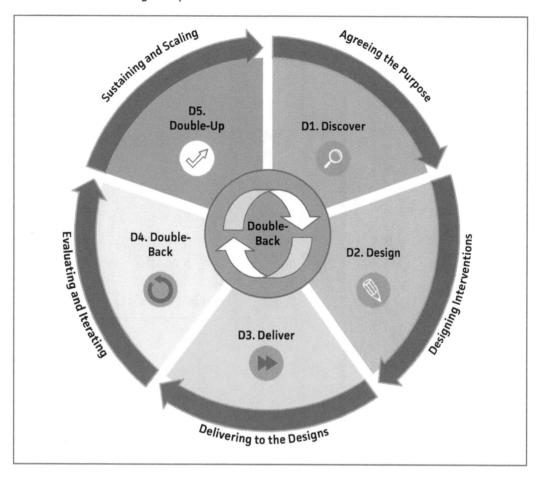

Yes, we agree that a gargantuan act of will is required to implement these implementation processes with fidelity. Hence, this is why we suggest that there is a missing role in schools and systems—the implementation specialist or even scientist (for what we are proposing is indeed a science-based approach). However, not having one is no excuse to put systematic approaches to implementation on hold as you wait patiently for your fully trained specialist to arrive.

In fact, we suspect that you (sort-of) use some version of some of these processes already. In your personal lives, you likely balance and choose between competing goals (e.g., whether to save more money for the future or whether to spend on enjoyment). Then come decisions about the type of enjoyment, with many of us opting, for example, to take a vacation. These decisions are essentially a form of (D1) *Discover* activities. Next, we decide where to go and what to do, which has many of us reviewing travel blogs and Tripadvisor and carefully interrogating what we read because so many of these reports are apparently planted by shills (i.e., we

FIGURE 0.4 Unpacking the *Building to Impact 5D* Stages

D1 DISCOVER	D2 DESIGN	D3 DELIVER	D4 DOUBLE-BACK	D5 DOUBLE-UP
Agree on ONE Education challenge that's worth progressing above ALL else	**Systematically search and agree on high-probability interventions to START and to STOP**	**Implement and de-implement AGREED designs**	**Monitor and evaluate your delivery chain and agree on PRIORITY actions**	**Maintain and grow your IMPACT**
1.1 Establish a Backbone Organization	**2.1** Explore Options in the Design Space	**3.1** Lock the Delivery Approach and Plan	**4.1** Monitor your Evaluation	**5.1** Sustainability Considerations
1.2 Decide the Education Challenge	**2.2** Build Program Logic Model(s)	**3.2** Undertake Delivery	**4.2** Monitor your Delivery	**5.2** Scaling Considerations
1.3 Explain the Education Challenge	**2.3** Stress Test Logic Model(s)	**3.3** Collect Monitoring and Evaluation Data	**4.3** Evaluate Your Delivery and Agree on Next Steps Using the Step 2.1–2.4 Tools	
1.4 Agree on What Better Looks Like	**2.4** Agree on What to STOP		**4.4** Evaluate your Evaluation!	
	2.5 Establish a Monitoring and Evaluation Plan			

168

are exploring options in the design space). Once we have agreed on the place, we then have further decisions to make: the mode of travel, the accommodation, and whether we will build our own itinerary or outsource it to professionals (all of which is *Design* (D2) and focused on program logic modeling, mapping design features and setting levels). After the plan is set, we get going (*Deliver*, D3). This also usually includes taking time off work (i.e., agreeing what to stop), because there aren't 48 hours in a day.

There are also, inevitably, real-time adjustments (e.g., the flight gets canceled, the museum isn't open on Mondays, the wind is too strong for jet skis, etc.). So, we have to iterate and agree with our travel partners on what's next. During the trip, we collect photos, record videos, and perhaps also write Tripadvisor reviews of our own. Some of us keep trip scrapbooks, with a mixture of diary entries and glued-in ticket stubs and maps. Then at the end comes the consideration of whether it was money well spent. Did the trip meet its objectives? Will you go on another vacation? And will it be the same type of trip and with the same people? (All of this is D4 *Double-Back*.)

We are suggesting that *every* decision that we make in our lives leverages mental processes that have some similarities with *Building to Impact 5D*. However, there are key differences:

1. **The level of codification.** When you make decisions in your head, you might not always be aware of the exact processes or criteria you are using. You are acting implicitly rather than explicitly, by a rule of thumb or heuristics. That's fine for deciding between a latte or a flat white but not for tracking vs. detracking or open-space vs. traditional classrooms. For important decisions like this, we *need* you to be thinking deeply, procedurally, systematically, and meta-cognitively.

2. **Optimal stopping.** When you make moment-by-moment decisions, you are more likely to think fast and act quick. You might look at only one or two alternatives before making your selection. However, we want you to think longer and look longer before making your choice. How long and at how many options is still a judgment call between the urgency for action, the reversibility of the action, and the scale of your ambition. A burning school building requires swift action to call the fire department: there isn't time for your backbone organization to sketch multiple Rube Goldberg machines. Equally, if you are using these processes as part of a professional learning community and your scale is a few classrooms in a single school, you will also want to be more agile in terms of the speed at which you leverage each process to decide your preferred option, before just getting on. Whereas if you are operating at the whole-school level or at multiple schools and/or seeking to implement things that will subsequently

be difficult to undo, it is better to think slow and map all the viable options in the design space, their probabilities, and the side effects (i.e., you need to make a local choice between rigid, iterative, and fluid modes of delivery).

As you leverage *Building to Impact 5D*, we also want you to be on the lookout for *process fetishism*. This is the false belief that simply by using the specific tools, filling in the boxes, and making the plan look pretty, there will be impact. The tools, processes, and templates are not an end in themselves. They are a means to impact. The value is in how they drive you to ask better questions, gather more systematic data to generate better answers, design and stress test high-probability interventions, deliver, and systematically enhance by thinking and acting like an improvement scientist.

Why does this matter so much? Because education has always been a bridge to the future. It is a crucial conduit between the living, the dead, and the yet-to-be-born.

As global populations rise to an estimated 10 billion in 2057, from 6 billion at the start of the century, and as automation wrestles control of more routine roles, people will need more education than ever. This means being numerate, literate, tolerant, and increasingly global in outlook and having cultural capital and reasoning skills. The alternative—a world where legions of people do not have the skills to hold their own—is unthinkable.

Education is the best antidote to the bad and the best accelerator of the good. What you do in your classrooms, schools, and districts is *fundamentally* transformative to lives and life chances. It comes with a *major* responsibility; so, we need to get this thing right.

Time to dig deep. Time to implement with rigor.

Appendix 1

Summary of 50 Reviewed Implementation Models

IMPLEMENTATION MODEL	DESCRIPTION	DEPLOYMENT CONTEXTS
Agile Ashmore and Runyan (2014)	Iterative project management methodology that is principally used in software development. Key areas of focus include (1) iterative and incremental implementation, with short feedback loops; (2) efficient communication; and (3) quality focus.	Software development projects
Appreciative Inquiry (AI) Cooperrider et al. (2014)	Centers on identifying, celebrating, and leveraging existing strengths rather than searching for problems to fix and deficit theorizing. Proposes a 4D approach: (D1) Discover, (D2) Dream, (D3) Design, and (D4) Destiny.	Range of commercial and public sector deployments globally
Balanced Scorecard Lawrie and Cobbold (2004)	A strategy performance management tool that supports monitoring and evaluation of progress that assess data across four quadrants: (1) customer, (2) finance, (3) processes, and (4) learning and growth.	Various business and public sector contexts
Collective Impact Kania and Kramer (2011)	Proposes five key criteria for impact: (1) Common Agenda, (2) Shared Measurement, (3) Mutually Reinforcing Activities, (4) Continuous Communication, and (5) Backbone Organization.	Social impact programs in the United States
COM-B (Capability, Opportunity, Motivation and Behaviour) Michie et al. (2011)	A framework devised in medical implementation science to support adoption decision-making. Posits that the success of implementation is strongly influenced by contextual fit linked to (1) local capability to implement the agreed intervention, (2) motivation to implement, and (3) opportunity/capacity to implement.	Health care explanatory model

(Continued)

(Continued)

IMPLEMENTATION MODEL	DESCRIPTION	DEPLOYMENT CONTEXTS
Communities That Care (CTC) Hawkins and Weis (1985)	A community-collaboration model that involves grass-roots stakeholders: (1) Get Started, (2) Get Organized, (3) Develop a Community Profile/Identify a Need, (4) Create a Plan, and (5) Implement and Evaluate.	Youth problem behaviors
Concerns-Based Adoption Model (C-BAM) Hall and Hord (2011)	Focuses on the cognitive concerns/barriers to implementation among educators for programs that are being implemented/scaled. Also provides a range of evaluative tools to measure attitudes and adoption levels among target stakeholder groups. Key dimensions include (1) Stages of Concern, which relate to the personal/affective aspects of implementation; (2) Innovation Configuration, which relates to the level of fidelity/adaptation in implementation; and (3) Levels of Use, which relates to the degree of implementation by stakeholders.	Education sector, high-income countries
Consolidated Framework for Implementation Research (CFIR) Damschroder et al. (2009)	A conceptual framework with 39 constructs that are postulated to improve implementation/outcomes. These constructs sit across five domains: (1) Intervention Characteristics, including intervention complexity, stakeholder characteristics; (2) Inner Setting, including organizational variables such as implementation climate and leadership engagement; (3) Outer Settings, including external policy and incentives to implement); (4) Individual Characteristics, including beliefs and knowledge about the interventions; and (5) Implementation Processes, including selection and evaluation protocols.	Health care explanatory model
CostOut Levin et al. (2018)	Program adoption decision tools that support the estimation of financial costs of implementation and maintenance of different interventions and the comparison of cost vs. probability and depth of impact.	Education financial modeling, US
Deliverology Barber et al. (2011)	Designed for scaling agreed interventions and includes processes related to (1) agreeing on success criteria, (2) establishing accountability structures and metrics, (3) creating local implementation targets, (4) performance tracking, (5) robust accountability dialogue, and (6) rewards and consequences.	Public policy implementation in high- and middle-income countries
Design Thinking Liedtka et al. (2013)	Employs a range of processes, including (1) context analysis to identify wicked issues, (2) ideation and solutions generating, (3) modeling and prototyping, and (4) testing and evaluating.	Range of commercial and public sector deployments globally

IMPLEMENTATION MODEL	DESCRIPTION	DEPLOYMENT CONTEXTS
Diffusion of Innovations Rogers (2003)	A theory of adoption model that seeks to explain how innovations spread through systems and achieve critical mass. Posits a five-stage decision process: (1) knowledge, (2) persuasion, (3) decision, (4) implementation, and (5) confirmation.	Theory of spread
Double Diamond Design Council (2021) and Nessler (2018)	A design thinking–oriented approach that traverses these stages: (1) Discover, (2) Define, (3) Develop, and (4) Deliver. Also provides a methods bank of tools and approaches.	Various
Dynamic Adaption Process Aarons et al. (2012)	Medical implementation model with a core focus on adapting the evidence-based protocols to local contexts. Posits four stages of implementation: (1) Exploration Phase, (2) Preparation Phase, (3) Implementation Phase, and (4) Sustainment. Many features overlap with the EPIS model, with an adaptation/localization lens.	Health care sector
Dynamic Sustainability Framework Chambers et al. (2013)	Focuses on maintaining and sustaining evidence-based protocols in health care settings. Key dimensions relate to maximizing the fit between the intervention, implementation setting, and wider ecological system (e.g., policy, regulation, and market forces) over time.	Health care sector
Eight-Step Process for Leading Change Kotter (2012)	Generic framework for the successful activation of change programs: (1) Create a Sense of Urgency, (2) Build a Guiding Coalition, (3) Form a Strategic Vision and Initiatives, (4) Enlist a Volunteer Army, (5) Enable Action by Removing Barriers, (6) Generate Short-Term Wins, (7) Sustain Acceleration, and (8) Institute Change.	Range of commercial and public sector deployments globally
Exploration, Preparation, Implementation, Sustainment (EPIS) Moullin et al. (2019)	Medical implementation model with four key stages: (1) Exploration (i.e., evaluating local need and appropriate evidence-based programs), (2) Preparation (i.e., developing implementation plans), (3) Implementation, and (4) Sustainment.	Health care sector
Getting to Outcomes (GTO) Wandersman (2014)	A 10-stage results-based approach for getting to agreed outcomes: (1) Focus, (2) Target, (3) Adopt, (4) Adapt, (5) Resources, (6) Plan, (7) Monitor, (8) Evaluate, (9) Improve, and (10) Sustain. A key focus is on organizational readiness for the identified/agreed program.	Wide ranging, including health care, community improvement, and military
Hexagon Tool Blase et al. (2013)	A six-part planning/exploration tool for schools to identify local needs and then evaluate prebuilt programs and their suitability for the local context. Focus areas are (1) Need, (2) Fit, (3) Resources, (4) Evidence, (5) Readiness, and (6) Capacity.	Education sector, high-income countries

(Continued)

(Continued)

IMPLEMENTATION MODEL	DESCRIPTION	DEPLOYMENT CONTEXTS
Human-Centred Design (HCD) IDEO (2015)	Participatory action-research approach that involves (1) immersion, (2) community brainstorming, (3) modeling/prototyping, and (4) implementing.	Range of commercial and public sector deployments globally
Iowa Model Brown (2014)	Eight-step model of evidence-based improvement: (1) identify context where improvement is required; (2) determine whether the improvement is a priority; (3) form a team to develop, implement, and evaluate the improvement; (4) review literature on the change area; (5) critique and synthesize the research; (6) stop and decide whether to proceed; (7) implement change in a pilot program; and (8) evaluate results.	Nurse practitioners in health care settings
Kaizen Graban and Swartz (2012)	Japanese quality improvement philosophy that is strongly aligned to Lean. Focused on improvement to existing processes rather than the development or implementation of new activities or "product lines." Key principles include the following: (1) every process can be improved, (2) continuous improvement is essential, (3) errors are usually the result of flawed processes not people, (4) everyone in an organization must implement improvements, and (5) incremental changes can result in significant impact.	Global, multisector
Knowledge-to-Action Framework (KTA) Graham et al. (2006)	Focused on contextualizing health care research prior to implementing, to adapt protocols to better fit local context. Key steps include the following: (1) identify the problem; (2) adapt knowledge to local context; (3) assess barriers/enablers to implementation; (4) select, tailor, and implement interventions; (5) monitor; (6) evaluate; and (7) sustain.	Health care implementation
Lean Improvement Womak and Jones (2013)	A continuous improvement process focused on increased efficiency. Involves (1) defining customer/stakeholder value, (2) mapping the existing value stream, (3) identifying process efficiencies, (4) implementing, (5) evaluating, and (6) beginning again.	Commercial manufacturing and service sectors
Leaning to G.O.L.D. Hamilton and Hattie (2022)	Framework for education improvement in developing countries. Combines Lean processes to identify activities and programs to de-implement and then testing and scaling, with design thinking–oriented approaches for implementation: (1) Goal Hunting, (2) Opportunity Seeking, (3) Liftoff, (4) Double-Back, and (5) Double-Up.	Education systems in developing countries

IMPLEMENTATION MODEL	DESCRIPTION	DEPLOYMENT CONTEXTS
Learning to Improve (LTI) Bryk et al. (2017)	LTI offers a framework for (1) the identification of areas for improvement, (2) improvement hypothesis development, and (3) Agile-oriented improvement cycles.	Education sector, high-income contexts
Logical Framework Approach (LFA) World Bank (2000)	Used to support program design prior to implementation and for the monitoring and evaluation of live initiatives. Enables the development of theories of change and action by outlining the inputs, activities, and outcomes and how these are expected to translate into short-, medium-, and longer-term impact	International development projects in low-income countries
Perpetual Beta	Software development paradigm that involves the release of minimal viable product, reviewing user data and adding new features in light of user experience data. Aligns with Agile methodology.	Software development
Plan, Do, Study, Act (PDSA) Deming (1986)	An action-research protocol to undertake local iterative improvement activity by (1) Planning (i.e., agreeing on what to implement), (2) Doing (i.e., putting it into practice), (3) Studying (i.e., evaluating the Impact), and (4) Acting on the evidence to decide next steps.	Global, multisector
Positive Deviance LeMahieu et al. (2017) and Pascale et al. (2010)	A framework for grass-roots exploration and fact finding, to detect positive outliers or "deviants" that buck whatever issue stakeholders seek to resolve. The idea is to catalog positive outlier behaviors that can be replicated and scaled.	Community-led initiatives
Practical, Robust Implementation and Sustainability Model (PRISM) Feldstein and Glasgow (2008)	Extension of the RE-AIM model and inclusion of Six Sigma processes. Key areas of focus include (1) creating infrastructure to encourage spread, (2) sharing best practices, (3) observing impact and adjusting protocols, and (4) adapting protocols to fit new environments.	Health care sector
PRECEDE-PROCEED Freire and Runyan (2006)	Health care implementation framework with two key baskets of protocols: (1) PRECEDE, which centers on contextual diagnosis prior to implementation to ensure fit; and (2) PROCEED, which focuses on implementation and process, impact, and outcome evaluation.	Health care sector
PRINCE2 Axelos (2017)	A structured project management process with seven key themes: (1) Business Case, (2) Organization, (3) Quality Management, (4) Product-Based Planning, (5) Risk Management, (6) Change Control, and (7) Progress Tracking.	Range of commercial and public sector deployments globally

(Continued)

(Continued)

IMPLEMENTATION MODEL	DESCRIPTION	DEPLOYMENT CONTEXTS
Problem-Driven Iterative Adaptation (PDIA) Andrews et al. (2017) and Pritchett et al. (2013)	Design thinking–oriented approach that provides explicit protocols for (1) identification of "problems", (2) root cause analysis, (3) searching for "solutions" in design space, (4) implementing high-probability interventions, (5) evaluating, and (6) iterating.	International development projects in low-income countries
Project Management Body of Knowledge (PMBOK) Project Management Institute (2021)	Catalogs a range of generic project management process for: (1) initiating, (2) planning, (3) executing, (4) monitoring and controlling, and (5) closing.	Range of commercial and public sector deployments globally
Promoting Action on Research Implementation in Health Services (PARIHS) Harvey and Kitson (2016)	Posits that successful implementation (I) is a function of Evidence (E), Context (C), and Facilitation (F).	Health care
Putting Evidence to Work Sharples et al. (2019)	Developed specifically for the education sector, this outlines a four-stage process: (1) Explore, (2) Prepare, (3) Deliver, and (4) Sustain.	Education improvement, UK
Quality Enhancement Research Initiative (QUERI) Braganza and Kilbourne (2021)	Framework for the implementation of effective programs to support US military veterans. Stages include (1) Pre-implementation, agreeing on goal, stakeholders, and searching for best practices; (2) Implementation, including adaptation strategy; and (3) Sustainment.	Army veterans, US
Quality Implementation Framework (QIF) Meyers et al. (2012)	Proposes 14 key actions across four phases: (1) Initial Considerations Regarding the Host Setting, (2) Creating a Structure for Implementation, (3) Ongoing Structure Once Implementation Begins, and (4) Evaluation	Health care implementation
RE-AIM (Reach, Effectiveness, Adoption, Implementation, Maintenance) Glasgow et al. (2019)	Medical sector framework from translating statistical significance into real-world clinical significance. Key areas of focus: (1) Reach (i.e., how is the target population engaged and onboarded), (2) Effectiveness (i.e., confirming that the intervention will generate positive impact for target group), (3) Adoption (i.e., processes for implementing and adapting the protocols), (4) Implementation (i.e., ensuring fidelity within the permitted adaptation parameters), and (5) Maintenance (i.e., institutionalizing as part of routine practice).	Health care rollout of new innovations at scale

IMPLEMENTATION MODEL	DESCRIPTION	DEPLOYMENT CONTEXTS
Reduce Change to Increase Improvement Robinson (2018)	Four-phase approach to implementation: (1) Agree on the Problem to be Solved, (2) Inquire into Relevant Theories of Action, (3) Evaluate the Relative Merit of Current and Alternative Theories of Action, and (4) Implement and Monitor a New, Sufficiently Shared Theory of Action.	Education sector, high-income countries
Replicating Effective Programs (REP) Kilbourne et al. (2007)	An initiative by the US Centers for Disease Control and Prevention to codify and productize the essential features of a range of health care programs, so that new providers can adopt them out of the box/on a turn-key basis. Each protocol was field-tested in a range of contexts and then translated into everyday language to facilitate adoption in next settings.	Scaling productized health care programs
Scaling Up Education Reform Bishop et al. (2010)	Proposes the GPILSEO framework of: (1) Goals, (2) Pedagogies, (3) Institutions, (4) Leadership, (5) Spreading, (6) Evidence, and (7) Ownership.	Education improvement, New Zealand
Six Sigma Pyzdek and Keller (2009)	A methodology for process improvement. Key processes include the following: (1) Define goals, (2) Measure and identify critical quality characteristics, (3) Analyze to identify alternatives, (4) Design alternative, and (5) Verify the Design.	Range of commercial and public sector deployments globally
Spiral of Inquiry Timperley et al. (2014)	Provides educators with six processes to enhance student learning outcomes: (1) Scanning, (2) Focusing, (3) Developing a Hunch, (4) Learning, (5) Taking Action, and (6) Checking. Designed for short and local cycles of inquiry and implementation.	Education sector, high-income contexts
Strategic Consulting Chevallier (2016) and Rasiel (2001)	A set of tools used by management consultants on business/public service improvement initiatives. The kitset includes processes for (1) Problem Framing, (2) Root Cause Identification, (3) Determining Actual Causes, (4) Identifying Potential Solutions, (5) Selecting Solution, (6) Selling the Solution to Principal Stakeholders, (7) Implementing and Monitoring the Solution, and (8) Dealing with Complications.	Range of commercial and public sector deployments globally
Stetler Model Stetler (2001)	Designed for use by individuals, teams, or organizations to identify and implement appropriate evidence-based practices for the local context. The five phases are: (1) Preparation, with focus on purpose and context; (2) Validation, with focus on reviewing interventions and their evidence base; (3) Decision-making, with focus on deciding which intervention to progress; (4) Translation/Application, with focus on developing an implementation plan, including any required adaptations; and (5) Evaluation.	Nurse practitioners in health care settings

(Continued)

(Continued)

IMPLEMENTATION MODEL	DESCRIPTION	DEPLOYMENT CONTEXTS
Teaching Sprints Breakspear and Jones (2020)	Process for teaching teams to (1) Prepare (i.e., identify focus area and intervention), (2) Sprint (i.e., implement), and (3) Review (i.e., reflect on effectiveness and agree next steps).	Education improvement, Australia
Understanding-User-Context Framework Jacobson et al. (2003)	Framework for the translation/application of knowledge/programs to new contexts. Focus areas include (1) User-Group Considerations, (2) the Research, (3) Research-User Relationship, and (4) Dissemination Strategy.	Health care implementation
Waterfall Royce (1970)	Linear project management model that traverses: (1) Requirements, (2) Design, (3) Implementation, (4) Verification, and (5) Maintenance	Range of commercial and public sector deployments globally

Appendix 2

Key Areas of Divergence Across 50 Implementation Models

Across the 50 models, we have identified a range of differentiators (adapted and extended from Hamilton & Hattie, 2022):

- **Adding vs. Subtracting.** The former is about implementing a new/additional activity in order to enhance outcomes. The latter is about removing activities, either wholesale or by chiseling away at program features to enhance efficiency or to free up time. Most of the 50 frameworks have a tendency toward adding, aside from Lean and Six Sigma.

- **Innovation Scaling vs. Local Needs Driven.** The former operates from the perspective of a product innovator and provides tools and processes to get innovations widely adopted. The latter is explicitly lensed from the perspective of the adopting institution and usually includes processes that support them in the identification of suitable programs. *Diffusion of Innovations* is an example of the former and *Communities That Care* the latter.

- **Top Down vs. Bottom Up.** Top-down frameworks support regional or national-level organizations to replicate a single program or policy with fidelity across multiple contexts. Bottom-up frameworks are more for use in local settings to identify and respond to local needs. *Deliverology* is an example of the former and was designed to establish national delivery units that drive change. Most of the other methodologies are compatible with either stance.

- **Individual vs. Group.** The former provides protocols for use by individual practitioners to identify personal enhancements. The latter is intended for use either by teams or whole organizations. The *Stetler Model* was designed for use directly by individual nurse practitioners and collectively by a group of practitioners. Most of the other models implicitly or explicitly orient toward group usage.

- **Linear vs. Adaptive Implementation.** Linear models move sequentially from one stage to the next and do not circle back or undo previously made decisions. They also tend to spend more time analyzing and deciding before moving to the next stage. Adaptive models move backward as well as forward. They implement, evaluate, and iterate. *Waterfall* is an example of a linear model and *Problem-Driven Iterative Adaptation* is an example of the latter.

- **Implicit vs. Explicit Design.** The latter provides tools and protocols for searching the design space to either identify and localize or build programs. The former treats design as a Black Box and provides no specific support for this element. *PRINCE2* is an example of implicit design and *Design Thinking* is an example of explicit design.

- **Slow vs. Fast.** Slow methodologies emphasize careful and considered design prior to implementation and are more likely to be utilized where the change, once implemented, is difficult to reverse. Fast approaches "plant a thousand seeds," spending little time on each and evaluating which should be watered further. Most of the methodologies are compatible with either stance; however, *Agile* is explicitly fast and *Waterfall* explicitly slow.

- **Rigid vs. Adaptive.** The former is about the rollout of a productized intervention with fidelity, whereas the latter provides tools and processes to explicitly map how the program/activities can be localized to fit the new context. *Replicating Effective Programs* is more oriented toward the former, although there are still elements of permitted adaptation. Most of the other methodologies are implicitly adaptive and some, including *RE-AIM* and the *Dynamic Adaption Process*, are explicitly adaptive and focus heavily on contextual fit.

- **Blank Sheet vs. Off the Shelf.** The former focuses on designing new interventions from scratch, whereas the latter assumes that the selected intervention will almost always be prebuilt. *Design Thinking* is an example of the former and the *Hexagon Tool* of the latter.

- **Wide Lens vs. Narrow Lens.** The latter focuses on one aspect of the implementation process, whereas the former seeks to provide an end-to-end process. Examples of a narrow lens include *CostOut* and *Balanced Scorecard*, which focus on financial modeling and quality assurance, respectively. Most of the other methodologies cover multiple stages of implementation from initial discovery to design, delivery, double-back, and double-up.

- **Governance vs. Beliefs Focused.** The former places more emphasis on governance and organization processes, accountability, and formalized communication and monitoring systems. The latter focuses more on "softer" aspects related to local beliefs and culture and the degree to which these are compatible with the proposed activities. Note that these are not mutually exclusive categories; however, *Deliverology* and PRINCE2 are more oriented toward the former and *Reduce Change to Increase Improvement* is most oriented toward the latter.

- **Problem Driven vs. Strengths Based.** The latter is more focused on appreciating and celebrating the existing progress and capabilities within the organization and leveraging these. The assumption is that banishing deficit theorizing and blame from the discourse results in more positive and generative dialogue and thinking. The former is explicitly focused on the search for and remediation of problems. The assumption is that only problems are worth the time investment and that strengths-based inquiry generates the danger of embarking on "happy projects" that do not address real needs. *Appreciative Inquiry* is an example of a strengths-based framing and *Problem-Driven Iterative Adaptation* is an example of a methodology that explicitly seeks problems.

- **Implementing vs. Sustaining.** The latter places a strong emphasis on how to maintain and grow what has been implemented; whereas the former does not explicitly address these longer-term questions and dimensions. *PRISM* and the *Dynamic Sustainability Framework* are examples of methodologies with explicit sustainability dimensions/processes.

Appendix 3

Key Areas of Similarity Across 50 Implementation Methodologies

Across the 50 methodologies we have identified 5 (relatively common) phases and 23 (relatively common) processes.

PHASE 1: PROBLEM/NEED/GOAL IDENTIFICATION (A.K.A. DISCOVERY)

1. Conduct a problem/needs/goals diagnostic assessment.
2. Build a theory of the cause of the problem/need (i.e., map the causal drivers and/or map existing strengths).
3. Agree on what success looks like (i.e., the success map or results framework).
4. Commence an evaluation plan related to this success.
5. Gain authorization and resources to proceed to Phase 2.

PHASE 2: SOLUTION/ACTIVITY DESIGN (A.K.A. DESIGN)

6. Scan for inductive solutions/opportunities (i.e., identify prebuilt programs that could be deployed).
7. Develop deductive solutions/opportunities (i.e., use a program logic framework to build multiple intervention/activity models from scratch).
8. Rank solutions, for example, by capability to implement, cost-benefit, ease of implementation, whether solutions/opportunities engage vs. bypass stakeholder beliefs, possibility for adaptation, or early vs. late adopter potential.

9. Stress-test preferred designs by mapping the various possible design features and setting levels and different dosage and fidelity levels.

10. Agree on preferred solutions/opportunities, including design features and setting levels.

11. Identify potential enablers and barriers to implementation, and the risk mitigations to these.

12. Build implementation capacity (e.g., recruit and train a central backbone team).

13. Develop a full monitoring and evaluation plan, including developing ways to assess fidelity of implementation and being particularly focused on local adaptations and their effects.

14. Gain authorization and resources to proceed to Phase 3.

PHASE 3: IMPLEMENTATION (A.K.A. DELIVERY)

15. Create implementation plans.
    a. Agree implementation approach e.g., rigid vs. flexible vs. fluid
    b. Develop project/program plan
    c. Develop product/output descriptors and acceptance criteria.

16. Create implementation teams, ensuring a mixture of research, evaluation, project management, and local context expertise.

17. Undertake implementation using program management processes.

18. Monitor implementation (i.e., milestones, products, budget, timelines, outputs, outcomes) and collect evaluative data.

PHASE 4: EVALUATION (A.K.A. DOUBLE-BACK)

19. Check that evaluative impact data has been collected during implementation, in line with the monitoring and evaluation plan.

20. Identify and agree on areas to iterate, including crawl and learn (or agreement to stop) and dosage, fidelity, adaptation, and quality (using Phase 2 processes).

21. Go back to Phase 3 and/or forward to Phase 5.

PHASE 5: REITERATING, SCALING, AND SUSTAINING (A.K.A. DOUBLE-UP)

22. Develop a plan to reiterate, scale, and/or sustain using data from steps 18–20 and tools and processes from steps 6–13.

23. Go back to Phase 3.

Source: Adapted from Hamilton and Hattie (2022).

Appendix 4

Findings From Selected Meta-Analyses and Systematic Reviews of Implementation

RESEARCHERS	RESEARCH TYPE	DESCRIPTION AND KEY FINDINGS
Daniels et al. (2021)	Systematic review	• Reviewed 74 studies on implementation of workplace health and well-being programs. Identified the following key implementation variables: plan continuation, learning/evaluation, and effective governance.
DuBois et al. (2002)	Meta-analysis	• Reviewed 55 mentoring studies, finding that **the single step of monitoring the level of implementation resulted in significantly higher impact effect sizes (0.18 vs. 0.06)**.
Meyers et al. (2012)	Systematic review	• Reviewed 25 implementation frameworks to identify 14 common variables, including needs/fit assessment, adaptation assessment, establishing an implementation organization, buy-in and communication strategies, developing implementation plans, process evaluation, and learning from experience.
Micheli et al. (2018)	Systematic review	• Reviewed 104 studies on key features for successful use of design thinking–based approaches. These include abductive reasoning, design-oriented tools, interdisciplinary collaboration, and welcoming ambiguity in the design process.
Moullin et al. (2015)	Systematic review	• Reviewed 49 articles on health care implementation methodologies. Suggests that the frameworks that are suitable for researchers to market and scale their innovations are different from those suitable for organizations to select and implement programs that support their needs.
Moullin et al. (2020)	Conceptual article	• Proposed 10 factors for effective implementation, including issue/goal definition, logic modeling, evaluation methodology selection, detailed implementation planning, localization of interventions to context, and iteration based on feedback.

(Continued)

(Continued)

RESEARCHERS	RESEARCH TYPE	DESCRIPTION AND KEY FINDINGS
Nilsen and Bernhardsson (2019)	Systematic review	• Reviewed 67 studies of 17 health care implementation frameworks from the perspective of contextual fit. The most frequently postulated important contextual variables were organizational support, financial resources, social relations and support, leadership, and organizational culture and climate.
Rojas-Andrade and Bahamondes (2019)	Systematic review	• Reviewed 31 studies on the fidelity of implementation in school-based mental health programs. Identified the following key variables: adherence, quality of the intervention, exposure to the intervention, and receptiveness.
Smith et al. (2004)	Synthesis	• Reviewed 14 whole-school antibullying programs. While finding that none were highly effective, they identified that **the settings that rigorously monitored implementation generate 2 times the effect size**.
Tobler (1986)	Meta-analysis	• Reviewed 143 adolescent drug-prevention interventions, finding that **well-implemented programs generated an effect size 0.36 MORE than less well-implemented programs**.
Weeks (2021)	Systematic review	• Reviewed 24 studies related to child welfare intervention implementations. Identified the following key implementation variables: funding, collaboration with external stakeholders, staff capacity and capability to implement, leadership support, stakeholder buy-in vs. resistance, clarity of the intervention (e.g., purpose and mechanisms), and establishment of implementation teams.
Wilson et al. (2003)	Meta-analysis	• Reviewed 221 programs, involving 56,000 participants, focused on reducing aggressive behaviors in schools, concluding that **implementation processes were the most important variable that influenced outcomes**.

Glossary

5D: a shorthand term used for the overarching *Building to Impact 5D* methodology. 5D refers to the fact that each of the five stages in the approach are *D* words: Discover, Design, Deliver, Double-Back, and Double-Up.

Abductive reasoning (abduction): drawing a provisional conclusion from what you currently know (e.g., Arran did not arrive on time today, maybe there was unusually bad traffic, or he forgot to set his alarm clock).

Backbone organization: a temporary organization structure established at the system, district, or whole-school level to bring about deep and sustained impact via the 5D methodology.

Black-Box evaluation: an approach to impact evaluation that involves collecting pre- and postintervention data to determine whether there has been improvement but without "lifting the lid" on the school/classroom to understand *why* the intervention was or wasn't effective (i.e., a Black Box).

Breakdown structure: a method for defining the key characteristics of an education challenge with a high level of granularity (i.e., by *breaking down* the key elements into their constituent parts or subcomponents).

Clear-Box evaluation: an approach to impact evaluation that collects *rich* qualitative and quantitative data to understand why the selected intervention was or wasn't effective and how it could be further improved/iterated to enhance impact.

D1: Discover: the stage of 5D that focuses on identifying an appropriate education challenge to progress, building a theory of the present, and setting provisional improvement goals (i.e., deciding what you want to improve the most and by how much).

D2: Design: the stage of 5D that focuses on identifying, agreeing, sequencing, and stress testing activities and interventions ready for implementation. This stage also involves establishing a monitoring and evaluation plan.

D3: Deliver: the stage of 5D that focuses on implementing the agreed designs and the collecting of monitoring and evaluation data.

D4: Double-Back: the stage of 5D that focuses on reviewing the collected monitoring and evaluation data to decide what to do next. This can include continuing, iterating, or stopping.

D5: Double-Up: the stage of 5D that focuses on sustaining and scaling your impact.

Deductive reasoning (deduction): drawing a conclusion based on widely accepted and available facts and information (e.g., to be at class by 9 a.m., I will have to leave the house by 8:15 because the travel time takes 45 minutes).

Design features and setting levels: a twin-axis mapping tool that enables you to identify all the ways that a proposed activity/intervention could be varied during implementation. The *design features* axis refers to the things that could be varied, including dosage, duration, target group, and fidelity. The *setting levels* dimension describes each of the possible variation *increments* (e.g., for time, those increments could be from minutes to hours to weeks to years, etc.).

Education challenge: the key goal or problem area that you have decided to prioritize and progress above all else. Other commonly used terms for this include key priority, compelling cause, just cause, core mission, crusade, burning platform, wicked issue, and so on (i.e., the thing that keeps you up at night).

Evaluation: checking whether your actions have generated sufficient impact and then deciding what to do next (e.g., plan continuation, plan iteration, or stopping). We distinguish between Black-Box, Clear-Box, and Gray-Box evaluations, also described in this glossary.

Gantt chart: a graphical tool invented by Henry Gantt, which enables you to show tasks and activities, including the time duration and linkages or dependencies between the tasks.

Gray-Box evaluation: an approach to impact evaluation that collects *some* qualitative and quantitative data to understand why the intervention was or wasn't effective and how it could be further improved. However, these data might not be strong enough to generate robust conclusions.

Highlight report: a dashboard-style report used to update key stakeholders on project progress and current risks and issues.

Implementation: in the context of 5D, implementation is much bigger than "just" implementation! It refers to the end-to-end process of *discovering* an appropriate education challenge, *designing* high-probability interventions, *delivering* to the design (i.e., what is commonly thought of as implementation), *doubling-back* to evaluate and iterate, and *doubling-up* to sustain, scale, or stop.

Inductive reasoning (induction): drawing a conclusion by observing a phenomenon or by seeing a pattern in some data (e.g., Arran has previously always arrived at class on time, so we can assume that he will also do so today).

Influence bubble: this refers to a variable/ node on a path analysis diagram that is hypothesized to be a causal driver of your identified education challenge.

Kanban board: a project management tool used to visualize (1) work in progress, (2) work completed, and (3) work still to do. Often these three are drawn on a whiteboard as columns and project tasks are written on sticky notes that are transferred across the columns as they are completed.

Lagging indicator: an observable change that takes time to happen and that can only be measured after a significant delay. For example, if we deliver teacher professional development, it will likely take several months (or more) before we see any noticeable improvements in student learning outcomes (i.e., there is a lag).

Leading indicator: a measure that can be used to predict future change in another area before it occurs. For example, if we have lesson observation data showing that teachers are implementing a new practice with fidelity, we might then predict that student learning outcomes will also go up in the future.

Matthew effect: a social phenomenon linked to the ideas that "the rich get richer and the poor get poorer," which is named after a Bible verse in the Gospel of Matthew.

Monitoring: the act of checking that you have done the things you originally set out to in terms of time, budget, and outputs.

Opportunity sketches: this refers to high-level lists of initiatives, activities, and/or programs you *could* implement (e.g., an intelligent tutoring system, a Response to Intervention program, a blended phonics program, etc.) but without getting into the detail of how you could/would bring this to life in your local context (i.e., it's just a *sketch* and not a detailed plan!)

Optimal stopping considerations: this is about deciding how long you should spend searching, analyzing, and exploring options, opportunities, and risks before just getting on and implementing *something*. The key tension is in balancing the *time-cost* of analyzing all your potential options in detail vs. the *impact-cost* of choosing the wrong thing and being stuck with the consequences.

Path analysis: a tool developed by Sewall Wright to hypothesize the relationship between different variables. In *Building to Impact 5D*, we use it to develop and test theories of the present (i.e., root cause analysis).

Positive outliers: stakeholders (e.g., schools, educators, students) who already achieve above-average outcomes in the agreed education challenge area. Mapping, codifying, and replicating what these stakeholders do differently is one of the strong pathways to impact.

Professional learning community: a type of within-school improvement model, often employing a communities-of-practice approach that facilities inquiry within a grade-level/year group or subject department. This involves the convening of meetings to agree on priority focus areas, the undertaking of improvement-oriented inquiry, and the evaluation of impact.

Program logic model: a graphic roadmap that shows the path from the present to an improved future (i.e., from means to ends). This contains baseline data about the present and activities/initiatives that will be implemented, including details of the required resources, actions, assumptions, and outcomes. It also maps the intended short-, medium-, and long-term outcomes and how these will be measured (i.e., the impact).

Project Management Body of Knowledge (PMBOK): this is a codified and widely agreed-on set of project management tools and processes that help to ensure successful implementation.

Project plan: a concrete roadmap for how you are going to execute your program logic model (i.e., your anticipated journey from getting from A to B to C to impact).

Ringelmann effect: the tendency for groups to become less productive the bigger they get.

Rube Goldberg machine: a type of cartoon drawing named after the American cartoonist Rube Goldberg. Usually, these cartoon machines consist of a series of unrelated but connected devices that generate a chain reaction, eventually culminating in an intended goal (i.e., A pushes B onto C, resulting in D). We suggest Rube Goldberg cartoons as an alternative way of presenting (and thinking through) a program logic model.

School district–level improvement: here, we refer to use of the 5D methodology by a backbone organization that has responsibility for the management and improvement of multiple schools, usually within the same local geography. In the United States, Canada, and parts of Australia, this type of support is often undertaken by a school district. In England, it is often provided by a multiacademy trust (MAT); in Scotland, by the local authority; and in New Zealand, by a community of learning (Kāhui Ako).

School system–level improvement: here, we refer to use of the 5D methodology by a backbone organization that operates at regional, state, or even national level. System-level stakeholders are normally responsible for hundreds to tens of thousands of schools and often work in organizations called the department of education, ministry of education, or education services area/district.

Schoolwide improvement: here, we refer to the use of the 5D methodology by a backbone organization that operates at whole-school level. This would involve progressing initiatives to improve outcomes for all students across the whole school and would involve steering and support from the school leadership team.

Stress testing: the process of identifying and mitigating everything that *could* go wrong in the implementation of your selected program logic model and the development of aligned mitigation plans.

Systematic review: a type of study that uses a systematized and reproducible methodology to identify and analyze all the relevant studies on a particular research question (i.e., a systematic study of studies). A meta-analysis is a type of systematic review that synthesizes studies that have quantitative data that can be converted into an effect size.

Theoretical best practice: activities, interventions, and/or programs that have extremely positive findings in systematic reviews. They are *theoretical* best practice because they highlight things that have been highly effective in other places; and, therefore, they should *theoretically* be good bets for impact in your context!

Theory of action: a detailed description of how your theory of improvement will build from the present to improve the future (i.e., a microlevel description of how you plan in bringing your theory of improvement to life. First, we will do A, then B, then C, etc.).

Theory of improvement: your high-level theory of what you will do to improve outcomes in the area of your education challenge. It explains the high-level mechanisms through which an opportunity sketch generates impact (i.e., a meso description). A strong theory of improvement builds on a strong theory of the present.

Theory of the present: your validated explanation about why your education challenge exists (i.e., what drives it, what is the root cause, and what is the path analysis?).

Within-school improvement: here, we refer to the use of the 5D methodology by a professional learning community, for example, that progresses improvement initiatives across a team of teachers working within the same grade/year level or within the same subject teaching team.

References

Aarons, G. A., Green, A. E., Palinkas, L. A., Self-Brown, S., Whitaker, D. J., Lutzker, J. R., Silovsky, J. F., Hecht, D. B., & Chaffin, M. J. (2012). Dynamic adaptation process to implement an evidence-based child maltreatment intervention. *Implementation Science, 7*, 32. https://doi.org/10.1186/1748-5908-7-32

Adams, G. S., Converse, B. A., Hales, A. H., & Klotz, H. (2021). People systematically overlook subtractive changes, *Nature, 592*, 258–261. https://doi.org/10.1038/s41586-021-03380-y

Adelman, H. S., & Taylor, L. (1997). Addressing barriers to learning: Beyond school-linked services and full-service schools. *The American Journal of Orthopsychiatry, 67*(3), 408–421. https://doi.org/10.1037/h0080243

Altinok, N., Angrist, N., & Patrinos, H. A. (2018). *Global data set on education quality (1965–2015)* (Policy Research Working Paper No. 8314). World Bank Group.

Andrews, M., Pritchett, L., & Woolcock, M. (2017). *Building state capability evidence, analysis, action.* Oxford University Press.

Arkes, H. R., & Blumer, C. (1985). The psychology of sunk cost. *Organizational Behavior and Human Decision Process, 35*(1), 124–140. https://doi.org/10.1016/0749-5978(85)90049-4

Ashmore, A. S., & Runyan, K. (2014). *Introduction to Agile methods* (1st ed.). Addison-Wesley Professional.

Aubusson, P., Aubusson, P., Harrison, A. G., & Ritchie, S. M. (2006). *Metaphor and analogy in science education.* Springer Publishing.

Axelos. (2017). *Managing successful projects with PRINCE2* (6th ed). The Stationary Office.

Baierlein, R. (1999). *Thermal physics.* Cambridge University Press.

Barber, M., Moffit, A., & Kihn, P. (2011). *Deliverology 101: A field guide for educational leaders.* Corwin.

Barfield, T. (1989). *Perilous frontier: Nomadic empires and China.* Blackwell.

Bauer, M. S., Damschroder, L., Hagedorn, H., Smith, J., & Kilbourne, A. M. (2015). An introduction to implementation science for the non-specialist. *BMC Psychology, 3*(1), 32. https://doi.org/10.1186/s40359-015-0089-9

Bernstein, B. (1970, February 26). Education cannot compensate for society. *New Society, 15*(387), 344–347.

Berra, Y. (1998). *The Yogi book: I really didn't say everything I said.* Working Man.

Bishop, R., O'Sullivan, D., & Berryman, M. (2010). *Scaling up education reform: Addressing the politics of disparity.* NZCER Press.

Bjork, R.A. (1994). Institutional impediments to effective training. In R. A. Bjork & D. Druckman (Eds.), *Learning, remembering, believing: Enhancing human performance.* National Academies Press.

Blase, K., Kiser, L., & Van Dyke, M. (2013). *The hexagon tool: Exploring context.* National Implementation Research Network, Frank Porter Graham Child Development Institute, University of North Carolina at Chapel Hill.

Boynton, A. (2016). *Nine things that separate the leaders from the managers.* https://www.forbes.com/sites/andyboynton/2016/03/31/want-to-be-a-leader-not-just-a-manager-do-these-nine-things/?sh=506a23ec51e0

Braganza, M. Z., & Kilbourne, A. M. (2021). The quality enhancement research initiative (QUERI) impact framework: Measuring the real-world impact of implementation science. *Journal of General Internal Medicine, 36*(2), 396–403, https://doi.org/10.1007/s11606-020-06143-z

Breakspear, S., & Jones, B. R. (2020). *Teaching sprints: How overloaded educators can keep getting better.* Corwin.

Brinkley, D. (2019). *American Moonshot: John F. Kennedy and the great space race.* Harper.

Brookover, W. B., & Lezotte, L. W. (1977). *Changes in school characteristics coincident with changes in student achievement.* Michigan State University College of Urban Development.

Brown, C. G. (2014). The Iowa model of evidence-based practice to promote quality care: An illustrated example in oncology nursing. *Clinical Journal of Oncology Nursing, 18*(2), 157–159. https://doi.org/10.1188/14.CJON.157-159

Bryk, A. S., Gomez, L. M., Grunow, A., & LeMahieu, P. G. (2017). *Learning to improve: How Americas schools can get better at getting better.* Harvard Education Press.

Carpenter, M. J., Jardin, B. F., Burris, J. L., Mathew, A. R., Schnoll, R. A., Rigotti, N. A., & Cummings, K. M. (2013). Clinical strategies to enhance the efficacy of nicotine replacement therapy for smoking cessation: A review of the literature. *Drugs, 73*(5), 407–426.

Cauthen, L. (n.d.). Just how big is the K–12 Ed tech market? *EdNewsDaily.* https://www.ednewsdaily.com/just-how-large-is-the-k12-ed-tech-market/

Chambers, D. A., Glasgow, R. E., & Stange, K. C. (2013). The dynamic sustainability framework: Addressing the paradox of sustainment amid ongoing change. *Implementation Science, 8,* 117, https://doi.org/10.1186/1748-5908-8-117

Chevallier, A. (2016). *Strategic thinking in complex problem solving.* Oxford University Press.

Chitty, C. (1997). The school effectiveness movement: Origins, shortcomings and future possibilities. *The Curriculum Journal, 8*(1), 45–62. https://doi.org/10.1080/09585176.1997.11070761

Christian, B., & Griffiths, T. (2017). *Algorithms to live by: The computer science of human decisions* (Reprint ed.). Picador.

Clarke, J. & Dede, C. (2009). Design for scalability: A case study of the river city curriculum. *Journal of Science Education and Technology, 18*(4), 353–365.

Cohen-Vogel, L., Tichnor-Wagner, A., Allen, D., Harrison, C., Kainz, K., Socol, A. R., & Wang, Q. (2015). Implementing educational innovations at scale: Transforming researchers into continuous improvement scientists. *Educational Policy, 29*(1), 257–277. https://doi.org/10.1177/0895904814560886

Coleman, J. S. (1966). *Equality of educational opportunity.* US Department of Education.

Cooperrider, D. L., Whitney, D., & Sobczak, D. (2014). *Appreciative inquiry: A positive revolution in change.* Berrett-Koehler Publishers.

Cuban, L. (1984). *How teachers taught: Constancy and change in American classrooms, 1890-1980.* Longman.

Cuban, L. (1990). Reforming again, again, and again. *Educational Researcher, 19*(1), 3–13. https://doi.org/10.3102/0013189X019001003

Currie, J., & Aizer, A. (2016). Program report: Children. *National Bureau of Economic Research.* https://www.nber.org/reporter/2016number4/program-report-children

Damschroder, L. J., Aron, D. C., Keith, R. E., Kirsh, S. R., Alexander, J. A., & Lowery, J. C. (2009). Fostering implementation of health services research findings into practice: A consolidated framework for advancing implementation science. *Implementation Science, 4,* 50. https://doi.org/10.1186/1748-5908-4-50

Daniels, K., Fida, R., Stepanek, M., & Gendronneau, C. (2021). Do multicomponent workplace health and wellbeing programs predict changes in health and wellbeing? *International Journal of Environmental Research and Public Health, 18,* 8964. https://doi.org/10.3390/ijerph18178964

Dawkins, R. (1976). *The selfish gene.* Oxford University Press.

Deming, E. D. (1986). *Out of the crisis.* Massachusetts Institute of Technology Center for Advanced Engineering Study.

Derzon, J. H., Sale, E., Springer, J. F., & Brounstein, P. (2005). Estimating intervention effectiveness: Synthetic projection of field evaluation results. *Journal of Prevention, 26*, 321–343. https://doi.org/10.1007/s10935-005-5391-5

Design Council. (2021). Eleven lessons. A study of the design processes. *Design Council.* https://www.designcouncil.org.uk/sites/default/files/asset/document/ElevenLessons_Design_Council%20(2).pdf

DuBois, D. L., Holloway, B. E., Valentine, J. C., & Cooper, H. (2002). Effectiveness of mentoring programs for youth: A meta-analytic review. *American Journal of Community Psychology, 30*, 157–197. https://doi.org/10.1023/A:1014628810714

DuFour, R., & Reeves, D. (2016). The futility of PLC lite. *Phi Delta Kappan, 97*(6), 69–71.

Dunst, C. J., & Trivette, C. M. (2012). Capacity-building family-systems intervention practices. In G. H. S. Singer, D. E. Biegel, & P. Conway (Eds.), *Family support and family caregiving across disabilities* (pp. 33–57). Routledge.

Durlak, J. A., & DuPre, E. P. (2008). Implementation matters: A review of research on the influence of implementation on program outcomes and the factors affecting implementation. *American Journal of Community Psychology, 41*(3–4), 27–50.

Edmonds, R. (1979). Effective schools for the urban poor. *Educational Leadership, 37*(1), 18–24.

Elmore, R. (1996). Getting to scale with good educational practice. *Harvard Educational Review, 66*(1), 1–27. https://doi.org/10.17763/haer.66.1.g73266758j348t33

Ericsson, K. A., Krampe, R. T., & Tesch-Römer, C. (1993). The role of deliberate practice in the acquisition of expert performance. *Psychological Review, 100*(3), 363–406. https://doi.org/10.1037/0033-295X.100.3.363

Ericsson, K. A., & Harwell, K. W. (2019). Deliberate practice and proposed limits on the effects of practice on the acquisition of expert performance: Why the original definition matters and recommendations for future research. *Frontiers in Psychology, 10*, 2396. https://doi.org/10.3389/fpsyg.2019.02396

Feldstein, A. C., & Glasgow, R. E. (2008). A practical, robust implementation and sustainability model (PRISM) for integrating research findings into practice. *The Joint Commission Journal on Quality and Patient Safety, 34*(4), 228–243. https://doi.org/10.1016/s1553-7250(08)34030-6

Feynman, R. (1974). Cargo cult science. Some remarks on science, pseudoscience, and learning how to not fool yourself. *Caltech's 1974 Commencement Address.* https://calteches.library.caltech.edu/51/2/CargoCult.htm

FINA. (2019). *FINA high diving rules: 2017-21.* Retrieved January 11, 2021, from https://resources.fina.org/fina/document/2021/01/19/a0abae86-9074-41e3-9cb0-4c001c355513/2017-2021_high_diving_13082019_0.pdf

Fishman, B., Penuel, W. R., Allen, A., & Cheng, B. H. (Eds.). (2013). *Design-based implementation research: Theories, methods, and exemplars.* National Society for the Study of Education Yearbook (Vol. 112, Issue 2, pp. 136–156). Teachers College Record.

Fixsen, D. L., Naoom, S. F., Blase, K. A., Friedman, R. M., & Wallace, F. (2005). *Implementation research: A synthesis of the literature.* University of South Florida.

Forsyth, D. R. (2014). *Group dynamics* (6th ed.). Wadsworth Cengage Learning.

Freire, K., & Runyan, C. W. (2006). Planning models: PRECEDE–PROCEED and Haddon Matrix. In A. C. Gielen, D. A. Sleet, and R. J. DiClemente (Eds.), *Injury and violence prevention: Behavioral science theories, methods, and applications* (1st ed., pp. 127–158). Jossey-Bass.

Fullan, M. (2000). The return of large-scale reform. *Journal of Educational Change, 1*, 5–28.

Galai, D., & Sade, O. (2006). The "Ostrich Effect" and the relationship between the liquidity and the yields of financial assets. *Journal of Business, 79*(5), 2741–2759. https://doi.org/10.1086/505250

Gawande, A. (2010). *The checklist manifesto: How to get things right* (1st ed.). Picador.

Gibson, R., & Zillman, D. (1994). Exaggerated versus representative exemplification in news reports: Perception of issues and personal consequences. *Communication Research, 21*(5), 603–624.

Glasgow, R. E., Harden S. M., Gaglio, B., Rabin, B., Smith M. L., Porter, G. C., Ory, M. G., & Estabrooks, P. A. (2019). RE-AIM planning and evaluation framework: Adapting to new science and practice with a 20-year review. *Frontiers in Public Health, 7,* 1–9. https://doi.org/0.3389/fpubh.2019.00064

Graban, M., & Swartz, J. E. (2012). *Healthcare Kaizen engaging front-line staff in sustainable continuous improvements.* Productivity Press.

Graham, I. D., Logan, J., Harrison, M. B., Straus, S. E., Tetroe, J., Caswell, W., & Robinson, N. (2006). Lost in knowledge translation: Time for a map? *Journal of Continuing Education in the Health Professions, 26*(1), 13–24.

Grant, J., Green, L., & Mason, B. (2003). Basic research and health: A reassessment of the scientific basis for the support of biomedical science. *Research Evaluation, 12,* 217–224.

Greenhalgh, T., Robert, G., Macfarlane, F., Bate, P., & Kyriakidou, O. (2004). Diffusion of innovations in service organizations: Systematic review and recommendations. *The Milbank Quarterly, 82*(4), 581–629. https://doi.org/10.1111/j.0887-378X.2004.00325.x

Guskey, R. T. (2020). Flip the script on change: Experience shapes teachers' attitudes and beliefs. *The Learning Professional, 41*(2), 18–22. https://learningforward.org/wp-content/uploads/2020/04/flip-the-script-on-change.pdf

Guskey, T. R. (2000). *Evaluating professional development.* Corwin.

Haddadin, Y., Annamaraju, P., & Regunath, H. (2021). *Central line associated blood stream infections.* StatPearls Publishing.

Hagger, M. S., Wood, C., Stiff, C., & Chatzisarantis, N. L. (2010). Ego depletion and the strength model of self-control: A meta-analysis. *Psychological Bulletin Journal, 136*(4), 495–525.

Hall, G. E. (1979). The concerns-based approach to facilitating change. *Educational Horizons, 57*(4), 202–208.

Hall, G. E., & Loucks, S. F. (1977). A developmental model for determining whether the treatment is actually implemented. *American Educational Research Journal, 14*(3), 263–276. https://doi.org/10.2307/1162291

Hall, G., & Hord, S. (2011). *Implementing change: Patterns, principles, and potholes* (3rd ed.). Allyn and Bacon.

Hamilton, A., & Hattie, J. (2021). *Getting to G.O.L.D.: The Visible Learning approach to education improvement.* Corwin.

Hamilton, A. & Hattie, J. (2022). *The lean education manifesto: A synthesis of 900+ systematic reviews for Visible Learning in developing countries.* Routledge.

Harris, S. (2010). *The moral landscape: How science can determine human values.* Free Press.

Harvey, G., & Kitson, A. (2016). PARIHS revisited: From heuristic to integrated framework for the successful implementation of knowledge into practice. *Implementation Science, 11, 33.* https://doi.org/10.1186/s13012-016-0398-2

Hattie, J. (2012). *Visible learning for teachers: Maximizing impact on learning.* Routledge.

Hattie, J. & Hamilton, A. (2020a). *As good as gold? Why we focus on the wrong drivers in education.* Corwin.

Hattie, J., & Hamilton, A. (2020b). *Real gold vs. fool's gold: The Visible Learning methodology for finding what works best in education.* Corwin.

Hattie, J., & Larsen, S. N. (2020). *The purposes of education: A conversation between John Hattie and Steen Nepper Larsen.* Routledge.

Hattie, J., Bustamante, V., Almarode, J. T., Fisher, D., & Frey, N. (2020). *Great teaching by design: From intention to implementation in the visible learning classroom* (1st ed.). Corwin.

Hawkins, J. (2021). *A thousand brains: A new theory of intelligence* (1st ed.). Basic Books.

Hawkins, J. D., & Weis, J. G. (1985). The social development model: An integrated approach to delinquency prevention. *Journal of Prevention*, 6, 73–97. https://doi.org/10.1007/BF01325432

Heath, C. (1995). Escalation and de-escalation of commitment in response to sunk costs: The role of budgeting in mental accounting. *Organizational Behavior and Human Decision Processes*, 62, 38–38.

Heffernan, N. (2019). Backtalk: Don't eliminate homework. Make it more effective. *Phi Delta Kappan*, 100(6), 80–80. https://doi.org/10.1177/0031721719834038

Herold, D. M., & Fedor, D. B. (2008). *Leading change management: Leadership strategies that really work.* Kogan Page.

Hofmann, W., Gschwendner, T., Friese, M., Wiers, R. W., & Schmitt, M. (2008). Working memory capacity and self-regulatory behavior: Toward an individual differences perspective on behavior determination by automatic versus controlled processes. *Journal of Personality and Social Psychology*, 95(4), 962–977. https://doi.org/10.1037/a0012705.

Holyoak, K. J. (2012). Analogy and relational reasoning. In K. J. Holyoak & R. G. Morrison (Eds.), *The Oxford handbook of thinking and reasoning* (pp. 234–259). Oxford University Press.

Hughes, J. R., Keely, J., & Naud, S. (2004). Shape of the relapse curve and long-term abstinence among untreated smokers. *Addiction*, 99(1), 29–38. http://doi.org/10.1111/j.1360-0443.2004.00540.x

Husén, T. (Ed.) (1967a). *International study of achievement in mathematics: A comparison of twelve countries* (Vol. 1). John Wiley & Sons.

Husén, T. (Ed.) (1967b). *International study of achievement in mathematics: A comparison of twelve countries* (Vol. 2). John Wiley & Sons.

IDEO. (2015). *The field guide to human centred design.* IDEO.

Ishikawa, K. (1968). *Guide to quality control.* Union of Japanese Scientists and Engineers.

Jacobson, N., Butterill, D., & Goering, P. (2003). Development of a framework for knowledge translation: Understanding user context. *Journal of Health Services Research & Policy*, 8(2), 94–99. http://doi.org/10.1258/135581903321466067

Jencks, C., Smith, M., Acland, H., Bane, M. J., Cohen, D., Gintis, H., . . . Michelson, S. (1972). *Inequality: A reassessment of the effect of family and schooling in America.* Basic Books.

Joyce, B. R., & Showers, B. (2002). *Student achievement through staff development* (3rd ed.). ASCD.

Kahneman, D. (2013). *Thinking, fast and slow.* Farrar, Straus and Giroux.

Kania, J., & Kramer, J. (2011). Collective impact. *Stanford Social Innovation Review*, 9(1), 36–41.

Kelly, B., & Perkins, D. F. (Eds.). (2012). *Handbook of implementation science for psychology in education.* Cambridge University Press. https://doi.org/10.1017/CBO9781139013949

Kilbourne, A. M., Neumann, M. S., Pincus, H. A., Bauer, M. S. & Stall R. (2007). Implementing evidence-based interventions in health care: Application of the replicating effective programs framework. *Implementation Science*, 2, 42. https://doi.org/10.1186/1748-5908-2-42

Kiritsis, E. (2019). *String theory in a nutshell* (2nd ed.). Princeton University Press.

Kirkpatrick, D. (1993). *Evaluating training programs: The four levels.* Berrett-Koehler Publishers.

Knoster, T. (1991, June). *Factors in managing complex change.* Material presentation at TASH conference, Washington, DC. The Association for People with Severe Disabilities.

Kohn, A. (2006). *The homework myth: Why our kids get too much of a bad thing.* Da Capo Press.

Kotter, J. P. (2012). *Leading change: Why transformation efforts fail.* Harvard Business Review Press.

Kwasnicka, D., Dombrowski, S. U., White, M., & Sniehotta, F. (2016). Theoretical explanations for maintenance of behaviour change: A systematic review of behaviour theories. *Health Psychology Review*, 10(3), 277–296.

Lawler, J. M. (1978). *IQ, heritability and racism: A Marxist critique of Jensenism.* Lawrence & Wishart.

Lawrie, G., & Cobbold, I. (2004). Third-generation balanced scorecard: Evolution of an effective strategic control tool. *International Journal of Productivity and Performance Management, 53*(7), 611–623. https://doi.org/10.1108/17410400410561231

Leinwand, P., & Mainardi, C. (2011). *Stop chasing too many priorities.* Retrieved November 14, 2021, from https://hbr.org/2011/04/stop-chasing-too-many-prioriti

LeMahieu, P., Nordstrum, L., & Gale, D. (2017). Positive deviance: Learning from positive anomalies. *Quality Assurance in Education, 25*(1), 109–124. https://doi.org/10.1108/QAE-12-2016-0083

Lentz, E. W. (2021). Breaking the warp barrier: Hyper-fast solitons in Einstein–Maxwell-plasma theory. *Classical and Quantum Gravity, 38,* 075015. https://doi.org/10.1088/1361-6382/abe692

Levin, H. M., Bowden, A. B., Shand, R., McEwan, P. J., & Belfield, C. R. (2018). *Economic evaluation in education: Cost-effectiveness and benefit-cost analysis.* Sage.

Liedtka, J., King, A., & Bennett, K. (2013). *Solving problems with design thinking: 10 stories of what works.* Columbia Business School Publishing.

Mackenbach, J. D., Rutter, H., Compernolle, S., Glonti, K., Oppert, J. M., Charreire, H., De Bourdeaudhuij, I., Brug, J., Nijpels, G., & Lakerveld, J. (2014). Obesogenic environments: A systematic review of the association between the physical environment and adult weight status, the SPOTLIGHT project. *BMC Public Health, 14,* 233.

Marshall, K. (2008). Interim assessments: A user's guide. *Phi Delta Kappan, 90*(1), 64–68.

Means, B., & Penuel, W. R. (2005). Research to support scaling up technology-based educational interventions. In C. Dede, J. P. Honan, & L. C. Peters (Eds.), *Scaling up success: Lessons from technology-based educational improvement* (pp. 176–197). Jossey-Bass.

Mencken, H. L. (1917/1949). The divine afflatus. In H. L. Mencken (Ed.), *A Mencken chrestomathy* (pp. 442–449). Alfred A. Knopf.

Meyers, D. C., Durlak, J. A., & Wandersman A. (2012). The quality implementation framework: A synthesis of critical steps in the implementation process. *American Journal of Community Psychology, 50*(3–4), 462–480.

Micheli, P., Wilner, S. J., Bhatti, S. H., Mura, M., & Beverland, M. B. (2018). Doing design thinking: Conceptual review, synthesis, and research agenda. *Journal of Product Innovation Management, 36*(2), 124–148.

Michie, S., van Stralen, M. M., & West, R. (2011). The behaviour change wheel: A new method for characterising and designing behaviour change interventions. *Implementation Science, 6,* 42. https://doi.org/10.1186/1748-5908-6-42

Moos, R. & Moos, B. (2006). Rates and predictors of relapse after natural and treated remission from alcohol use disorders. *Addiction, 101,* 212–222. https://doi.org/10.1111/j.1360-0443.2006.01310

Morel, R. P., Coburn, C., Catterson, A. K., & Higgs J. (2019). The multiple meanings of scale: Implications for researchers and practitioners. *Educational Researcher, 48*(6), 369–377. https://doi.org/10.3102/0013189X19860531

Morris, Z. S., Wooding, S., & Grant, J. (2011). The answer is 17 years, what is the question: Understanding time lags in translational research. *Journal of the Royal Society of Medicine, 104*(12), 510–520. https://doi.org/10.1258/jrsm.2011.110180

Moullin, J. C., Dickson, K. S., Stadnick, N. A., Albers, B., Nilsen, P., Broder-Fingert, S., Mukasa, B., & Aarons G. A. (2020). Ten recommendations for using implementation frameworks in research and practice. *Implementation Science Communications, 1,* 42. https://doi.org/10.1186/s43058-020-00023-7

Moullin, J. C., Dickson, K. S., Stadnick, N. A., Rabin, B., & Aarons, G. A. (2019). Systematic review of the exploration, preparation, implementation, sustainment (EPIS) framework. *Implementation*

Science, 14, 1. http://doi.org/10.1186/s13012-018-0842-6

Moullin, J. C., Sabater-Hernández, D., Fernandez-Llimos, F., & Benrimoj, S. I. (2015). A systematic review of implementation frameworks of innovations in healthcare and resulting generic implementation framework. *Health Research Policy and Systems*, 13, 16. https://doi.org/10.1186/s12961-015-0005-z

Mullis, I. V. S., Martin, M. O., Foy, P., & Hooper, M. (2017). *PIRLS 2016: International results in reading*. TIMSS & PIRLS International Study Center, Lynch School of Education and Human Development, Boston College and International Association for the Evaluation of Educational Achievement.

Mullis, I. V. S., Martin, M. O., Foy, P., Kelly, D., & Fishbein, B. (2020). *TIMSS 2019: International results in mathematics and science*. TIMSS & PIRLS International Study Center, Lynch School of Education and Human Development, Boston College and International Association for the Evaluation of Educational Achievement.

Murphy, P. (2020). *COVID-19: Proportionality, public policy and social distancing*. Palgrave.

Murre, J. M. J., & Dros, J. (2015). Replication and analysis of Ebbinghaus' forgetting curve. *PLoS ONE*, 10(7), e0120644. https://doi.org/10.1371/journal.pone.0120644

NASA. (2021). *NASA technology transfer program*. Retrieved November 1, 2021, from https://spinoff.nasa.gov/

Nessler, D. (2018). How to apply a design thinking, HCD, UX or any creative process from scratch. *Medium*. Retrieved November 1, 2021, from https://medium.com/digital-experience-design/how-to-apply-a-design-thinking-hcd-ux-or-any-creative-process-from-scratch-b8786efbf812

Newport, C. (2016). *Deep work: Rules for focused success in a distracted world*. Grand Central Publishing.

Newport, C. (2021). *A world without email: Reimagining work in an age of communication overload*. Penguin Publishing Group.

Nickerson, R. S. (1998). Confirmation bias: A ubiquitous phenomenon in many guises. *Review of General Psychology*, 2(2), 175–220. https://doi.org/10.1037/1089-2680.2.2.175

Nilsen, P., & Bernhardsson, S. (2019). Context matters in implementation science: A scoping review of determinant frameworks that describe contextual determinants for implementation outcomes. *BMC Health Services Research*, 19(189). https://doi.org/10.1186/s12913-019-4015-3

Nordgren, L., & Schnonthal, D. (2021). *The human element: Overcoming the resistance that awaits new ideas*. Wiley.

O'Donnell, C. L. (2008). Defining, conceptualizing, and measuring fidelity of implementation and its relationship to outcomes in K–12 curriculum intervention research. *Review of Educational Research*, 78(1), 33–84. https://doi.org/10.3102/0034654307313793

Ohno, T. (1988). *Toyota production system: Beyond large-scale production*. Productivity Press.

Organization for Economic Cooperation and Development. (2019). *PISA 2018 results (Volume I): What students know and can do*. OECD Publishing.

Organization for Economic Cooperation and Development. (2020). *TALIS 2018 results (Volume II): Teachers and school leaders as valued professionals*. OECD Publishing. https://doi.org/10.1787/19cf08df-en

Oster, E. (2020). *COVID-19, learning loss and inequality*. Retrieved November 14, 2021, from https://emilyoster.substack.com/p/covid-19-learning-loss-and-inequality

Papay, J. P., & Kraft, M. A. (2015). Productivity returns to experience in the teacher labor market: Methodological challenges and new evidence on long-term career improvement. *Journal of Public Economics*, 130, 105–119. https://doi.org/10.1016/j.jpubeco.2015.02.008

Pascale, R. T., Sternin, J., & Sternin, M. (2010). *The power of positive deviance: How unlikely innovators solve the world's toughest problems*. Harvard Business Press.

Pearl, J., & Mackenzie, D. (2020). *The book of why: The new science of cause and effect* (Reprint ed.). Basic Books.

Pinker, S. (2019). *Enlightenment now: The case for reason, science, humanism, and progress* (Reprint ed.). Penguin Books.

Pritchett, L., Samji, S. & Hammer, J. (2013). *It's all about MeE: Using structured experiential learning ("e") to crawl the design space* (CGD Working Paper 322). Center for Global Development. https://www.cgdev.org/publication/its-all-about-mee

Project Management Institute. (2021). *A guide to the project management body of knowledge (PMBOK® guide)—Seventh edition and the standard for project management.* Project Management Institute.

Pyzdek, T. & Keller, P. A. (2009). *The Six Sigma handbook* (3rd ed.). McGraw-Hill.

Ranganathan, P., Pramesh, C. S., & Buyse, M. (2015). Common pitfalls in statistical analysis: Clinical versus statistical significance. *Perspectives in Clinical Research*, 6(3), 169–170. https://doi.org/10.4103/2229-3485.159943

Rasiel, E. M. (2001). *The McKinsey mind.* McGraw-Hill.

Reeves, D. (2013). *Finding your leadership focus: What matters most for student results.* Columbia University Teachers College Press.

Reeves, D. (2019). *Five skills colleges really want now.* Retrieved June 30, 2020, from https://www.creativeleadership.net/blog/five-skills-colleges-really-want-now

Reeves, D. (2020a). *Achieving equity and excellence: Immediate results from the lessons of high-poverty, high-success schools.* Solution Tree Press.

Reeves, D. (2020b). *How to stop the coming dropout time bomb.* Retrieved October 28, 2020, from https://www.creativeleadership.net/blog/how-to-stop-the-coming-dropout-time-bomb.

Reeves, D. (2021a). *Deep change leadership: A model for renewing and strengthening schools and districts.* Solution Tree Press.

Reeves, D. (2021b). *The learning leader: How to focus school improvement for better results* (2nd ed.). ASCD.

Reeves, D. B. (2009). *Leading change in your school: How to conquer myths, build commitment, and get results* (1st ed.). ASCD.

Rice, J. K. (2013). Learning from experience? Evidence on the impact and distribution of teacher experience and the implications for teacher policy. *Education Finance and Policy*, 8(3), 332–348. https://doi.org/https://doi.org/10.1162/EDFP_a_00099

Ringelmann, M. (1913). Recherches sur les moteurs animés: Travail de l'homme. *Annales de l'Institut National Agronomique*, 12 (2nd series), 1–40.

Robinson, V. M. J., Hohepa, M., & Lloyd, C. (2009). *School leadership and student outcomes: Identifying what works and why. Best evidence synthesis.* Ministry of Education.

Robinson, V. M. J. (2018). *Reduce change to increase improvement.* Corwin.

Rogers, E. (2003). *Diffusion of innovations* (5th ed.). Simon and Schuster.

Rojas-Andrade, R., & Bahamondes, L. L. (2019). Is implementation fidelity important? A systematic review on school-based mental health programs. *Contemporary School Psychology*, 23, 339–350. https://doi.org/10.1007/s40688-018-0175-0

Roschelle, J., Feng, M., Murphy, R. F., & Mason, C. A. (2016). Online mathematics homework increases student achievement. *AERA Open*, 2(4). https://doi.org/10.1177/2332858416673968

Rosenthal, R. (1966). *Experimenter effects in behavioral research.* Appleton-Century-Crofts.

Roser, M., & Ortiz-Ospina, E. (2016). Literacy. *Our World in Data.* https://ourworldindata.org/literacy

Rothman, A. J., Sheeran, P., & Wood, W. (2009). Reflective and automatic processes in the initiation and maintenance of dietary change. *Annals of Behavioral Medicine*, 38(Suppl. 1), S4–S17.

Royce, W. W. (1970). *Managing the development of large software systems.* Proceedings of IEEE WESCON, Washington, DC. http://www-scf.usc.edu/~csci201/lectures/Lecture11/royce1970.pdf

Rutter, M., Maughan, B., Mortimore, P., & Ouston, J. (1979). *Fifteen thousand hours: Secondary schools and their effects on children.* Open Books.

Sarason, S. B. (1995). Foreword. In A. Lieberman (Ed.), *The work of restructuring schools: Building from the ground up* (pp. vii–viii). Teachers College Press.

Schneider, J. (2014). *From the ivory tower to the schoolhouse: How scholarship becomes common knowledge in education.* Harvard University Press.

Shannon, C. E. (1948). A mathematical theory of communication. *Bell System Technical Journal, 27*(379–423), 623–656. https://doi.org/10.1002/j.1538-7305.1948.tb01338.x

Sharot, T. (2011). The optimism bias. *Current Biology, 21*(23), R941–R945. https://doi.org/10.1016/j.cub.2011.10.030

Sharples, J., Albers, B., & Fraser, S. (2019). *Putting evidence to work: A school's guide to implementation. Guidance Report.* Education Endowment Foundation.

Simon, B., & Whitbread, N. (1974). Schools can make a difference. *Forum for the Discussion of New Trends in Education, 16*(2), 35, 44.

Sinha, T., & Kapur, M. (2021). When problem solving followed by instruction works: Evidence for productive failure. *Review of Educational Research, 91*(5), 761–798. https://doi.org/10.3102/00346543211019105

Sisken, L. S. (2016). Mutual adaptation in action. *Teachers College Record, 118*(13), 1–18.

Slavin, R. (2011). *Educational psychology: Theory and practice* (10th ed.). Pearson.

Sloane, F. C. (2005). The scaling of reading interventions: Building multilevel insight. *Reading Research Quarterly, 40*(3), 361–366.

Smith, J. D., Schneider, B. H., Smith, P. K., & Ananiadou, K. (2004). The effectiveness of whole-school antibullying programs: A synthesis of evaluation research. *School Psychology Review, 33*(4), 547–560.

Stetler, C. B. (2001). Updating the Stetler model of research utilization to facilitate evidence-based practice. *Nursing Outlook, 49*(6), 272–279. https://doi.org/10.1067/mno.2001.120517

Stith, S., Pruitt, I., Dees, J. E., Fronce, M., Green, N., Som, A., & Linkh, D. (2006). Implementing community-based prevention programming: A review of the literature. *The Journal of Primary Prevention, 27*(6), 599–617.

Straub, E. T. (2009). Understanding technology adoption: Theory and future directions for informal learning. *Review of Educational Research, 79*(2), 625–649. https://doi.org/10.3102/0034654308325896

Stringfield, S., & Datnow, A. (1998). Introduction: Scaling up school restructuring designs in urban schools. *Education and Urban Society, 30*(3), 269–276, https://doi.org/10.1177/0013124598030003001

Timperley, H., Kaser, L., & Halbert, J. (2014). *A framework for transforming learning in schools: Innovation and the spiral of inquiry.* Centre for Strategic Education.

Timperley, H., Wilson, A., Barrar, H., & Fung, I. (2007). *The teacher professional learning and development BES illuminates the kind of professional learning for teachers that strengthens valued outcomes for diverse learners.* Ministry of Education.

Tobler, N. S. (1986). Meta-analysis of 143 adolescent drug prevention programs: Quantitative outcome results of program participants compared to a control or comparison group. *Journal of Drug Issues, 16*(4), 537–567. https://doi.org/10.1177/002204268601600405

Tsai, A. G., & Wadden, T. A. (2005). Systematic review: An evaluation of major commercial weight loss programs in the United States. *Annals of Internal Medicine, 142*(1), 56–66. https://doi.org/10.7326/0003-4819-142-1-200501040-00012

Turing, A. M. (1937). On computable numbers, with an application to the entscheidungsproblem. *Proceedings of the London Mathematical Society, S2-42*(1), 230–265. https://doi.org/10.1112/plms/s2-42.1.230

Turkle, S. (2016). *Reclaiming conversation: The power of talk in a digital age.* Penguin Publishing Group.

Vincent, D. (2019). The modern history of literacy. In J. L. Rury & E. Tamura (Eds.), *The Oxford handbook of the history of education* (pp. 507–522). Oxford University Press.

Visible Learning Meta[x]. (2021). https://www.visiblelearningmetax.com/

Wandersman A. (2014). Getting to outcomes: An evaluation capacity building example of rationale, science, and practice. *American Journal of Evaluation, 35*(1), 100–106, https://doi.org/10.1177/1098214013500705

Weeks, A. (2021). Important factors for evidence-based implementation in child welfare settings: A systematic review. *Journal of Evidence-Informed Social Work, 18*(2), 129–154. http://doi.org/10.1080/26408066.2020.1807433

Weinstein, N. D., & Sandman, P. M. (1992). A model of the precaution adoption process: Evidence from home radon testing. *Health Psychology, 11*(3), 170–180. https://doi.org/10.1037/0278-6133.11.3.170

Wiliam, D. (2010). Standardized testing and school accountability. *Educational Psychologist, 45*(2), 107–122. https://doi.org/10.1080/00461521003703060

Wiliam, D. (2016). *Leadership for teacher learning: Creating a culture where all teachers improve so that all learners succeed.* Learning Sciences International.

Wiliam, D. (2018). *Creating the Schools our children need: Why what we are doing now won't help much (and what we can do instead).* Learning Sciences International.

Willingham, D. (2012). *When can you trust the experts? How to tell good science from bad in education* (1st ed.). Jossey-Bass.

Wilson, S. J., Lipsey, M. W., & Derzon, J. H. (2003). The effects of school-based intervention programs on aggressive behavior: A meta-analysis. *Journal of Consulting and Clinical Psychology, 71,* 136–149.

Wing, R. R., & Phelan, S. (2005). Long-term weight loss maintenance. *The American Journal of Clinical Nutrition, 82*(1 Suppl.), 222S–225S. https://doi.org/10.1093/ajcn/82.1.222S

Wiske, M. S., & Perkins, D. (2005). Dewey goes digital: Scaling up constructivist pedagogies and the promise of new technologies. In C. Dede, J. Honan, & L. Peters (Eds.), *Scaling up success: Lessons learned from technology-based educational innovation.* Jossey-Bass.

Womak, J., & Jones, D. (2013). *Lean thinking: Banish waste and create wealth in your corporation* (Revised and updated). Simon & Schuster.

World Bank. (2000). *The logframe handbook.* World Bank Group.

World Bank. (2018). *World development report (WDR) 2018: Learning to realize education's promise.* World Bank Group.

Wright, S. (1921). Correlation and causation. *Journal of Agricultural Research, 20,* 557–585.

Zaleznik, A. (1992). Leaders and managers: Are they different? *Harvard Business Review.*

Zhao, Y. (2017). What works may hurt: Side effects in education. *Journal of Educational Change, 18,* 1–19. https://doi.org/10.1007/s10833-016-9294-4

Zhao, Y. (2018). *What works may hurt: Side effects in education.* Teachers College Press.

Zhao, Y. (2020). Two decades of havoc: A synthesis of criticism against PISA. *Journal of Educational Change, 21,* 245–266. https://doi.org/10.1007/s10833-019-09367-x

Index

Build your Visible Learning® library!

GREAT TEACHING BY DESIGN

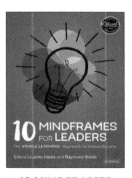

VISIBLE LEARNING FEEDBACK

COLLECTIVE STUDENT EFFICACY

10 MINDFRAMES FOR VISIBLE LEARNING

10 MINDFRAMES FOR LEADERS

DEVELOPING TEACHING EXPERTISE

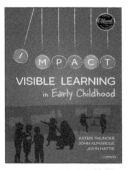

VISIBLE LEARNING IN EARLY CHILDHOOD

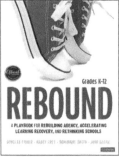

REBOUND

LEADING THE REBOUND

Visit corwin.com/vlbooks

DEVELOPING ASSESSMENT-CAPABLE VISIBLE LEARNERS,
Grades K–12

VISIBLE LEARNING FOR LITERACY,
Grades K–12

VISIBLE LEARNING FOR MATHEMATICS,
Grades K–12

TEACHING LITERACY IN THE VISIBLE LEARNING CLASSROOM,
Grades K–5, 6–12

TEACHING MATHEMATICS IN THE VISIBLE LEARNING CLASSROOM,
Grades K–2, 3–5, 6–8, and High School

VISIBLE LEARNING FOR SCIENCE,
Grades K–12

VISIBLE LEARNING FOR SOCIAL STUDIES,
Grades K–12

CORWIN

A SAGE Publishing Company

Helping educators make the greatest impact

CORWIN HAS ONE MISSION: to enhance education through intentional professional learning.

We build long-term relationships with our authors, educators, clients, and associations who partner with us to develop and continuously improve the best evidence-based practices that establish and support lifelong learning.